Transforming Schools— Empowering Children

Arun Kapur

SAGE Publications
New Delhi ▪ Thousand Oaks ▪ London

First published in 2007 by

 Sage Publications India Pvt Ltd
B 1/I 1 Mohan Cooperative Industrial Area
Mathura Road
New Delhi 110 044
www.sagepub.in

Sage Publications Inc
2455 Teller Road
Thousand Oaks, California 91320

Sage Publications Ltd
1 Oliver's Yard
55 City Road
London EC1Y 1SP

Published by Vivek Mehra for Sage Publications India Pvt Ltd, typeset in 10.5/13.5 pt Aldine 401BT and printed at Chaman Enterprises, New Delhi.

Library of Congress Cataloging-in-Publication Data

Kapur, Arun, 1954–
    Transforming schools—empowering children / Arun Kapur.
        p. cm.
    1. Schools. 2. Education. I. Title.

LB41.K37   371.2—dc22   2006   2006037710

ISBN: 978-0-7619-3563-6 (Pb)   978-81-7829-723-1 (India-Pb)

Sage Production Team: Gasper Desouza, Roopa Sharma, Sigi Peter, Mathew and Santosh Rawat

Transforming Schools—
Empowering Children

To my daughters, Ritika and Anjalika,
who mean the world to me

&

To Rekha and Aroon Purie,
for providing me the space and opportunity to learn and grow
as well as create a dynamic learning environment

Contents

List of Figures		viii
Preface		xiii
Acknowledgements		xvii
Introduction		xviii
1.	Purpose of Schools	1
2.	Learning	8
3.	Curriculum	31
4.	Assessment	52
5.	Wholistic Learning	74
6.	Technology	86
7.	Teachers	103
8.	Teacher Curriculum	130
9.	Lesson Planning	154
10.	Teaching for Diversity and Inclusion	181
11.	Parents	196
12.	Management	211
13.	Leadership	238
About the Author		254

List of Figures

1.1   Each child has a different potential   5

2.1   A school gradually lowers the fencing around its students   9
2.2   A school provides a dynamic and multi-dimensional
      experience to its students   10
2.3   A great school provides experiences that enable students
      to explore the outside world and teaches them to find
      connections between these and their inner self   12
2.4   An education system that is Learning Process-based   14
2.5   The three cornerstones of the Learning Process are Joy,
      Ownership and Decision Making   15
2.6   Vertical Integration over the years   21
2.7   No field of study exists in isolation and all are parts
      of the big picture   22
2.8   There are two main aspects of student empowerment: one
      is 'understanding' and the other is 'developing abilities'   23
2.9   Howard Gardner broke away from the common notion
      of a single number that depicts the 'intelligence' of a
      human being   25
2.10 Various theories of cognition have a certain commonality   27

3.1   Schools can either accept a given board-based
      curriculum or interact with the world outside to
      create their own curriculum   32
3.2   Flaws of the three aspects of the curriculum prescribed
      by Indian board   35
3.3   The process of reform itself is severely flawed   36
3.4   There are varied reasons for a curriculum   38
3.5   Curricula have been traditionally designed in a
      linear and disconnected fashion   39
3.6   The curriculum develops through the dynamic
      interaction of action and reflection   41
3.7   Outcomes can be categorised as Individual, Societal
      and Spiritual   44

3.8   At the core is the vision for the curriculum   45
3.9   An evaluation based on the assessment of only content
       knowledge degenerates into a vicious cycle of
       memorisation exercise and examination orientation   48
3.10 The curriculum web consists of the four main
       components of the curriculum   50

4.1   The Assessment Cycles   54
4.2   The assessment basket needs to incorporate several
       different types of tools in order to capture the true
       capabilities of the student   56
4.3   There can be two roles for examinations   57
4.4   Examinations must not be isolated and independent
       events in the lives of students   58
4.5   The examination reform process cannot be set off without
       taking into account all aspects of the learning process 61
4.6   A true assessment gives us an authentic picture of the
       student who is being assessed and not a set of
       meaningless statistics   64
4.7   The assessment development cycle answers questions
       on the design of the different elements of assessment   71
4.8   Guidelines for combining benchmarks in the four
       wheels with personality traits to define acceptable
       and not acceptable levels of achievement   72
4.9   The four wheels of assessment each have different
       parameters for measurement   72

5.1   The learning process consists of steps leading to the
       creation of new knowledge and its application in
       different environments   74
5.2   Academic curriculum usually concentrates on truth.
       Holism implies inclusion of all aspects of life including
       Beauty and Ethics   76
5.3   It is not just the scholastic content of the course that
       is designed wholistically   78
5.4   The chief characteristics of the first year of the course 80
5.5   Year 2 sees greater inter-dependence between
       activities and greater independence for students   82
5.6   The third year is the year of the student   84

6.1 Attitudes of an educational institution to change
    can be dynamic or static   87
6.2 Changes are taking place in several domains that
    affect the learning process   87
6.3 Learning through technology impacts the quality, style
    and reach of the learning process   90
6.4 Behind every reason given as a drawback against the
    use of technology is a new skill that needs to be learnt   94
6.5 Every course in the curriculum must link these skills
    together in the learning process   98
6.6 A web of possibilities using ICT to develop fundamental
    learning skills   100

7.1 Each of the six fundamental qualities of a teacher has
    a different type of impact on her ability to be effective   104
7.2 The teacher ensures that assessments are a cycle of
    continuous feedback and all her actions related
    to student learning are based on this feedback   111
7.3 A great teacher is not a passive acceptor of a given
    environment—she actively contributes to different
    types of environments in the school   119
7.4 The edifice of the complex learning structure that is
    required for a student rests on the actions of teachers   122
7.5 The poor quality of teachers is a consequence of
    the working conditions—low pay, few promotions,
    stress and tedium   126

8.1 Training ensures that teachers develop wider perspectives
    and awareness of their subject specialisation in perspective   133
8.2 Schools train teachers on implementing learning and
    assessment techniques that are based on the school
    philosophy   134
8.3 Teachers are trained to understand both social interactions
    and child psychology that affect the behaviour of
    individual children as well as groups of students   136
8.4 Schools enhance teacher productivity by training them
    to manage knowledge and to communicate effectively   138
8.5 Leaders in communication skills get different
    levels of responsibility depending on their ability   141

8.6 Examples of tasks for teachers with good
     organisational abilities   142
8.7 Teachers with good inter-personal skills can have a
     strong influence on the behaviour of other teachers   143

9.1 Lesson plans need to capture both conceptual
     understanding as well as the learning process   155
9.2 The conventional lesson plan sequence   157
9.3 A simplified, sample matrix that teachers can use   176
9.4 A teacher learns from other teachers of the same subject
     and discipline   177
9.5 Teachers of different classes can co-ordinate the vertical
     integration of lessons   178
9.6 A database is a powerful tool for (w)holistic learning   179
9.7 Sharing of ideas has no limits   179

10.1 Individualised learning in great schools leads to
      recognition of diversity   181
10.2 The two aspects of a teacher's attitude: empathy and
      objectivity   186
10.3 Teachers need to use both active and passive methods
      to influence student attitudes   188
10.4 Multi-dimensional planning is a very crucial part of the
      learning-teaching process   190
10.5 Networking, diversity-friendly systems and infrastructure
      facilities are the three important factors that make
      the management of diversity and inclusion effective   192

11.1 Government control over fees and finances of schools
      has a detrimental effect on the parent–school relationship 197
11.2 Parent–school interaction enables sharing of strengths   198
11.3 Balanced parenting requires an appropriate mix of
      different parenting styles to meet the needs of different
      situations, family backgrounds and child needs   199
11.4 Schools expect parents to have certain basic qualities
      that have a positive influence on their child's ability to
      learn and adjust to the school programme   201
11.5 Parents want to participate in an effective learning
      programme for their children   203

11.6 While parents want schools to reinforce core values they
do not want interference in their personal way of life   205

11.7 Parents want their child to be recognised as unique and
to be nurtured by the school in a manner that is most
appropriate to her as an individual   206

11.8 Parent–school interactions relate both to communication
and to participation   208

12.1 The organisational structure of a school has effectively
two layers   212

12.2 A school creates a positive learning environment to
deal with challenges of managing clients and employees   213

12.3 Conflicts are caused due to differing perceptions of
stakeholders and due to limits in resources—time,
finances and people   216

12.4 Some examples of systems and subsystems in a school   218

12.5 The problems in implementation of financial systems   219

12.6 Systems, both new and old, need to be measured
against four basic benchmarks   220

12.7 Developing the system process is only one step in the
development of a new system   223

12.8 The first step in creating a new system to assess
the success of a school   228

12.9 Each success parameter is measured using a specific
instrument   231

12.10 The steps in the development of the system for
measuring the success of a school are closely related
to the steps for the development of most systems   235

13.1 While all members of the school community contribute
to and learn from the learning process, the leader of
the school and leadership by the school give the right
direction to this process   239

13.2 Proactive citizenship   240

13.3 The research centre connects all types of organisations
in a community that are interested in education and
learning from each other   249

13.4 Each research centre connects to several other centres
to widen the base of shared learning   250

Preface

I started my career in education at the Doon School, Dehradun, where I spent 13 years of my life. I had never planned to be a schoolteacher and had no professional degree in education. However, from an early age, I have been very curious to know how the mind works, how a person learns. At college, I came across some people who had a photographic memory or who could learn by rote without understanding the subject matter. It was then that I started making a distinction between understanding—actually knowing something—and reproducing others' words without understanding and contributing anything of one's own. At Doon School, I met some amazing members of the staff from whom I learnt a lot. All my learning about how learning takes place in the classroom came from people who practised this for several years. Doon School gave me a perspective that learning does not take place only inside the classroom, but also outside it—that geography is learnt on the mountains and at the riverside, that history is learnt by talking to people who lived through it.

The desire to know more about how one learns led me to undertake many courses in the science of learning, pedagogy, classroom climate, curriculum development, varied learning and teaching styles, stages of child development, thinking and problem-solving skills. An international conference on creative thinking at MIT gave me an opportunity to meet Howard Gardner, Professor of Cognition and Education at the Harvard Graduate School, and other experts in the field. All this convinced me that one could actually teach creativity.

I went to teach in a co-educational school in England for a year and came back to join the British School, New Delhi, as Principal. I am currently the Director of Vasant Valley School, where my association with the school began much before it was set up. As the head of the institution, I used the collective wisdom of teachers, who came from different teaching backgrounds, to incorporate composite teaching methodologies. The hallmark of our success is that a school that started from scratch, operated from the very first day like a well-established institution founded on the ethos of open-mindedness, constant learning and adaptation. There was no experimentation with students. The systems that were put into place in school had been thought through and discussed by the core group of teachers for many months before the students actually came in the school.

I distinctly remember one of the first things we did when we were setting up Vasant Valley School: We shared our memories as children— what we hated about our schools, what we loved about our schools, the teachers we liked, the teachers who inspired us. It helped us in putting together a blueprint out of which emerged the dynamic learning environment of Vasant Valley School—vision, philosophy and practice, innovative teaching methodologies, sensitisation to diverse learning needs and abilities, and most important of all, an open and positive environment.

From the very beginning we believed that every child was special— the term we used was '*differently abled*'. No child is disabled or handi-capped or incapable: those words bothered me, so we started talking about how we were all differently abled, and therefore some were great footballers, some were great mathematicians, some could read—they were all good in one area or another. If one is not good at any thing, it was only because their potential has not been realised for one reason or another. We also realised that the onus of breaking through this barrier was on us—as an institution and as teachers building the insti-tution. Though we were aware that safety nets had to be in place because we were talking about children here, we were very clear that these safety nets had to be invisible ones, so that the children grew unfettered.

Discipline is always necessary, a boundary is necessary, but within the boundary you could do what you wanted to, and we realised with experience that in such an environment *students rose to the levels of our expectation*. If we have low expectations from students they rise to a low height; if we have high expectations they rise high. *This is the combination that is at the foundation of our system—our expectation levels, our sense of discipline, our understanding that each child was different, our understanding that the environment makes a huge difference.*

There is a lot that a school can do; however, one cannot discount the fact that a significant amount of learning takes place at home as well. This is especially true in the realm of values. Though it is the responsi-bility of the school to inculcate certain values in children, schools can do little if these do not get reinforced at home. A child might grow differently if the school could provide the tools for independent think-ing, and would be lucky to go to a school that provides these tools. A school should not attempt to force students to change their thinking but it can play a crucial role in shaping a child's response to ideas by providing the tools that would enable them to think independently.

A good education provides the tools to improve the quality of one's decisions. One could learn '2 plus 2' in mathematics and about 'steam' in physics anywhere, but what distinguishes one school from another is the tools it provides to facilitate the learning and create new knowledge. A good education empowers a person to make the best of all situations and opportunities and, more important, inspires one to be constantly in the learning mode.

My experience as a teacher has taught me two things: first, the mission of any school should be to empower children to actualise their potential. Second, the purpose of education ultimately is to prepare a new generation to take over from the older generation that is dying. If every generation had to reinvent how to generate electricity or rediscover penicillin, then humanity would not get anywhere and there would be no progress. The whole idea is to internalise the knowledge gathered by the earlier generations, learn with the tools developed to receive that knowledge and then, through institutions like the school, transfer this knowledge to students and provide them with tools to filter the irrelevant from the relevant and, above all, provide them the tools to create new knowledge.

In this context, teacher training acquires paramount importance. Teaching is the lowest-paid profession in the world and wrongly perceived as a job anyone can do. No wonder, when a teacher is interacting with a student, the parents do not think twice about criticising the teacher, criticising the methods of the teacher, or saying, 'I can do it better, and my teachers were better.' When parents do this, they are negating the impact the teachers have on the students. Moreover, teachers today have to work in a completely different environment that is marked by a tremendous explosion in the fields of media, communication and information technology. Students now are exposed to diverse sources from which they can collect information and also learn. Industries such as market research employ bright, creative youngsters and have huge budgets at their disposal to conduct research to find ways to influence children's minds. Advertising agencies bank on this research to create 'moods' and influence buying by tempting children and generating needs in their minds that have to be satisfied instantaneously! Attractive images and presentations tell a whole story in 45 seconds! It is also done very intelligently, and on careful observation one would notice that a programme that a child may be watching is not of so much consequence as the commercials that come during the intervals. The programme between advertisements is being designed to fit into the structure and sequencing of the advertisements, and so it is no longer just a good programme but a whole package that is being offered, and when I, as a teacher, go into a classroom, that is what I am competing with. I have to vie for the attention of a child whose mind has been fed on a rich diet of beautifully created images—images crafted with lights and sound and music and costumes. This I have to do with a chalk and a blackboard!

A teacher needs to be empowered. She needs to understand the world that children today are growing up in. She needs to understand the power of multimedia and use it in her classroom, and for that she needs to be lucky enough to be in a school that has access to such facilities. However, this does not mean that teachers should now become 'ad men', but they do need to approach it from a position of strength. They need to know their match, the domain knowledge and should be excited about learning more and enhancing their skills.

A school is as good as the quality of interactions between teachers and students. No matter how good the school infrastructure is, it is not a great school if the quality of interaction is not high. An essential requirement for bringing about this interaction is how one trains a teacher to be passionate about her subject. One can have a great school under a tree and a mediocre school in the best infrastructure. What is required is the ability to match great infrastructure with great teachers. It becomes necessary that in our planning of a great school, there be a parallel structure for growth of a teacher. Therefore, teachers' development becomes absolutely crucial.

The teacher development programme can be multi-layered. There can be in-house workshops, or training and exchange programmes within and outside the country with an in-built option that gives the teachers the flexibility to choose the course/programme that matches their interests and needs. The leader of a school must be proactive and organise professional development regularly. In the school I head, I organise such sessions myself in a room we call 'Return to School' where teachers return to school as students. It creates a space for them to discuss, debate new ideas and innovate, and it allows them to introspect, assess themselves and set targets for each year and strive to excel in their areas of responsibility.

I must add that no aspect of Vasant Valley School was inflexible; we are constantly evolving, learning new ideas, reflecting on our experiences and responding to rapidly changing environment. I look at the school as work in progress that is committed to a lifelong learning journey. It is a source of pride and deep satisfaction to me that in a short span of time, Vasant Valley School has become one of the most sought-after institutions in the country.

Acknowledgements

First and foremost, I would like to thank Nitya Ram, my colleague at Vasant Valley School and Learn Today, for her immense contribution to this book. Her creative and critical inputs enabled me to place my arguments on a firmer foundation of rigorous logic. All the figures in the book have been created by her. Thanks are also due to Shalini Advani who was the first to notice the faint glimmer of a book after reading the first of the manuscript.

I would like to express my deep gratitude to the young people I have interacted with and learnt from at the Doon School, Dehra Dun; Vasant Valley School, New Delhi; and the numerous young people who are outside the formal school system in places like the Tihar Jail, New Delhi; Ritinjali's Second Chance School, Mahipalpur; and Ritinjali's Night School at INA Market, New Delhi. All these bright young minds have inspired me through conversations and interactions and provided me unique insights on the complexity of the learning process and in the institution of schooling.

My thanks are also due to my colleagues at the Vasant Valley School, Ritinjali and Pallavan who reviewed large parts of the manuscript and looked at the finer points of the book. Here the role that Dilreen Kaur played needs to be underlined.

I would like to thank all the teachers and parents who I have interacted with over the years. They have indeed strengthened my belief that the process of growth is never-ending.

I could not have grown without the love, support and encouragement that I constantly got from my parents, Usha and Ascharj Nath Kapur. Their ability to adapt positively to all circumstances always amazed me and I salute them and all that they stand for. It was their ability to always be relevant that set me on this path. And of course, my daughters Ritika and Anjalika through whose eyes I try and see life as it should be. Thank you.

Introduction

Schools of yesterday had a 'one size fits all' curriculum as they were expected to prepare students for an industrialised economy based on mass production that had rigid social layers. In those times, people belonging to different professions, social classes or ethnic groups did not interact much among themselves. Schools also reflected this reality as they remained isolated from each other and continued with systems that had in place for several generations. However, as a result of increasing mobility people of different backgrounds, cultures and abilities are no longer separated by geographical or social barriers and social distinctions are becoming increasingly fluid.

The workplace too has become very complex, as organisations today are on the look-out for people with different skills and backgrounds. To meet these challenges, schools today are changing and developing new systems. There is an increasing tendency towards greater individualisation of education with an emphasis on a broad-based education. It is no longer enough to excel in board examinations; students need to develop other skills and interests—in academics, arts, sports or in community interactions. Schools at the cutting edge, those that keep up with new challenges, offer almost any combination of subjects that interests the student. They offer courses in newly emerging subjects and fields of specialisations. Schools that could anticipate such a future 20 years ago and change their systems to keep pace with these developments are the ones that have produced the most successful students. These were the great schools of yesterday that were less isolated from the world outside than others around them.

In a similar manner, great schools today are looking towards meeting the challenges of the future. They know that systems and learning must constantly change to keep pace with changes in the outside world. In the chapters that follow, I have woven my expertise and experience together to offer insights into 'what makes a great school'. Two perspectives, in particular, are discussed throughout the book: first, the recognition that learning is an innate ingredient of our very humanity and second, how we can actively facilitate a shift in the learning and teaching environment to better serve the needs of diverse learners and communities in the context of a changing world.

In addition to outlining the characteristics of a great school, this book provides concrete tools and abundant resources for directing a school on its journey with a growth plan for all the stakeholders—students, teachers, administrators and parents. I must mention here my strong belief that great schools are not created only from prescriptive lists, policies and procedures. They are created locally, and work from professional knowledge, decisions, judgments and relationships, where local school people (staff, students, administrators, parents and community partners) are empowered to share in the choices and responsibilities of making the school a better place.

Regardless of the varied contexts within which they are located, schools across the world still struggle with the familiar issues of how to learn about teaching, how to strike a balance between teaching and research and how to evaluate both teaching and learning, besides the curricular, pedagogical and other issues. This book attempts to show ways on how to generate meaningful dialogue among all the stakeholders about teaching and learning and how to create a forum for productive inter-disciplinary conversations about the art and practice of teaching. The perspectives discussed in the book attempt to provide readers a new outlook on everyday concerns and introduce new thoughts on teaching and learning.

Chapter 1 looks at how our understanding of the existence of the institution called 'school' has changed over the past century. It also outlines the design for a new school, using the technologies that are currently available for learning.

Chapter 2 defines the core purpose of a school, which is to enable students to learn how to prepare for life. The emphasis is on the process of learning rather than the content or the outcomes, aiming at multi-dimensional learning and long-lasting outcomes. The chapter also deals with questions and issues such as these: What is the process by which learning actually takes place in the minds of children (and adults)? What is the best and most efficient process by which educators can guide students to become independent learners?

Chapter 3 looks at the curriculum as a dynamic set of processes that continuously interact with one another. It also discusses the significant issues in formulating a curriculum that integrates all the needs of the student and meets the goals of preparation for life.

Chapter 4 discusses alternatives to the 'examinations as assessment' and sets forth a model of assessment based on the premise that the purpose of assessment is to increase the dynamic potential of a student by putting her through a learning process that is appropriate for her needs. This assessment model creates an intricate and interconnected grid of nano-assessments that join to form a true picture of the student being assessed.

Chapter 5 includes a 'wholistic' course spread over three academic years that specifically takes students through a critical thinking learning process that will teach them how to learn. The emphasis once again is on creating courses for students that develop their skills to cope with and stay ahead of change in an increasingly fluid world.

Chapter 6 discusses the impact of technology on teaching and the emergence of information and communication technology as an important agent for bringing about change in schools.

Chapter 7 provides the key to a great school, which is summed up in the following words: 'A school is great only if it has great teachers.' The chapter elaborates on the fundamental qualities of a great teacher and links it to the four basic ways by which these qualities are developed—planning, assessment, creating the right environment and continuous learning.

Chapter 8 stresses on the need for constantly developing the potential and abilities of good teachers and provides a curriculum for teachers to help them understand the school vision and to ensure that they always remain in the learning mode.

Chapter 9 defines an effective lesson plan and briefly discusses all the elements of the learning process—horizontal integration, vertical integration, cutting edge learning techniques and individualised.

Chapter 10 elaborates on the concept of celebrating diversity as an extension of a school's philosophy of individualised learning.

Chapter 11 talks about how schools complement parenting. It also discusses how school-parent interaction enables sharing of strengths—schools help parents to become more objective, parents help schools to give better individual attention.

Chapter 12 gives an outline of the organisation structure in a school, the role of management in implementing efficient systems for the running of the school and developing new systems to determine the success of a school.

While all members of the school community contribute to and learn from the learning process, the leader of the school and leadership by the school give the right direction to this process. Chapter 13 talks about the two meanings of leadership in the context of a great school. One refers to the leader of the school who guides the school along the path that will lead it to greatness. The second refers to the leadership provided by a great school to other schools.

The book also contains inspiring examples, passionate stories and case studies written by teachers on the teaching–learning process and challenges they face in classrooms.

One final note: All of us involved in the field of education have to keep going back to this fundamental question, 'Is this the way that education should continue into the future?' We need to re-orient ourselves to the reason why we are doing what we are doing, in the schools. This is germane to the entire process of learning, teaching and growing. This also calls for a commitment to view ourselves not only as educators but also as learners who must, while implementing change, actively engage in a process of continuous interaction, reflection and re-definition of positions. The starting point for making a great school thus lies in our willingness to change ourselves.

Purpose of Schools 1

The millennium is a few years old and people everywhere are caught up in a world of change that is changing much faster than anyone had ever anticipated. The pace of change is itself increasing at an exponential rate, and obsolescence is almost instantaneous. Both adults and students need to cope with this world. All civilisations have growing up rites for children to prepare them for adulthood—in the modern world this rite is called schooling, a long drawn out ritual—it starts much earlier and takes much longer to complete.

Schools as we know them were designed more than a century ago. In those times, schools were almost the last place for change, and in fact changed only after the change was established in the society outside. Schools were a place where adults led the learning; they directed and controlled 'child-centred' activities. Today, this type of a school is no longer relevant. The entire concept and structure of a school needs to change. Revamping the existing education system with small changes will not serve the purpose. A freshly repaired vintage car that works perfectly is not what is needed—a totally new model that is built for the needs of this constantly changing future needs to be designed. In their efforts to reform, educationists now are beginning to realise that instead of fine-tuning a time-worn system, there should be an endeavour to build a new process altogether—a process that is in tune with the changed environment that we live in today.

Educationists also need to look ahead. They should attempt to build 'cybernetic' systems incorporating the latest advances in technology, concepts and ideas to build institutions/processes that not only meet the needs of the world as it is now, but also anticipate the future.

What does this new school look like? Here we need to go back to the rationale for the existence of the institution called the 'school' and based on this develop the design for the new school, using the technology and science of learning that is available.

Schools ensure the survival of the fittest

According to Darwin, only the fittest of a species survive. What is survival? For the simplest of creatures, 'survival' is merely being able to live long enough to reproduce offspring to replace the individuals of the species that will die. Survival also includes taking care of the offspring and ensuring their survival at least till they are old enough to reproduce. As a species becomes more complex and advanced, parenting becomes important.

For the human species, survival goes beyond this. For humans, who have the power of rational thinking, survival is not just the survival of the body, but also of the mind. An increasingly fertile mind has to satisfy far greater hunger, thirst and aspiration in order to survive. Parents want each aspect of their child's life to be perfect and are willing to invest all they can to help their children to survive in the fittest manner.

If survival has a different meaning for humans, does fitness too mean something more than physical fitness?

Fitness for humans mean vigour in everything—the intellect, physical body, emotions, spiritual nature and the vitality of the society and the environment that they live in. If fitness is not restricted to good physical health, how do we recognise a person who is fit in all these different dimensions? In the human context, being the fittest means being a leader—the fittest humans are the ones who lead in various aspects of life.

For all other species, being fit implies that they are perfectly adapted to the environment in which they live. The human species, however, is not wholly dependent upon the environment around it. Humans modify their environment in order to survive in the fittest manner, and create, through this constant modification, an increasingly complex world that suits their needs for fitness and survival.

> While for all other species, the definition of 'fittest' belongs to the physical realm, for the human species, the definition of fitness spans many dimensions.

Schools are needed to deal with complexity

The complex and multi-faceted world we live in today has been created as a result of this pursuit of fitness and modification of the environment by the human species. Yet, as the world becomes increasingly intricate, parents often do not have all the skills required to help their children to emerge as leaders or even become fit enough to survive.

They therefore entrust their children to people who are experts in various fields, and gradually the concept of acquiring learning from places outside the home emerges.

The place of learning progressively evolves from a small amoeba-like structure to become a large and complex cellular organisation because no single person is capable of possessing all the skills required to help children develop their multifarious strengths year after year. Thus, from a small group the large school structure emerges.

Therefore, schools provide a structure to the students, a kind of scaffolding within which students need to grow, learn and evolve. Since the potential that each student possesses is not only different but also dynamic, the scaffolding that the school provides to the students also needs to be individualised and be ever-changing and growing. This process of constant monitoring, changing the scaffold and growing happens in a systematic and scientific manner in well-organised schools. In the age of fast changes and new knowledge being created every day, a school is one place where students can be exposed to advancements in all fields under a single roof.

Schools must be networked to industry and other fields—arts, music, and research—and to advances in higher learning and the world of work. Schools can no longer work in isolated ivory towers as before; they need to become bridges to the world outside.

Schools are needed to deal with freedom

One of the consequences of the increasing complexity in the world is increased access to different types of information, knowledge and wisdom. This has led to the spread of greater awareness and freedom.

In such an environment, it is no longer sufficient for us to understand and know the immediate physical and social reality that we live in, but also to understand the people and cultures very different from our own. For this exposure to happen in an organised fashion it is necessary for children to have appropriate systems that will act as a window to the big world outside.

People today have far more freedom than they have ever had in the history of human civilisation. An important aspect of living in a free world is to be able to understand and appreciate this freedom. Many political theorists have said that there can be nothing called absolute freedom: for freedom to be enjoyed, we need boundaries and limits.

3

A school in many ways helps students to understand the meaning of freedom within boundaries. A school helps to bring discipline in the lives of the students and also helps them to understand and appreciate freedom.

Schools are needed to give a sense of identity to deal with diversity

Despite educators often quoting Socrates' phrase 'Know Thyself', most schooling does not encourage deep self-knowledge. At best, Socrates' phrase translates into 'Develop some personal opinions' or 'Realise that you are a citizen of a democratic country', but not 'Develop informed awareness how you are situated in the worlds of power, knowledge-making, possibility, creativity, resources, people, places and things'.

One of the important goals of a school should be to help students acquire the knowledge, attitudes, and skills needed to function effectively in a pluralistic democratic society and to interact, negotiate and communicate with people from diverse groups. A school, therefore, first needs to develop students' skills for knowing and appreciating their own culture in order to develop a sense of belonging while enabling integration with and appreciation of other communities and the wider world.

Schools are needed to develop student potential

The statement, 'It is necessary for children to have some systems and discipline' has unfortunately acquired negative connotations in the minds of people. Many believe that discipline is a suppression of natural freedom, that discipline means repression of the individual.

On the other hand, there is a positive interpretation of discipline. Discipline is the force that enables a person to fulfill their desires. It creates a channel for use of their energies and talents in the right manner. This type of discipline prevents chaos and provides the focus required to attain the highest of goals.

The difference between the negative discipline and the positive one is twofold. The source and purpose of the two are different. The negative form of discipline seeks to achieve the convenience of the person who imposes it from the outside. The positive type of discipline is

Figure 1.1 Each child has a different potential represented by the circles— the child on the left started with greater inner potential, but received less of the 'stretch' that good education gives

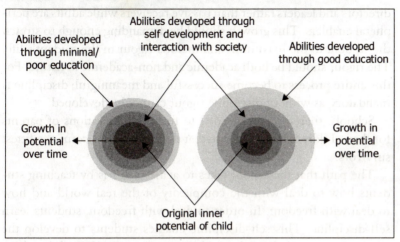

Abilities developed
through minimal/
poor education

Abilities developed through
self development and
interaction with society

Abilities developed
through good education

Growth in
potential
over time

Growth in
potential
over time

Original inner
potential of child

essential to help a person to stretch to the limits of their potential from within, it is uplifting and it is self-driven rather than externally imposed. Students need this self-discipline in their lives to understand and appreciate freedom to reach their true potential.

An enlightened educator understands that all students have a potential, which is dynamic, and that the purpose of the school experience is to bring out this potential in all students. It is only when this potential is tapped and honed that they can help students fully develop their abilities.

The process of learning should be such that it hones this potential in all students and ensures that this process of honing leads to the growth of the student. For that to happen, students can no longer be receivers of education. Today information is equally available to both teacher and student. So a school needs to be a place where students do things and adults react to what they do. As language and numerical skills are provided, students direct the move forward and set the course of the movement. The adults provide the pre-knowledge required for the direction that the student will take. In this scenario, the amount, speed and depth of what is to be learnt is fluid. But the process will enable them to cover everything that is relevant to their educational needs; that which is irrelevant will be left out.

Assessments will follow the same pattern—what will be assessed now will be rigour, ability to take risks, ability to stay till the end, sense of confidence, adaptability, commitment, thoroughness in research, awareness, connectedness and networking of knowledge. Schools need to focus on multi-skill building. In this school, students are dynamic directors and leaders rather than passive receivers while adults are peripheral enablers. This growth should be demanding enough to stretch the student to the maximum and include rigour in the student's life. The rigour should be both academic and non-academic in nature. For this entire process to become successful and meaningful, discipline is mandatory, as without discipline rigour cannot be developed.

Schools, therefore, are needed to fulfil the aspirations of parents for their children. Parents desire that their children become the fittest survivors.

The path that the school takes to achieve this is by teaching students how to deal with the complexity of the real world and how to deal with freedom. In order to deal with freedom, students learn self-discipline. This self-discipline enables students to develop the rigour that is needed to achieve their true potential. By helping them achieve their true potential, schools ensure that their students are the fittest survivors.

Throughout this process, schools need to remember at every stage in the child's development that they are only standing in for the parents. Schools exist as an institution because parents have entrusted their children to them. They exist because parents have this overwhelming need to nurture children who will be the very best.

In other words, *schooling needs to be a total experience*!

Summary

- The world is changing much faster than anyone ever anticipated. The pace of change, too, is increasing at an exponential rate, and obsolescence is almost instantaneous. Both adults and students need to cope with this rapidly changing world.
- Schools as we know them now were designed more than a century ago for that different age. In those times, schools were almost the last place for change, and in fact changed only after the change was established in the society outside.
- The entire concept and structure of a school needs to change. Revamping the existing education system with small changes will not serve the purpose.
- Now, educationists need to look ahead. They should attempt to build 'cybernetic' systems incorporating the latest advances in technology,

concepts and ideas to build institutions that not only meet the needs of the world as it is now, but also anticipate the future.

- Humans modify their environment in order to survive in the fittest manner, and through this constant modification create an increasingly complex world that suits their needs for fitness and survival.
- Schools provide a structure to the students, a kind of scaffolding that the students need to grow, learn and evolve.
- A school helps to bring discipline in the lives of the students and also helps them understand and appreciate freedom.
- Schools are needed to give a sense of identity to deal with diversity.
- School needs to be a place where students do things and adults react to what they do.
- In assessing students, schools need to focus on rigour, ability to take risks, sense of confidence, adaptability, commitment, thoroughness in research, ability to stay till the end, awareness, connectedness and networking of knowledge. The emphasis should be on multi-skill building.
- Schools can no longer work as ivory towers as before; they need to become bridges to the world outside. Schools must be networked to industry and other fields—arts, music and research—and to advances in higher learning and the world of work.
- Schools need to remember at every stage in the child's development that they are only standing in for the parents. Schools exist as an institution because parents have entrusted their children to them. They exist because parents have this overwhelming need to nurture children who will be the very best.

2

Learning

The learning process

A great school develops the learning abilities of its students

The purpose of a school is to provide an individualised education to its students—one that is relevant, develops critical thinking skills and stretches the potential of the student. The most important interactions in a school are the learning interactions of its students. Students are the sole reason for its existence. This existence is not just for the routine tasks of teaching the three R's to students—*the school caters to the students' individual as well as collective needs.*

In order to create successful human beings—success being defined as having the knowledge base, skills and attitudes to lead a fulfilled life and effectively engage in multiple adult roles such as that of a community leader, parent, worker—schools need to develop each student as a human being who can cope with and conquer life's challenges, both external and internal.

Great schools apply all their energy to development of a student into such a person. This development covers all aspects of the students' personality as well as their knowledge of the skills required to succeed in life. Even the focus on developing the other individuals in the school—teachers, administrators—is ultimately to benefit the students and to create a climate that is conducive to their growth. It is like what John Dewey talked about a Copernican revolution in which 'all the appliances of schooling would revolve around the child'. The fact that in a great school all members of the school move along a path of growth is one of the positive by-products of this focus on the students.

> A great school never forgets that it exists for the all round growth and development of its students and that all systems in the schools are created only for this aim.

Students learn in a protected environment

Schools therefore provide the scaffolding within which students are given exposure to learning experiences in a structured manner to achieve this optimal development. Schools ensure a protected environment where students are nurtured and gradually exposed to the real world in order to make them strong enough, and when the time comes, to stay ahead in the real world. This nurturing is a crucial quality of the schooling process.

Every gardener knows that a sapling needs to be initially protected and fenced within shielding boundaries. Once this sapling grows strong enough to survive by itself, the fences are removed and this young plant can now be moved to a setting where it will thrive. A great school not only performs this function of nurture, but also identifies for each of its students the environment where they will flourish once they leave the protective boundaries of the school. It is within the walls of this school that students will transform into successful and good citizens and find their rightful place in society.

Figure 2.1 A school gradually lowers the fencing around its students as they grow strong enough to manage on their own

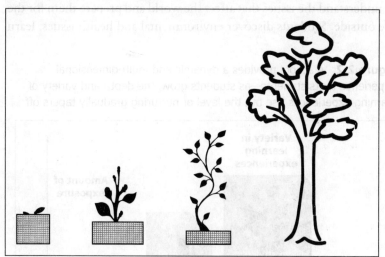

The fence that schools build around their students not only protects them from the outside world but also helps them develop their inner strengths. As part of the nurturing process, students learn to look within themselves and develop self-knowledge. They build self-confidence and faith in their talents. Each student recognises that they are in their own unique way a great and complete person who is learning how to make the most of her strengths and how to conquer her weaknesses. This understanding goes hand in hand with a student's understanding of the 'content' of academics, sports, various arts and the environment and society around her.

Students learn through gradual exposure to the external world

The nurturing and protective function of school does not mean that it does not expose students to the real world, but rather that this exposure happens within controlled circumstances through a variety of learning experiences. Students in a great school are made aware of a variety of aspects of the outside world that is appropriate for their age.

This may take the form of a visit to a factory for the youngest of the children and a short-term working session in that factory for the older ones. The protective walls of the school are gradually let down to expose children to the real world as and when they are physically, intellectually and emotionally prepared for this experience.

This shielded exposure to the real world progressively helps students to understand the issues that affect the world and prepare them for the life outside. Students discover environmental and health issues, learn

Figure 2.2 A school provides a dynamic and multi-dimensional experience to its students—as students grow, the depth and variety of learning experiences rise but the level of nurturing gradually tapers off

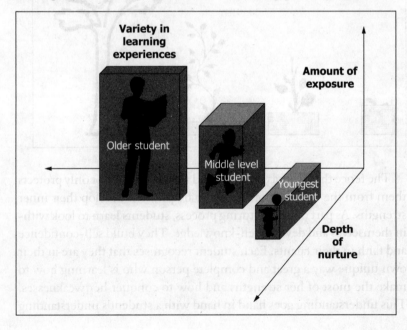

about the society, the community and the nation they live in, and inter-act with the privileged and the less privileged and with people from all walks of life. A great school introduces students to actual experiences and interactions in a manner that they can relate to and understand. This could entail something as basic as a visit to a market by ten-year-olds wherein they are asked to research about different products available in the shops, their prices, make comparisons and learn about money transactions.

Students learn by connecting the inner self with the outside world

The interactions with the real world are not only for the pure pursuit of information and experience for a successful career, but also a part of the pursuit of the inner self. Through their interactions with other communities, religions and philosophies of life, with the lesser privileged and those with special needs, students find connection and develop compassion and character.

Students explore questions regarding their self and higher purpose in life. They develop a craving of delight when encountering beauty, power, grace and love and the sheer joy of being alive. Students feel the awe and mystery of creating and creativity. They have an urge for transcendence—to go beyond their perceived limits in the mystic and real world. This connection with the inner self and introspection gives each student the ability not only to recognise both her own strengths and weaknesses, but also to face challenges with confidence.

A great body of research suggests that attention, learning, perform-ance, retention and recall all diminish when anxiety is high. Students

Ananya Lamba, a Class XII student, was very passionate about music. Her academic scores did not place her among the top scorers of the school. She was under tremendous pressure from home to improve her scores, which resulted in high anxiety about writing her pre-board psychology exam. Her school recognised her love for music and allowed her to blossom, while at the same time creating space for her to take an open book exam as an exercise to reduce her anxiety. This flexibility shown by the school gave a boost to her confidence. She pursued her music even more vigorously and became the Head of Art Council at her school. She also managed to get scores that got her into a good college in the city. Great schools provide such an environment by encouraging students to search for their own unique perceptions and new knowledge.

therefore need to learn and develop as human beings in an environment that reduces this anxiety—in surroundings that enable them to find inner peace and joy in new discoveries, yet simultaneously sublimating all inner discontent into a quest for achievements at the very limits of their abilities. In my more than two decades of teaching career, I have come across numerous positive instances where schools have nurtured talent.

Figure 2.3 A great school provides experiences that enable students to explore the outside world and teaches them to find connections between these and their inner self

Students learn to learn

A great school knows that there are no destinations—there are only temporary wayside halts in the journey of life. This journey is called learning, and the goal of learning is learning itself. An important goal of a great school, therefore, is the development of lifelong learners, people who seek out and create knowledge and understanding throughout their lives.

Every member of the school family needs to understand this principle and live according to it. By surrounding students with learners from all occupations, whether they are teachers or accountants or gardeners, the school sends a message to students that they will always be learners, and that adulthood does not mean an end to learning.

A great school deliberately and constantly reminds itself that it is here because it is in the business of learning and that every individual in the school needs to be a role model to the students by being a learner herself. More than the sciences or the arts that a student learns, this message of self-empowerment through learning is perhaps the most important.

We are not talking about the learning that comes out of textbooks, but about the process of learning how to become learners, a process that is far more complex than the academic content delivered by a school to its students.

If teachers act initially as facilitators who create a problem and provide the resources to solve the problem, students will come to find learning dynamic and exciting. Eventually, students will begin to define their own problems. They will be experimenting with and examining questions that are of interest to them. Learning will get an immediate purpose and meaning for students.

Students learn by doing things or making a discovery

In a great school, the student is actively involved and not just sitting and listening. The case study given here illustrates learning by doing or discovery learning. One student made a discovery about two colours mixing to form a new colour. Many students explored other colours to make new discoveries. They charted them and posted the chart so they could use it for a reference. They learnt by doing.

Karishma and Aman are painting at the easel in the art room. Each of them has a jar of blue paint and a jar of yellow paint. Suddenly Aman says, 'Look, Karishma, I made green!' 'How did you do it?' asks Karishma. 'I put yellow paint on top of my blue paint—yellow and blue put together make green!' says Aman. Other students gather around to watch and ask for a turn. The teacher wonders aloud what would happen if they mixed other colours. She allows the students to explore colours and help her chart their colour discoveries with words and colour samples.

Students also learn by seeing/observation, experimenting and memorising.

Elements of the learning process

Schools need to focus on the process involved in learning and schooling. They are so deeply set in their routines that they begin to lay more emphasis on the outcome than the teaching learning process itself. This is perhaps the reason why they have started accepting technical efficiency over a whole host of other efficiencies in school.

When schools begin to understand that outcomes are not as important as the process of learning, they will be able to impart multi-dimensional learning. Increasing the importance of the learning process does not lead to lesser outcomes, but leads to multi-dimensional outcomes.

Figure 2.4 An education system that is learning process-based and stresses outcome requires more effort and co-ordination among the teaching, managerial and administrative levels, and ultimately achieves multi-dimensional outcomes for students. A system that is based on routine and focuses more on outcomes requires less effort and no role for administration in the learning routine and leads to single dimensional outcomes.

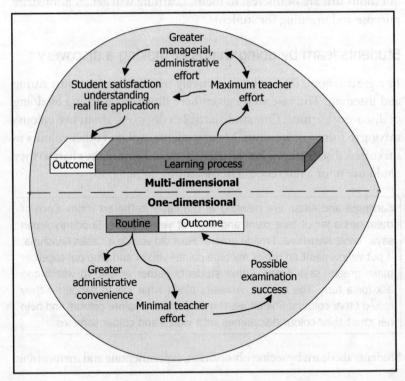

Joy

A school's aim should be that out of 100 per cent in any given performance, the process should carry a weight of 95 per cent and the outcome should carry a weight of 5 per cent. The difference between the emphasis on the process and the performance is the same as between learning for the joy of learning vis-à-vis learning for a test. Learning for the joy of learning gives students conceptual clarity and the ability to transfer theory into practical life. This learning and teaching is more difficult than learning and teaching for a test but is surely more satisfying.

Figure 2.5 The three cornerstones of the learning process are joy, ownership and decision making. The effects of these are all are interlinked—the outcomes have multiple roots.

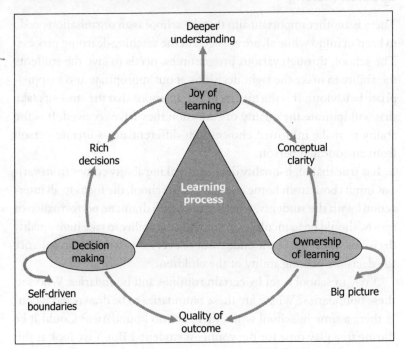

This is true not only in the field of academic achievement but in every sphere of learning that is involved in the school. For example, when a school puts up a music or drama performance for parents, teachers who are already carrying a full load of academic and other routine school work are given the additional responsibility for reaching the target of the performance. This target needs to be achieved through the difficult way of emphasising on the process and not through the easy option of just preparing for the final show without having the children learn from the process. What also needs to be noted is that the only compensation the teachers get from this exercise is the satisfaction of having done a great job. This reminds me of a history teacher who made her students learn about the historical monuments in the city through a project. She divided the class into groups of three and assigned a monument each to all the groups. Each group was expected to research on the history, architecture, ideology, culture and literature of the period and make presentations to the class. Then the class was taken out to visit the monuments, with each group acting as a guide to the class for the particular monument assigned to them.

Decision making

There is another important aim that the school as an organisation needs to keep in mind while all are engaged in the teaching-learning process. The school, through various programmes, needs to give the students the ability to make the right decisions about appropriate and inappropriate behaviour. It is the quality of the decisions that the students take that will indicate the quality of education they have received. It is the ability to make informed choices that differentiates a literate person from an educated person.

It is true that high-quality decision-making ability comes from various inputs both from home and school. In school, the focus in all interactions with the students, whether in class, a dramatic performance or sports, should be to inculcate in students the ability to take high-quality decisions. It should be the endeavour of every single teacher to enhance the decision-making ability of the children.

A day in school is set by certain routines and boundaries. Who sets these boundaries? Where are these boundaries to be drawn and when? Is there a time in school when there are no boundaries? Could it be during free play time for the youngest students? But if we look at this time closely, we find that even here boundaries are being drawn, even for the youngest students. There are norms of behaviour that are followed—and enforced, if necessary.

Does the 'authority' or the teacher necessarily set these boundaries? Can this be reversed sometimes? Can we—should not we—expect students to draw their own boundaries? Are boundaries only physical—in terms of behaviour? What about attitudinal boundaries? How should these be inculcated?

The boundaries here are of two kinds, the tangible and the intangible. Both are as important as the other. Just as the teacher's setting boundaries is important, students too need to set their own boundaries. As they grow, they need to rise to higher levels of self-driven attitudes and behaviour and lower levels of need for explicit guidance or boundary setting from teachers.

The process of learning must therefore bring forth in each student their ability not only to take informed decisions but also to take decisions that might not be popular. The process must empower students not to let a handful of people force them into action which they would not otherwise be a part of. The ability to take the best decisions, no matter how unpopular, distinguishes students in a good school from the lemmings who make up most of the world.

The lack of decision-making ability has led to most of the ills of the society. A handful of fanatics today in their misguided zeal for religion are holding the rest of the world to ransom, and it is the inability of the silent majority to stop this minority that's leading our world into a state of lawlessness. This is so often represented in our classrooms as well when a handful of students disrupt the classroom and the majority, who might internally not approve, sit silently and allow their precious time to be wasted.

If a school can develop students' ability to make informed choices that reflect what they really believe in, then it would have done a great job. For this, the school needs to create spaces in the school system to enable their students to take decisions. In the school where I teach, we have a 45 minutes slot—*Infinity slot*—four days a week where students can choose the activity they wish to do. The activities could include remedial classes, academics, sports, laboratory work, art, music, and library, question banks, chess, film making, recycling paper and interacting with one another. Besides, the students are free to choose their hobbies and specialisations, and the senior school students have the freedom to choose their summer internships. There is also an interactive life skills programme that builds their ability to make high-quality choices regarding their health, and risk behaviour. We also make use of a Reflection Sheet for the students to reflect on their actions and allow them to arrive at their own conclusions.

Students will take on the responsibility of making informed choices when they have a sense of ownership in the learning process. The process becomes meaningful when it can give a sense of ownership of the programme to the students, because in the long run that will pay off much higher dividends than having the students do something where they have no ownership. For this to happen successfully, the teachers

17

REFLECTION SHEET

Name of the Student .... Date ....

What I did: ....

....

....

Why I did it: ....

....

....

What Classroom Rule did I break? ....

....

....

What were my other options? ....

....

....

What effect did my behaviour have on my learning and on others' learning?

....

....

....

What will I do the next time? ....

....

....

What help/support do I need? ....

....

....

Signature of Student ....

Signature of Class Teacher ....

Signature of Tutor ....

will have to give up some of their teaching time to give the students the big picture. Once the picture is complete for the students then even with the truncated time, the outcomes will be reached in a much smoother fashion—and the quality of the outcome will be far better.

For example, the teacher asks the students to identify people who help us, instead of identifying the cobbler or the police officer as persons who help us. Going one step further, she asks students to bring their parents into the classroom. The parents tell the students how they are contributing to society as helpers. This would give even the youngest child entering school a sense of ownership to the new society in which she has now found a space. It would also help children look at their parents in a new and fulfilling way. In this way, the content has not been lost, but the process has evolved with the *bhagidari* (participation) of students. I remember a group of Class VIII students who were taken to visit a landfill site to understand the garbage disposal mechanisms. The students were horrified by the filth and squalor and the toxic fumes rising out of it and the fact that it was not an efficient system. On their way back to school, they discussed what they could do to improve the site's efficiency. They decided to take this as a challenge and address this issue before the Chief Minister (CM) of the state. They made a presentation to the CM on the basis of which the CM issued directions to the concerned authorities to act on the matter. Subsequently, the students sent a report to the CM and received a letter of appreciation from the CM for being responsible citizens.

The push and pull train

Teachers have become compartmentalised into their own pockets of teaching on the train of learning where the final station is the Class XII exam. Students are often but passengers on the train with the teachers being the engine pulling the different compartments along. However, learning should also have the 'push' factor in itself where the learners too guide the direction of learning. We need to examine whether the roles of the pusher and puller can be reversed from time to time. We also need to ask the question: would the process be the same if the eventual goal was changed?

Let us look at the process of learning. So far, the norm has been to define the content and the process is only a conveyer of this content. Why not reverse this mindset and have a content that serves the process? After all, it is the process that is supreme because it is without end. By and large, in most school systems the content that is learnt is

19

both necessary and sufficient: it is in the process of learning that major gaps remain.

For this process is the skill by which students will learn and continue to learn through their lives. Once they have internalised this process, whatever the content that they have to learn later in life, however much the world of knowledge may change, they will always be able to keep ahead. They know now how to learn. Whether it is to learn to read, listen, assimilate, disseminate, utilise and, most of all, create new information and knowledge. Of course, we need to have certain learning goals for students. But students themselves decide, based on the projects they are working on, how and for what the tools of learning are to be used and the direction of the movement. Teachers then set the processes that will help students reach those goals. As students reach higher levels of maturity in this learning process, they will learn to set goals for themselves and then plot a course to reach them.

Therefore on this 'push and pull train', students will do most of the 'pulling' themselves. Their ownership of the learning process, their ability to make informed decisions and their joy and satisfaction in what they are learning are the fuel that moves them forward. What is the role of the teacher then? Teachers do not 'push' content on to their students. They instead guide students through the learning process. The push is given through the implementation of a learning structure that enables students to work out their own routes and find their own way to their goals.

Continuity in the learning process

The learning goals that schools set are what they call the curriculum—academic, physical and emotional. In most schools, these goals are set at the beginning of the year and end with the academic year. At the beginning of every academic year, students move on to a new set of goals. There is currently in these schools a sense that the process of learning starts and ends every year, and therefore there is a sense of discontinuity. Learning cannot be efficient in such a scenario—it needs to have continuity.

At the same time, there also needs to be closure—students should be aware that they have accomplished some things, they have grown and they now need to move on to the next stage in their learning.

Often, a year is too short a time to complete a given process of learning before moving on to the next stage. It would be more effective to group years together. Two years of early childhood learning and the first year of regular school is when children learn to adjust to staying away from home. They also learn how to communicate, behave and interact with a larger set of people—teachers and peers. Year two is often a transitional year from the mainly socialisation skills of the early years and the moving on to more formalised academic processes of learning. Years 3 to 5, 6 to 8, 9 to 10 and 11 to 12 form cohesive groups of skill sets.

Learning goals therefore do not need to end every academic year but should flow through these age groups. There is now a longer time frame for putting goals and processes into place.

Figure 2.6 Vertical integration over the years—while the learning process needs to be a seamless process, gaining depth over the years, the other programmes need not end abruptly at the end of every academic or calendar year. The levels of continuity could be different for different programmes—and even for different subjects within a programme.

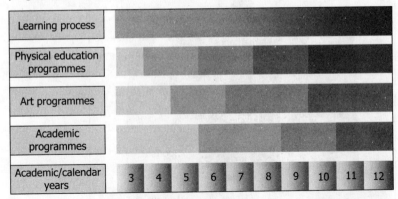

This kind of vertical integration of students across different years goes against the grain for many teachers who have taught in the conventional manner. Teachers will now need to look at not just their classes, but also co-ordinate with older and younger students and the teachers who are teaching them.

In order to make a success of such a system, a change is needed in the attitude of the teachers who will now need to work as teams rather than as individuals to take the process forward. After all, a teacher who is teaching components E, F, G of a process should have the confidence that the teacher before her has taught components A, B, C and D of that process. What this means is that, though divisions remain in a vertically integrated system, these divisions are more fluid than before.

Cohesiveness in the learning process

It is not only continuity that is needed in a learning process, but also cohesiveness and awareness of interrelationships. Often, a teacher imparts the knowledge of her specialisation to her students in isolation. When we move away from a system that teaches 'content' to a system that teaches 'processes', when a learning process therefore becomes more important than the content, then the teacher will no longer be teaching just a 'topic'. The process of learning implies that no content exists in isolation. Mathematics impacts a sportsperson as much as it impacts physics. Music is as closely linked with the biology of the brain as it is with the culture and history of a community.

Figure 2.7 No field of study exists in isolation and all are parts of the big picture. Stress on the learning process rather than on a 'subject' leads to an understanding of interconnections.

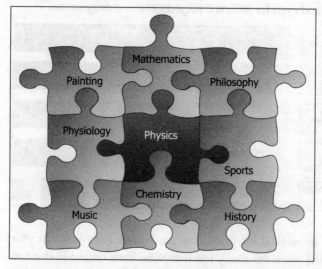

If the process that has to be learnt is, for example, the ability to research and collate information, for the process to be complete a student must be able to collate information not just on quantum physics, but also on its relationships with a variety of other disciplines, with technology as much as with philosophy. This is because in this learning scenario, it is not quantum physics that is important but the process of research and collation. If tomorrow the theories of quantum physics are rejected and replaced by some other theories, the student can use this same process to learn the new theory. Learning or memorising a single piece of content can only be useful in the short term—in the long term it can only lead to a dead end.

Therefore, the process of horizontal integration of learning across disciplines is as important as vertical continuity.

Horizontal integration too requires attitudinal change in teachers. Teachers need to be open to other disciplines and aware of changes and inter-linkages that keep emerging. A teacher teaching part B of a learning process needs to co-ordinate not just with those who teach A and C, but also with those who are teaching B1, B2 and B3 of the process.

A learning process is therefore not a point (content), nor is it linear (purely vertical or horizontal), but is actually a complex grid that stretches in all dimensions. Currently in many schools, different teachers teach single points in this grid, and the inter-linkages between these points are neglected. A school that teaches process rather than content, by teaching students the 'how' of learning, rather than the 'what' of learning, will enable them to discover and make effective use of these inter-linkages on their own.

In order to fulfil learning processes and goals and achieve self-empowerment, students need both to understand and to apply their understanding. The former is an introspective skill and it looks in-wards. The latter looks outwards at a practical world. Both skills need an awareness of and reliance on this grid of interdependencies. Both skills will develop when there is continuity in the learning process.

Figure 2.8 There are two main aspects of student empowerment: one is 'understanding' and the other is 'developing abilities'. What must be understood and the abilities that must be developed are all essential elements of the Learning Process.

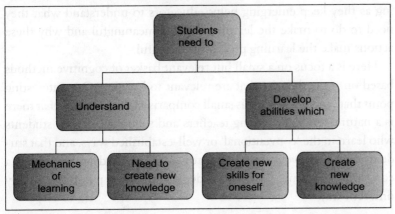

Learning and theories of cognition

Most of those involved in the field of education or genuinely interested in the overall development of students will definitely agree that the process of learning needs far more focus and attention in order to bring about this growth in the child. Students need to 'understand' and they need to 'develop abilities', but how do they go about it? What is the process by which learning actually develops in the minds of children (and adults)? What is the best and most efficient process by which educators can guide students to become independent learners?

These questions are not new. A vast amount of research has gone into understanding how people learn. Yet this continues to be an emerging field, and the abilities of the human brain will continue to surprise us for years to come. The field of cognitive science is very vast and very many theories abound, but at a practical level it is not possible for any school to apply each of these theories to the learning process that they follow in real life. While there is much that an educator can learn from studying this branch of knowledge of 'learning how to learn', and there are gems of wisdom in each of the various theories, yet there is also a lot of overlap between them.

Each school therefore needs to choose the theories of learning that suit the vision and philosophy of the school. This is a crucial decision and decision makers in the school system need to apply their mind to this task with all seriousness. Many schools just plunge into the task of schooling—get a curriculum, get some teachers and start the business.

Yet educators instinctively do know that this is not enough and add 'activities' to the curriculum to make it richer. Few think deeply about the reason for these activities. Studying the various theories of learning as they keep emerging helps educators to understand what they need to do to make the learning process meaningful and why these actions make the learning process meaningful.

Here is a focus on a small but relevant basket of cognitive methods based on some theories that are relevant to learning. One interesting point that emerges from this small comparison of theories is that there is a natural tendency among teachers and schools to favour students who learn in the 'conventional' or well-established ways, and that students who learn well—but differently—are at a disadvantage in such a conventional set-up. Each theory depicts this same point in a slightly different way.

Multiple intelligence theory

In his theory of Multiple Intelligences, Howard Gardner[1] postulated that there is no single 'intelligence' that can be measured by a single unified number, but rather that each child has a different way of perceiving and understanding the world. Gardner originally listed seven such Intelligences:

Figure 2.9 Howard Gardner broke away from the common notion of a single number that depicts the 'intelligence' of a human being. Different people have different intelligences and as a consequence learn differently and gain different types of mastery in different fields.

Verbal-Linguistic: *The ability to use words and language*	**Logical-Mathematical:** *Inductive and deductive thinking and reasoning, use of numbers and the recognition of abstract patterns*		**Traditional Academic**
Visual-Spatial *Visualise objects and spatial dimensions, and create internal images and pictures*	**Musical-Rhythmic** *Recognise tonal patterns and sounds, as well as a sensitivity to rhythms and beats*	**Body-Kinaesthetic** *The wisdom of the body and the ability to control physical motion*	**Vocational**
Interpersonal *The capacity for person-to-person communications and relationships*	**Intrapersonal** *The spiritual, inner states of being, self-reflection and awareness*		**Psychological**
Naturalistic *Ability to learn from the natural environment*	**Existentialist** *Asks questions and seeks answers about human existence*		**Philosophical**

Gardner has since added two more: *Naturalistic Intelligence* or the ability to learn from the natural environment and *Existentialist Intelligence* which is the intelligence that asks questions and seeks answers about human existence[2].

According to Gardner, people learn best when they use the intelligence that they favour. This is their 'learning style'. A musically gifted person will learn science better through activities that integrate music into the lesson. Any system of learning needs to strengthen not just

[1] Howard Gardner, *Frames of Mind: The Theory of Multiple Intelligences.*
[2] Howard Gardner, *Intelligence Reframed: Multiple Intelligences for the 21st Century.*

one or two types of intelligence, but rather all types of intelligence in order to develop balanced learning skills. A student, who uses a variety of intelligences to learn, will be better equipped to deal with different learning challenges.

It is very clear that a school needs to know the individual learning style of the student and to implement a two-pronged strategy. The first is when the learning process uses the particular intelligence that a student favours to make this student's learning more effective. The second strategy is to develop those intelligences in the student that are not her strengths so that she will learn in a balanced way and not be at a disadvantage when faced with situations that require different types of learning techniques.

Learning styles

David Kolb proposed another theory of learning styles that gives insight into the learning processes of the mind in his work on *Experiential Learning*[3]. He proposed these types of learners:

1. **Concrete and abstract perceivers**—Concrete perceivers absorb information through direct experience, by doing, acting, sensing and feeling. Abstract perceivers, however, take in information through analysis, observation and thinking.
2. **Active and reflective processors**—Active processors make sense of an experience by immediately using the new information. Reflective processors make sense of an experience by reflecting on and thinking about it.

Cognition and neuroscience[4]

These theories of cognition are based on the way the human brain learns and thinks. Research in neuroscience or the science of the brain and the nervous system has shown that there is a biological basis to perception, memory and learning. In the brain, the neo-cortex or thinking brain controls cognition, reasoning, language and higher intelligence.

[3] David Kolb, *Experiential Learning: Experience as the Source of Learning and Development*.
[4] Renate and Geoffrey Caine, *Making Connections: Teaching and the Human Brain*; Gerald Edelman, *Bright Air, Brilliant Fire: On the Matter of the Mind*; Bernice McCarthy, *The 4-MAT System: Teaching to Learning Styles with Right/Left Mode Techniques*.

Figure 2.10 Various theories of cognition have a certain commonality. They are all based on an understanding of how the brain works and show how minds work differently for different people and therefore learning too needs to be different for different people.

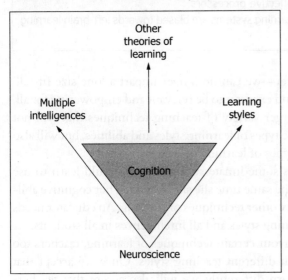

The brain is a very powerful parallel processor that processes both consciously and subconsciously, it processes wholes and parts and also processes information acquired through focussed attention as well as peripheral perception. The best learning happens when it is stored in natural spatial memory rather than in rote memory.

Most people do not use their entire brain to learn—most favour either the left or the right side. Those who favour the left brain are logical rational analytical objective, think sequentially and look at parts. Those who are right brained are intuitive, holistic, synthesizing subjective, think random thoughts and look at wholes.

Implications of these theories on human cognition

The most important implication of the theories of cognition is that the way learning happens is different for each individual.

As a consequence it becomes crucial that if learning has to be effective for everyone, then each individual needs to learn the way that is most comfortable for her. Each one of these very different theories have the

27

- Traditionally education has given most importance to just two types of intelligences—the Verbal-Linguistic and the Logical-Mathematical.
- Conventional education is biased towards people who are abstract perceivers and reflective processors.
- Most traditional learning systems are biased towards left-brain learning and rote memory.

same wisdom to offer—we can no longer impart a 'one size fits all' type of instruction and expect it to be relevant and empowering for all. We need to use a larger variety of teaching techniques that will not only appeal to diverse types of learning styles and abilities, but will also reinforce different types of learning in each individual.

Every student has some innate strengths and should learn to use these effectively; at the same time she should widen her cognitive abilities by learning many other techniques of learning. An educator needs to bolster up all learning styles and all intelligences in all students.

Just as students favour certain techniques of learning, teachers too are comfortable with different teaching styles. Once we accept that people think and learn differently, we will also accept that teachers need to teach differently. Allowing students to learn according to their individual needs empowers them; in the same way, allowing teachers to teach in their individual teaching styles empowers them too. Giving teachers the resources and the freedom to use different teaching styles sets them on the path to continuous learning and growth.

Roadblocks in implementing these cognitive theories

Even where educators understand how the brain works and how learning happens, instructional methods using this understanding are rarely implemented. Appropriate curriculum and instruction that leads to genuine learning and empowerment requires complex preparations and participation by educators. They need to give increased levels of individual attention to students. Other requirements are flexible structuring of curriculum, creating a wide variety of learning techniques and environments to reinforce the concepts through different ways and to give students a 'wholistic' perception.

Yet the entire schooling system works within several constraints— very large number of students, poor student–teacher ratio, need to cope with an inflexible and often outdated curriculum dictated by Education Boards, funds required to acquire experts and resources to support these instructional techniques, limitations of student time spent in school and not the least, need to motivate overworked teachers to put in the extra effort required.

Schools therefore need to tackle this issue on two fronts. First, development of positive attitudes towards the learning process—and to the hard work and effort required. A part of the process of developing the right attitude is through creating awareness about these techniques—how will teachers know that students learn differently if they have never heard of the Multiple Intelligence Theories? Given the state of teacher education programmes, it is entirely possible teachers have never heard of many of the theories of learning that are current today.

Second, the use by school of teaching and learning techniques that will actually make life easier for those who have to implement this process. There are many tools that are available today that can make learning a richer experience with a little planning and some extra effort. With various advances in the science and technology of learning, most educators realise now that much power is available to them today that was not available a generation ago.

Summary

- The core purpose of a school is to enable students to *learn* how to prepare for life.
- The school therefore nurtures its students and protects them until they are strong and independent enough to face the real world.
- It exposes students gradually to real-life experiences. As the fences around the students are gradually lowered, they learn about life in the outside world.
- Yet, in order to cope with the pressures outside, students also need to develop awareness of their inner self.
- Students thus need to learn that all knowledge—both within and outside—is linked. This makes the journey through which learning happens very important. This journey is the learning process.
- Stress on the learning process implies:
  - Multi-dimensional learning and long-lasting outcomes.
  - Joy in learning, therefore, greater depth of knowledge and better decision making.
  - Learning is not pushed onto the students—the students do the pulling instead.

Paraphrase!

29

- Learning does not happen in well-defined pockets—there must be continuity or vertical integration of learning.
  - Learning in any discipline is not isolated from other disciplines—there must be horizontal integration or cohesiveness in the process.
- Learning to learn leads to understanding and development of abilities.
- A child is strong enough to be prepared for life when she has the ability and strength to face tough situations and make tough decisions.
- Schools thus need to understand how the human mind learns. Various theories of cognition provide this knowledge.
- A crucial insight given by these theories is that though students learn differently, in real life, teaching systems teach only a few types of learners.
- Schools therefore need to consciously seek to use a variety of learning–teaching techniques and styles in order to reach out to every child and achieve the relevant education that is their most basic goal.

Curriculum

Great schools make education relevant

Schools need to provide relevant education. But what do we mean by 'relevant'? The curriculum for students in any school needs to prepare them for life; therefore, it needs to be relevant to what will be happening in the outside world when the student leaves school after several years. However, this question of relevance is often not part of the consciousness of schools at all. After all, any good school is affiliated to one Education Board or another, and the curriculum is therefore considered a given.

Relevance through proactive measures

Great schools do not take the easy way out. They develop their own systems to respond promptly to a rapidly changing society. These systems help their students cope with change without losing fundamental values. These schools do not follow a given board curriculum blindly. Great schools recognise the diversity in backgrounds, needs and aspirations of its students and develop a curriculum that meets these needs.

Most education boards provide a broad-based curriculum that deals more with the three R's than with life skills and citizenship. In most good schools, these gaps in the board curriculum are filled by special programmes developed by schools themselves. Great schools constantly seek ways to enrich the curriculum by offering more courses that supplement a strong academic programme.

Such schools take proactive measures to develop relevant curriculum. Curriculum in these schools is seen as an 'ongoing social process composed of the interactions of students, teachers, knowledge and milieu' (Catherine Cornbleth, 1990).They also closely interact with the industry and the economy to learn what skills the job market

Figure 3.1 Schools can either accept a given board-based curriculum and end their search there or interact with the world outside to create their own curriculum based on student needs

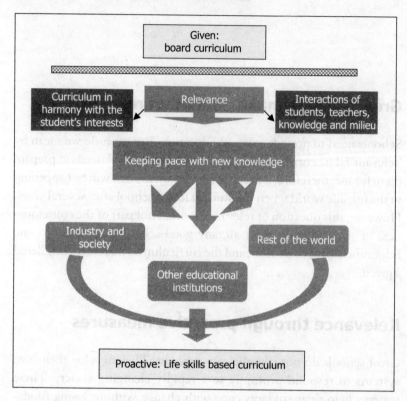

requires, and pass these on to their students. Great schools also do not function in isolation. They keep their doors and windows open to share and learn by interacting with other schools and students not only in the country but also in other parts of the world and thus increase the national and international awareness of their students.

Here, critical thinking skills and life skill development are closely integrated into the curriculum. Students have teacher mentors who advise and guide them in all aspects of their personal and career needs. Programmes to develop environment awareness, outreach programmes to teach social responsibility, camps for team building, career awareness programmes, summer placements and adoption of historical sites to develop national pride are some examples of steps that schools can and do take to make education a preparation for responsible and successful adulthood.

Integration of all student needs

Relevance of education is not therefore just about keeping pace with change. That is no doubt necessary for relevance—but it is not sufficient. Relevance implies a curriculum that is constantly updated with the knowledge that students will need when they leave school, with skills and values that will help them in adult life. It is a curriculum that implements all these in a scientific, efficient and productive manner. It is also a curriculum that has built-in flexibility to cater to the diverse needs, interests, talents and potentials of different students. Rigidly defined curricula can never be relevant to the large majority and often serve no one as they cater to the lowest common factor.

Right through our discussion, we have assumed that the curriculum prescribed by most Indian boards is neither sufficient nor relevant. What is the ground reality about Indian education systems? A closer look will help us to understand what a curriculum should not be, before we attempt to understand what it should be.

School curriculum issues

Indian schools are governed by several boards of education. Apart from national boards, such as the CBSE and the ICSE, there are several others with smaller jurisdiction—such as those at the state level.

Each one of these boards prescribes a curriculum that is given to schools to follow. Each of these conducts examinations at different points which is the basis for end of school certification and also serves as a gateway to institutions of higher learning—usually only within the jurisdiction of that board. A common thread that appears to run through all of these is the perception in the minds of most people that conduct of examinations is the paramount role of a board and the setting of the curriculum is the secondary role. This has led to an undue emphasis on examination. Students (as well as teachers and parents) believe that the entire purpose of education is to do well in examinations and failure is a major personal and social disgrace. In addition, this is also the cause for confusion of purpose—does a board exist to set curriculum, learning and teaching standards, or does it serve a purely certification role?

There is also a perception (but there are definitely qualitative variations between different boards) that the curriculum prescribed by many boards is outdated, irrelevant, full of inaccuracies and political distortions. It overloads the student with information merely to be memorised. The curriculum also lays almost no stress on pedagogy or the process of learning, being almost entirely focused on content. And where pedagogical instructions are given, they are obsolete. Schools have little or no flexibility in the content that must be taught, especially for Classes X and XII, and no significant or useful guidelines on the manner in which learning must take place. The last set of problems with the curriculum prescribed by boards is a consequence of the flaws in the system. Due to the poor quality of the curriculum and lack of trust in the system, the certificates issued by these boards carry very little value (ironically, given the stress on the examinations and the examination stress). They do not guarantee jobs and often are not even recognised in the higher education market.

Most students are compelled to seek other qualifications and therefore move in ever-larger numbers to degree courses even if they are not interested in higher education. This leaves a very large number of people over-qualified and under-skilled for the jobs that they seek. A direct consequence of this demand for degrees is the mushrooming of poor-quality colleges. The existing so-called vocational courses are poorly designed and lack prestige and have negligible recognition in the marketplace.

In addition, those who do wish to go in for quality higher education are forced in ever-increasing numbers to write additional examinations to seek admissions into the very few quality courses available to them. The lack of trust is reflected in all the quality institutions of higher education conducting their own admission test.

Reforms and the problem with reforms

In recent times, there has been a growing awareness of all these issues and many of the leading boards are in the process of revamping their curriculum and examination systems. The streams of reform are in a few distinct areas:

- Curriculum content revision (Modernisation and load reduction)
- New methods of learning (Experiential learning, project-based learning)
- Examination reform (from memorisation and comprehension skills to application skills and understanding)
- Teacher training

Figure 3.2 Each of the three aspects of the curriculum prescribed by Indian boards has many flaws. The learning process that needs to be central to the curriculum is neglected. Nor is there any certainty of purpose—do boards set the curriculum, or do they exist for conducting examinations?

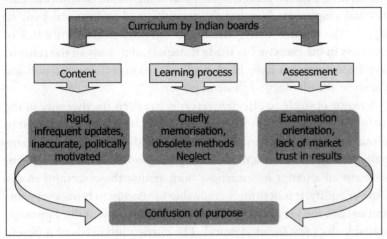

Though well intentioned, the common thread that runs through this entire reform process is a lack of 'wholism'. Each reform recommendation is made in isolation and without reference to the other aspects of the system. The content is revised by a different group of experts who have no link with the examination experts who, in turn, are working independently of the teacher trainers.

Given this scenario, pedagogical and learning process recommendations cannot be followed as the content requirements are usually in conflict with or totally unrelated to these. Many gaps remain, as reforms often do not even begin to touch on the aspects of the teaching-learning process. Planning, cross-integration of disciplines and defining processes for evaluating learning outcomes are some well-known gaps. An important drawback of this piecemeal approach is that nowhere has the purpose of the curriculum been clearly defined. The confusion over the certification versus learning skills role of the curriculum persists.

The reform process is also seen as a one-off course of action. While the students in the next few years may benefit due to currently modern content, given the rapid changes in knowledge, a few years later, the students will again be burdened by an obsolete curriculum. There is no in-built mechanism that looks at the need for continuous change and updates in curriculum content, let alone in the learning process.

It is said that sometimes the cure is worse than the disease—many of the reforms and changes have been made in a surreptitious and authoritarian manner. These have not been results of open discussion with leading experts, academicians, practicing teachers, students, parents and employers. Nor has the scientific and pedagogical basis (if any) for the reforms been shared with the public. The entire lack of openness in the exercise has made it suspect, and many of the reforms have been found to have been made to promote a specific political agenda or the ideology of those in power.

A major obstacle to effective reforms has been the diversity in the quality of students. From students in remote areas with the poorest of resources to students in metros with some of the best learning systems in the world, India has them all. Perhaps the biggest flaw of the reforms has been an attempt to somehow homogenise these sections in the name of equity. It is definitely creditable to attempt to bring every student to have the very best in curriculum and learning skills. However, equitable does not mean identical. The curriculum needs of different groups of students are different. What is needed is not 'one single size fits all' type of curriculum but several sets of curricula and in-built flexibility in each curriculum to suit the differences in students between and within groups. There has been no effort made to develop curricula

Figure 3.3 The process of reform itself is severely flawed—reforms of isolated elements of the curriculum have taken place, that too without any dynamic approach. Reforms have enforced unnecessary homogeneity and lack openness.

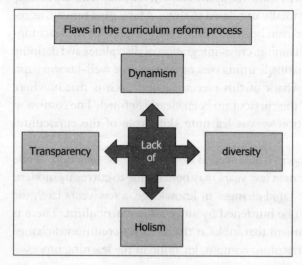

appropriate for different groups, and in fact it is considered politically incorrect to do so.

This survey of the ills in the current curriculum systems in this country does not provide us with any answers, but is a useful exercise as it raises some of the questions whose answers need to be found.

How should one design a curriculum? What should its purpose be? What should its structure be? What are the processes to be embedded in it? How can one make it flexible? How can one define different types of curricula? Is there anything that should be common to different types of curricula? How can we assess and evaluate the success of a curriculum? How can we make it dynamic?

Curriculum design

School curriculum over the years has had one characteristic. Every year they have a syllabus for each subject. Each syllabus is based on what is considered appropriate for a particular age group. Each subject is taught with little or no reference to other subjects, let alone the interrelationships between them. The sum of these syllabi is the curriculum. This is despite the fact that today we have a better understanding of what makes a good curriculum. We know that sets of unconnected linear subjects cannot be summed up to create a curriculum, however well the teaching of these may be. We also know that the curriculum is far greater than the sum of syllabi for different subjects or fields of knowledge. A syllabus is after all only a small part of the content of the curriculum.

What, then, is curriculum? The word 'curriculum' has its origins in the running/chariot tracks of Greece. In Latin, curriculum was a racing chariot; *currere* was to run. Curriculum is the sum of all activities, experiences and learning opportunities provided to the students under the auspices of a school. It develops through the *dynamic interaction* of action and reflection. Curriculum is, in fact, what actually happens in classrooms and includes informal contact between teachers and students as well as among the students themselves. It also includes what the teacher decides to do on the spur of the moment. So, there are three faces to a curriculum: the curriculum on paper; the curriculum in action; and the curriculum that students actually learn.

Before we design a curriculum, we need to ask a very crucial question: What is the purpose of the curriculum? Is it meant to provide a basic minimum certification? Should it prepare students for a vocation

37

straight after school? Should it enable students to compete for admissions to institutions of higher learning within the country? Should it enable students to seek admission anywhere in the world? Is it possible for a curriculum to be designed that meets all these purposes? Or is there some higher purpose for a curriculum? Are all these smaller parts, taken together, the main purpose of this curriculum?

Figure 3.4 There are varied reasons for a curriculum—yet all of them are just small elements of the chief purpose, preparation for life

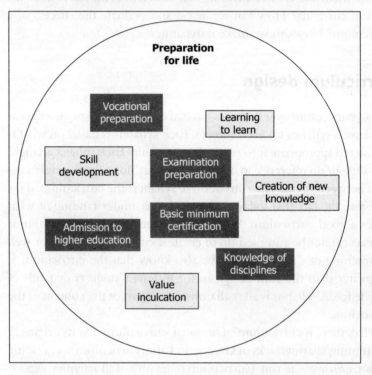

It follows then that in the constantly changing world, where knowledge is constantly becoming obsolete, a curriculum needs to lay more stress on the *process* of learning than on the *content* of learning.

The answer to the last question perhaps is closest to the truth. As noted earlier, a curriculum must prepare students for life: It needs to give them the skills, attitudes and values they need to meet the challenges when they leave school—whether these challenges relate to examinations, admissions or to becoming successful, responsible and productive citizens of the world.

A curriculum, therefore, needs to be designed not for the needs of today but for the needs of 15 to 20 years in the future.

Children learn in different ways—different groups of children with different backgrounds and experiences learn differently, and even within each (supposedly homogeneous) group, each student learns in a differ-ent manner. A curriculum needs to be flexible enough for each student to create her own process of learning and her own integrated learning web in a way that will be meaningful to her and yet meet both her content and outcome needs.

The process of curriculum design

The traditional process of curriculum design may be something like this:

Figure 3.5 Curricula have been traditionally designed in a linear and disconnected fashion. Each element exists independently and changes without affecting other elements.

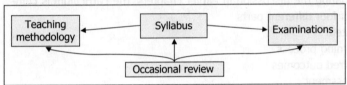

It is actually a set of four discontinuous and unrelated processes. A syllabus is created that defines the content to be taught in various inde-pendent disciplines. The methods of teaching this syllabus (blackboard, project work, homework and field trips) are laid out—either with or without linkage to the content. Examinations are designed based on the content of the syllabus. The syllabus, the teaching methodology and examinations in such a system are independently defined. The process of curriculum review is not a part of the system but happens whenever it becomes apparent that the current system is not working, or when protests against an 'obsolete curriculum' become too loud to ignore, or when political mileage can be extracted from change.

That there are major gaps in this process is evident, and many questions are left unanswered. The science of learning is dealt with at a very superficial level.

In this system, the purpose of:

The Syllabus: To teach students as much as possible about various disciplines, topics and concepts
Different Teaching Methods: To add variety to the syllabus
Examinations: To test students knowledge (and perhaps understanding) of the syllabus, to give a certificate

39

You may observe that the purpose of each component in the curriculum is different and more of an afterthought. Obviously, we cannot leave the curriculum development process at this level. The entire process of learning, teaching and evaluation needs to be interlinked at every step and constantly referred back to the purpose or vision of the curriculum.

Curriculum components

If we start with the premise that the purpose of a curriculum is to prepare students for life, then the design of the curriculum falls into place.

> Consolidating the discussion in earlier chapters, the curriculum is composed of four different parts
> - Content
> - Learning process
> - Desired outcomes
> - Assessment

Content

We have already seen that in an ideal curriculum, the content needs to be always at the *cutting edge*—students have to be prepared for life 15 to 20 years in the future to be at the forefront in any field/movement. The content also needs to be *broad-based*—today few people remain in the same profession for life. Broad-based content will enable students to make connections, to acquire skills that they can use for a variety of purposes, solve problems by looking at multiple perspectives and incorporate information from different fields, all of which will be an essential ingredient for success in the future. Finally, the content should also lead to an understanding of the *links* between different disciplines and concepts. The movement toward a global economy and international connections, as well as rapid changes in technology, is pushing learning toward integration. By linking subject areas, one can provide meaningful learning experiences that develop skills and knowledge, while leading to an understanding of conceptual relationships. For example, rather than studying maths or social studies in isolation, a class might study a unit called 'The Sea', using maths to calculate pressure at certain depths and social studies to understand why coastal inland populations have different livelihoods.

No profession exists in isolation today. As we change focus from industrialisation to services, greater productivity no longer means knowing more and more about less and less, but rather knowing how everything connects and how to utilise effectively these inter-connections. The content needs to be delivered to students in the form of non-linear content webs.

Figure 3.6 The curriculum develops through the dynamic interaction of action and reflection. The content of the curriculum needs to be innovative, inter-linked to all disciplines and therefore broad-based. In this curriculum, the actual disciplines are not defined separately but are a matter of choice.

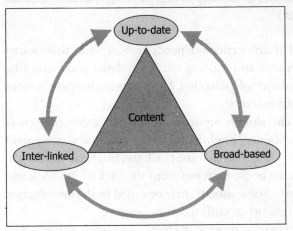

All this implies building in processes for continuous update of content in the curriculum. There are two ways of doing this. At present this update is external—committees and boards decide on what to update and when to update. If the board wishes to continue to keep total control over content, they could have an annual review and a system where it is compulsory to delete content—say 10 per cent in every discipline—every year and replace with the latest advances in this field. It is crucial to delete before adding, otherwise, the consequence as we have seen is just a greater load on the student. This method will require an increase in bureaucratic procedures and therefore may be acceptable!

The second method, which is likely to truly keep content relevant and at the cutting edge, is to give schools and teachers far greater autonomy in choosing content than is presently the norm. The role of a board would be to give guidelines to schools on how to decide the content and to ensure that standards are met, rather than actually spelling out the content chapter by chapter.

41

Learning and teaching processes

What are the guidelines and standards on which the course content of the curriculum is to be developed? In this scheme, we cannot define content independently from the learning and teaching process. The four cornerstones of this process, which we have discussed earlier, are:

- Individualisation in learning and teaching styles
- Continuity through vertical integration or continuity over time
- Cohesion between different disciplines through horizontal integration
- Cutting edge learning technology—using processes as discovered by research in the science of learning (critical thinking, relevance, creation of new knowledge)

Course material in any curriculum needs to incorporate these learning processes. Content and process are interrelated and cannot be developed independently of each other. How learning happens is more important than what is learnt.

In a traditional curriculum, students are taught various subjects—history, geography, science, English and so on. Each subject is taught in the same manner—a textbook, some chalk and blackboard classes to explain the text in the book, exercises from the back of the book and tests based on the text. Some subjects may be varied by the introduction of laboratory experiments or visits to a museum.

Essentially, the learning process is identical for each subject. The result is a tendency for students to memorise the contents of the textbook (and often the laboratory experiment procedure too!) There is no connection between history and physics or physical education and mathematics. What is learnt in one academic year is often forgotten the next year—there is no connection over the years, and every student is taught in the same manner.

Instead, a great school incorporates varied learning processes for each discipline (subject) or sets of disciplines that meets the diverse needs and aspirations of its students so that the curriculum is:

- Connected—topics within a discipline are connected.
- Sequenced—similar ideas are taught in concert, although subjects are different.
- Webbed—thematic teaching, using a theme as a base for instructions in many disciplines.
- Threaded—thinking skills, social skills, multiple intelligences and study skills are threaded throughout the disciplines.

- Integrated—principles that overlap multiple disciplines are examined for common skills, concepts and attitudes.
- Networked—student directs the integration process through selection of a network of experts and resources.

The curriculum itself could comprise:

- Language and communication
- Mathematical studies and applications
- Social and environmental studies
- Physical education
- Creative and aesthetic activities such as art and design, drama, music.
- Life skills education that includes critical thinking, problem-solving, decision-making and communication skills, conflict resolution, healthy relationships, self-esteem, positive thinking, time and stress management, goal setting, sexual and reproductive health, gender and so on
- Technological activities and applications
- Content appropriately related to the social and academic changes in the society
- Content necessary for students' entry to college or university
- Keeping abreast of workforce requirements and incorporating those skills in the curriculum
- Value the importance of multi-cultural education and encourage students to experience other cultures

The curriculum could be so structured that one course is learnt through classroom lectures, the second through an independent research paper, the third through a group project, the fourth through practical experimentation and the fifth through interactions with people in the real world.

There could be many more such *process-differentiated courses* and students could choose the five types that suit their learning styles and potential. Each course can deal with a different discipline or set of disciplines and students could choose which discipline to study in which style. Such a structure lends itself to different individual learning styles, to critical thinking, to creation of new knowledge. As the curriculum is not defined in terms of content but in terms of processes, the content would always be relevant and cutting edge.

The goal of such curriculum is to learn how to learn. Once different learning processes are defined in each course framework, they can be matched to the content that is relevant at that point in time. Each of these courses integrates different sets of disciplines at different levels

In this curriculum, we do not have five different sets of courses that are differentiated by the subject or discipline, but are otherwise structured exactly alike. Instead, we have different types of courses that are structured differently to enable learning through different types of learning processes.

43

of horizontal or vertical integration. Each uses different techniques for individualised learning. The structure of the course processes too may keep changing with advances in the science of learning.

Outcomes

We have said that content is not important; what is important is the learning process. But then what is the purpose of the learning process? We need to answer this question to decide where education is going to take us and which learning process to use in any course of study. To do this, we take the purpose of our curriculum—'preparation for life'—and break up this purpose into smaller learning outcomes.

Figure 3.7 Outcomes can be categorised as Individual, Societal and Spiritual. Yet many outcomes are a combination of these, for, as in other cases, no outcome can exist in isolation.

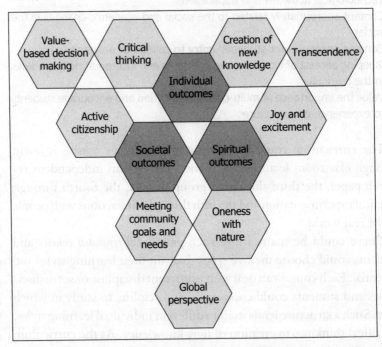

Those processes (or, in our lexicon, courses) are then chosen that enable students to reach these outcomes. While critical thinking and creation of new knowledge will form the common thread in all the courses of study, societal outcomes will come out of courses that lead to interactions with the outside world and to those where students work in groups and learn to interact with each other. Spiritual outcomes come from choice—students choose those disciplines or subjects that give them the greatest joy in learning and enable them to achieve transcendence.

> Thus, *outcomes* turn out to be our starting point and not the content, as was the case with the traditional curriculum. Outcomes are derived from the purpose and vision of the curriculum; the learning processes are chosen to achieve these outcomes and the content fits into these learning processes.

Figure 3.8 At the core is the vision for the curriculum—this could be different for different education boards. Based on the vision, we need to decide what the learning outcomes should be. The learning process is what achieves this vision and the learning outcomes. Content is part of an indefinable periphery as it is constantly in a state of change.

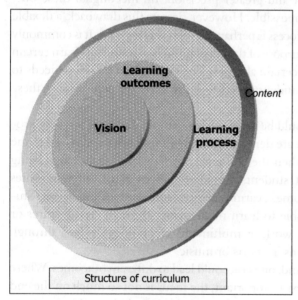

Outcomes and standards

There can be two ways of looking at a curriculum—the standards-based curriculum and the outcomes-based curriculum.

The standards-based curriculum applies minimum standards to every item in the curriculum—the content, the process and the out-comes. The end result in such a curriculum could be that it reduces all to the lowest common acceptable denominator. In every society, there will be certain members who do not reach minimum acceptable standards, and so there is a temptation (and perhaps political pressure) to lower standards to accommodate them.

How would we measure, in such a system, that the prescribed standards have been met? It can only be done through examinations. In this approach, examinations become all-important and end up becoming the entire purpose of the curriculum. Examinations become the standard by which the student and the curriculum are measured. Given that the entire process of setting standards is arbitrary, there is no way that an examination can be the only way to judge a student's abilities. Certainly examinations cannot be the purpose of the curriculum.

The outcomes-based curriculum[1] tries to overcome this by setting up a set of learning outcomes that all students must reach. A drawback of this method is the temptation to refine these learning outcomes to levels of greater and greater precision, till meeting all these outcomes becomes impossible. However, despite this drawback, a flexible outcomes-based process is perhaps the best way forward. It is commonly accepted that the purpose of the curriculum is that students learn certain skills and develop certain abilities. The curriculum therefore needs to design tasks that students need to do in order to demonstrate these abilities.

These tasks should be set in such a manner that both learning processes and content are demonstrated. Different tasks could lead to the same outcome: When the content knowledge and skill that is being learnt is important, students should be allowed to use different routes to reach this outcome. Learning basic mathematics is important. Students should be able to learn mathematics through class lectures or individual project work or multimedia technology or even through real-life applications in sports or music.

On the other hand, one task could lead to different outcomes. Where the learning process is important, the focus is not so much on the end content, but on learning a certain method or skill. Students need to learn how to stand in front of an audience and present an idea. They need to be able to use technology to make their presentation effective. It does not matter if this presentation is on soccer or the history of Jazz or advances in genetic technology.

---

[1] Outcomes are explicit statements of the knowledge, skills and understanding expected to be learnt by students.

Whether the focus is on content or process, the student is given choices to select the learning path that is individually most productive and joyful.

Evaluation

Any curriculum system needs to have built-in evaluation measures. Evaluation is seen as the end of the learning system. It is often wrongly assumed that evaluations are independent of all the elements of the system that went before it. This is a consequence of the 'linear' vision of a curriculum.

It is a fact that no curriculum is linear—it is always a cycle with several inter-dependent cogs turning within the cycle. Therefore, the design of the evaluation mechanism affects the learning outcomes, the process and the content. An examination that lays stress on memorisation will lead students to develop memorisation skills, to focus on content that needs to be remembered rather than understood or analysed. The outcome will be students who can repeat but cannot create knowledge.

If once again, we come back to the purpose of our curriculum—to prepare students for life, then, the purpose of evaluation is twofold:

- Can we measure if the curriculum does prepare students for life?
- Can we measure how well the students are prepared for life?

Student Evaluation

To evaluate student performance, a variety of evaluation methods will lead to a better assessment of her abilities and achievements. Evaluation methods need to be designed not only to test the content knowledge of the student, but also to check if the student has achieved the desired learning outcomes.

Does a student have critical thinking skills—the ability to apply, analyse and synthesise? How well prepared is she for the transition from school to college? What is her involvement with society? Does learning excite her? No single examination can answer these questions, however well designed.

The evaluation of a student thus needs to combine tests and examinations with projects, thesis and portfolios, tasks, performances and exhibitions, journals, experiments with interviews and discussions and

Figure 3.9 An evaluation based on the assessment of only content knowledge degenerates into a vicious cycle of memorisation exercise and examination orientation. Meaningful evaluation is possible only with the measurement of varied learning outcomes based on different assessment techniques and the built-in feedback completes a beneficial cycle.

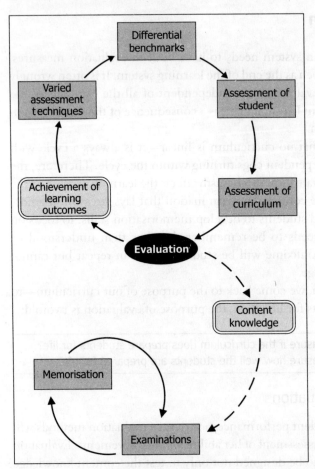

the perceptions of her teachers and peers. Besides this, a student evaluation needs to test the level of her fitness in each of these dimensions as well: rigour, ability to take risks, sense of confidence, adaptability, commitment, thoroughness in research, ability to stay till the end, awareness, connectedness and networking of knowledge.

Students also need to include their own perceptions of their abilities: in other words, a self-evaluation. Even young students need to learn how to evaluate themselves objectively, because no one knows them better than they do.

This is where the role of achievement standards comes in. Standards cannot exist independently, nor can they be ends in themselves. Standards as currently defined are just a basic minimum score that students must achieve in an examination.

Instead, standards need to be defined differently—as part of a system that integrates differential evaluation techniques to required learning outcomes. There is no single standard—for if there were, it would have to be the minimum standard. Instead, these standards are defined for different levels of progressively increasing challenges. They ensure that the measurement of learning outcomes is objective and fair and provides benchmarks for comparison.

Without standards, measuring learning outcomes can degenerate into a vague and subjective exercise that pulls everyone down, not up. Therefore, we need to exercise considerable caution with standards—both in terms of definition and application.

Curriculum evaluation

Measuring student performance is only one aspect of evaluation; the other is to evaluate the curriculum itself. A system of feedback is required for every component and every process in the curriculum. Without this, even the best-designed curriculum will become static, and sooner or later irrelevant. Any good curriculum design will have such a system of feedback built into the system.

In such a design, at every stage various stakeholders—students, teachers, parents, administrators and employers—will have access to a forum for giving their feedback. This feedback is then analysed and relevant changes are ploughed back into the system. In such a curriculum, changes do not happen only when external pressures become too strong to withstand, rather more due to internal built-in processes.

Just as there is a learning process for student learning, so also there are learning processes for all stakeholders in a school. It is part of the learning process of teachers to plough back the feedback on the successes and failures of earlier years into the curriculum of the future. Similarly, the management and the head of school too constantly review what went right and what could be made better, not just for the students, but for the teachers and the administration as well.

Change, in a well-designed curriculum, is therefore a consequence of well-planned action and not a hasty reaction to emergencies.

One of the crucial essentials for this process of evaluation to be successful is the gathering and analysis of data. In the earlier times this would have been an impractical and time-consuming procedure, but today we live in times of easy access to information technology and

Figure 3.10 The curriculum web consists of the four main components of the curriculum—learning outcomes, learning process, content and assessment. For the curriculum to be effective each of these elements must be linked to each other and a system of feedback needs to be intrinsic to the system.

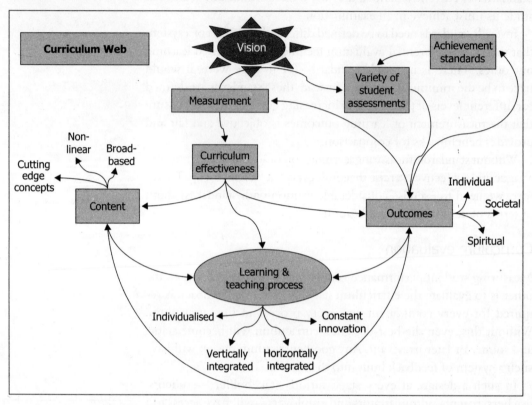

have several tools that make the analysis of any system possible based not on perceptions and beliefs but on actual data.

Technology can also speed up the time it takes for the analysis to happen and the results and conclusions to be ploughed back into the system. It can also speed up the links between the various elements of the curriculum system—the outcomes, the process, the content and the evaluation.

The four elements of the curriculum model set forth above can be seen to be a complex web of links with each other, unlike the conventional model where each element exists in isolation or relative isolation.

Here, changes in one part of the web leads to changes across the entire curriculum. Yet at the same time, this model has in-built feedback loops and flexibility for a dynamic process of improvement to avoid the stagnation trap of static one time updates to the curriculum that we see at present. These feedback loops also ensure that the system remains stable.

The question however remains: can such a system be implemented? This system is based on current wisdom and, given the will to do so, educational institutions and organisations the world over can implement such structures.

Summary

- Education needs to be relevant to real life, so schools need to interact and learn what is pertinent from the outside world.
- This relevance needs to be built into a curriculum that integrates all student needs.
- The main problems are irrelevant content, examination orientation and no role for the learning process.
- Though some reforms have taken place in recent time, these have been static, piecemeal, non-transparent and made with no recognition of diversity of student potential and needs.
- There is therefore a pressing need to formulate a curriculum that meets the goals of preparation for life and sees all other goals as smaller components of this goal.
- The focal point of this curriculum would be the learning process based on an understanding of learning outcomes.
- Content would be a consequence of learning and not the cause.
- Assessment will assess not only students, but the entire curriculum process.
- The curriculum thus becomes a dynamic set of different processes that continuously interact with each other—in other words, an inter-linked web.

4   Assessment

Great schools assess students 'wholistically'[1]

For many schools, assessment means measuring the student's success.
Often the chief indicator of this success is excellence in performance
at examinations. Great schools assess success by seeing if their students
are successful in their profession and are constructive members of the
society and good human beings.

In great schools, both the 'how' and 'why' of assessment are different
from the conventional understanding that holds that examinations alone
can assess student success.

The purpose of assessment is not just to measure success. Assessment
is an integral part of the learning process and meant to ensure that
learning goals are met. It is the crucial link between effective teaching,
student learning and learning outcomes and goals of students. Assessment is used to gather useful information on the particular knowledge
and abilities students have or have not developed in ways that will guide
further learning and the improvement of curriculum and instruction.
Assessment, thus, serves the purpose of enabling schools to chart a
future course of action for students, to make an Individual Education
Plan (IEP) for every student that will create an optimal future for them.
This IEP determines the curriculum of the students.[2]

*Thus, assessment becomes the first step in the learning process of the student
and not the last one.*

Assessments are not done in isolation—they are always linked to
the learning outcomes and the goals of the student. An examination

---

[1] The word holistic has 'hole' in it. A hole implies emptiness. The word is instead
spelt 'wholistic' in this book to stress that the schooling of students should be looked
at as a complete experience.

[2] A great school recognises that every student has special needs and requires an
IEP. This plan understands the student's past and looks at the student's current strengths
and weaknesses and then builds a future growth plan for them. The IEP is based on
the student's needs and not on the teacher's abilities or an education board's administrative convenience.

only evaluates what a student knows or does not know. The assessment evaluates what the student needs to know in order to succeed in life. It evaluates how much further the student needs to travel in order to reach the destinations of survival, fitness and leadership. The assessment, hence, helps students learn as well as document and evaluate their learning. It recommends the best path forward for this journey.

Assessments contain within them an evaluation of how much of a student's achievement is due to Nature and how much is due to Nurture. This is required because assessments.

Assessments consist in evaluating how much of a student's achievement is due to Nature and how much due to Nurture. This is required because assessments are also the engines that boost the student's dynamic potential. Every student has a dynamic potential, and this consists of her inner potential, the environment in which she lives and the learning inputs that she receives. Over time, even if a child did not go to a school, this potential would keep changing both as part of her inner growth as well as the changes in the environment.

In great schools, this dynamic potential of the student is constantly evaluated. The school then learns the student's strengths and weaknesses. It uses this feedback to reinforce the strengths and to eliminate or minimise the weaknesses.

A cyclical process is therefore generated, where assessments constantly influence the learning programme of the student. Programmes for reinforcements of strengths and remediation of weaknesses are developed for individual students based on this feedback.

As they grow older, children reach milestones of development in different areas at different times. These milestones do not change every year, but across a band of years. At some point during this band, almost every child will reach the milestone. The exact point of achievement within the band of time will vary for every child, based on her inner potential, multiple intelligence strengths and the effectiveness of the learning programme that has been devised for her learning styles. It is also a function of her attitudes and the level of effort she has put in. The assessment cycle, therefore, does not necessarily span just one academic year.

In consequence, assessment instruments need to be designed to judge if the student has reached her milestone within the band that has been defined for her age group. These milestones are the benchmarks for assessment.

Figure 4.1 The Assessment Cycles: Every child comes to school with an existing potential and from a given environment. She needs to go through several assessment cycles to increase her potential as much as possible.

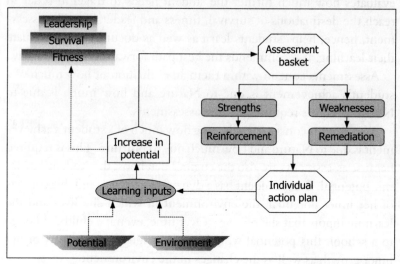

Thus, the purpose of assessment is not just to measure whether a student is successful or not, but to create an action plan that will definitely make the student succeed—at her own terms and according to her potential. I remember an instance where a math teacher identified two students in her class who were much ahead of others. While teaching 'determinants' to the rest of the class, she allowed them to practise 'integration' and monitored them individually, thereby honing their exceptional abilities.

Evaluation tools

Great schools monitor and evaluate students through varying assessment periods and in every aspect of the students' personality. They assess all aspects of the growth of the student—intellectual, physical, social and emotional.

The evaluation gives teachers and parents continuous feedback not only of achievements in academics, arts and sports, but also on character development profiles with strengths, weaknesses and attitudes of the student. The assessment gives suggestions for the future path of the student in each of these areas of development and growth. This feedback is then used to take actions that will increase the dynamic potential of the student.

The role of assessment, therefore, becomes critical for a learning plan that will affect the future development and growth of the student. The need for accurate assessments is crucial. How do we make these assessments accurate?

Assessments can be made accurate by ensuring that evaluations are elements of a process and not an isolated event, by ensuring that evaluation is not teacher-centric, and by using a variety of evaluation tools.

Just as learning is a process, so too assessments are a process. Just as learning is a student-led process that aims to meet the aspirations of parents, assessment is a process that requires student and parent participation. Self-assessment by students is an important part of the process.

Teachers collate their own assessments with the self-assessment of students as well as assessment inputs given by parents, to get an accurate picture that reflects the abilities and personality of the student.

For the same milestone or benchmark, there can be different perceptions of achievement. The yardsticks used by teachers to judge children will be different from those that parents and the children will use. All these different perceptions are critical for an accurate assessment.

The deviations and the concurrence in the separate measurements by teachers, students and parents need to be compared and analysed. The gaps and differences in these three inputs lead to introspection and this leads further to the development of an accurate learning plan for the child. This constant comparison of assessments iteratively leads to the most effective goals for the students and sets her learning path.

Thus, teachers, students and parents measure the student's achievement against set benchmarks. These are based on the concepts taught in the class in different learning areas. They also use a basket of instruments—assessment is not only one-dimensional examination. Great schools rely on a multiplicity of evaluation tools to measure and assess the learning of students. Great schools know that examinations are just one aspect of the feedback of the learning process. These schools use other evaluation systems in conjunction with examinations. Besides examinations, evaluation could include projects, thesis and portfolios, tasks, performances and exhibitions, journals, experiments, interviews, discussions and the perceptions of teachers and peers.

Assessments are therefore a combination of many types of evaluation—both short-term and long-term. There are quantitative and qualitative measurements. There are measurements that look at the perspective of the teacher, the student and the parents. These are held at different units of time and for different units of learning material and evaluate different approaches to learning.

Figure 4.2 The assessment basket needs to incorporate several different types of tools in order to capture the true capabilities of the student and to make diagnostic recommendations for her based on the evaluation

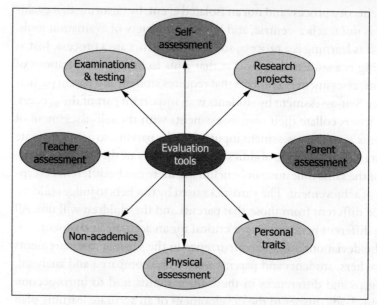

The variety and the different perspectives ensure accurate assessments that lead to an appropriate Individual Education Plan—and as each assessment leads to a better understanding of the student, it affects the IEP in a dynamic manner. Assessment is therefore a cyclical process that starts when the student enters the school and continues right through until she is ready to take on the world outside the walls of the school.

Examinations

We live in a society today that gives paramount importance to examinations. Right at the early childhood stage, toddlers are taught how to 'pass' the entrance examination of their nursery school and this preparation for examinations does not end at any part of the education process—whether it is board-level examinations in school or the examinations for admission to colleges and institutions and for jobs.

Does our education system today take the students through the pillars of equity, relevance and excellence to develop students' imagination, creativity, spirit of enquiry and adventure? On the other hand, does it only develop a limited part of the student towards examination, career and a job? Does this in turn develop only a limited part of their potential? The questions that we need to ask ourselves are: Does the board prescribe a syllabus? Do the objectives, learning outcomes and course material prepare the students to cope with the challenges of growing up? Alternatively, does it act as a filter to seek admission to colleges?

However, even though the focus should be on 'wholistic' assessment, given the current examination orientation in the society, and lack of reforms, schools cannot neglect to teach students examination skills. Examinations therefore do hold a special place among all evaluation tools—more for social and historical reasons than for cognitive or pedagogical reasons.

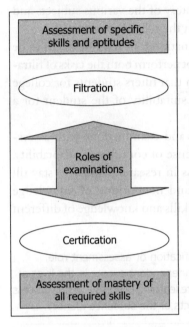

Figure 4.3 There can be two roles for examinations; each has its own structure

Great schools counsel students and parents (and teachers!) on examinations—and work towards changing the mindset that they are an end in themselves. They teach students how to maximise performance, and how to cope with examination pressure. Students and teachers attend workshops on time and stress management. Students are encouraged to choose one from a variety of examination boards—national, international or open school—that suits their aspirations and abilities best.

We can envisage two roles for examinations. One is the filtration role of examinations. This is the simpler role. The examinations are conducted to select students for further studies at the next rung of the ladder of education. Each stage in the education process has an

The ground reality in India is that board examinations purport to perform both filtration and certification roles—that of filters to college placements and a capping role that certifies that students have achieved the necessary standards in meeting the requirements of a prescribed syllabus.

examination that filters students who are then permitted to move onto the next stage.

The second role of examinations is that of *certification*. This examination assesses whether students who have followed the syllabus prescribed by a board have actually reached all the learning outcomes prescribed by the appropriate standards. Thus, this examination sets the standard of the student in her mastery of the various subjects and skills learnt during her participation in the school programme.

Obviously, the format of the examination for each role needs to be different—the same examination cannot perform both the tasks of filtration and assessment. The examination that filters students for college needs to take into consideration the suitability of the student for a specific course.

An evaluation that combines tests and examinations with assessment in rigour, ability to take risks, sense of confidence, adaptability, commitment, efficiency, thoroughness in research, ability to stay till the end, awareness, connectedness and networking of knowledge also assesses a wide variety of student skills and knowledge of different

Figure 4.4 In order to meet their certification or assessment role, examinations must not be isolated and independent events in the lives of students—they need to be part of the entire learning process and this process must be closely interwoven with all aspects of the student's identity

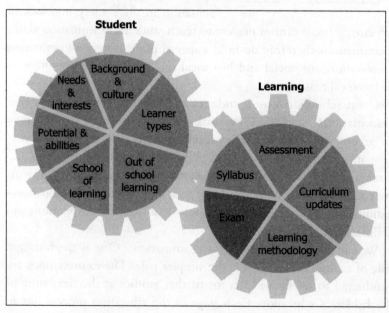

fields of learning and different skill sets. It is an overall assessment of the student's achievements, strengths, weaknesses, aptitudes and personality traits.

Certification role of examinations in India

Is the certificating role of examinations being met? There is a consensus that education systems have tended to be conceived as rigid and isolated entities. Learning in schools is seen as separate from and unconnected to the learning that takes place in non-formal and informal environments.

There is very little flexibility for catering to the specific differences of learners—individual personality, culture, language, learning style, family background, motivational level, interests and special needs. Furthermore, the system fails to take into account the physical, emotional, social and cognitive abilities of each learner. Curricula have been framed in tightly compartmentalised and fragmented disciplines, with content and material that tends to be irrelevant to most learners. It is based on examination results and not learning outcome or content. People who prepare textbooks have been isolated from the school system for several years.

The existing system of examinations does not provide sufficiently objective information about the knowledge and skills of learners. It only places emphasis on the recall of facts and memorisation by rote. The use of examination results as the most important indicator of school effectiveness ignores the other factors which contribute to performance. Focusing on examination results ignores many other important outcomes of schooling, such as the learner's personal, social and physical development, and the strengthening of their potentialities and skills, confidence, teamwork, initiative, interests, attitudes and values.

Filtration role of examinations in India

It is therefore clear that the certificating role of examinations is not being met. Are board examinations then fulfilling the other role—that of effective filters for admission to higher education?

Colleges need school grades and examination scores to grant admission with certain baseline assurances about the incoming class, but these scores do not provide direct evidence of many other attributes associated

59

with a successful student. They completely ignore critical attributes such as analytical ability and the knowledge of facts, processes, concepts, and skills that are vital for a student's success in college. The highest value must be attached to the cultivation of such habits as curiosity, independence, clarity and incisiveness of thought, tolerance for ambiguity and ability to manage time. Students will be poorly prepared for higher education if their success in secondary school is largely a result of memorisation.

> Examinations in India are serving neither the role of certification nor of filtration. Despite this, education has come to concern itself exclusively with examinations, high grades and achievements, and in the midst of all the gains that the education system has made in recent years, something vital has been lost.

As a result of this, almost all leading colleges and institutions of higher education in India (barring a few that admit students to general degree courses) have their own admission procedures for aspiring students seeking admission such as written examinations or interviews or group discussions. Therefore, the answer to the above questions may very well be that neither do education boards prepare new generations for adult life nor do they act as filters to get admission in colleges!

Need for wholistic reforms

What should be done to bridge the gap between school and college? Should we continue to perpetuate the tyranny of the syllabus- and examination-based system or make attempts to change it? We should consider how colleges and schools can find ways to work together.

The most crucial requirement in school education today is to facilitate a shift from the culture of schooling to a culture of learning. This implies situating learning beyond the conventional school-teacher-textbook modalities.

There is a need to appreciate that learners are different and require choice, while ensuring that they are exposed to a multiplicity of contexts. Therefore, it is of utmost importance that 'multiple intelligences' must lead to multiple learning styles.

To fulfil the multiplicity of these needs, it is critical also to look at the teaching styles. Reforms need to consider the changing requirements, to look at the curriculum of teacher training programmes and to understand the mindsets of teachers coming into a classroom.

Figure 4.5 The examination reform process cannot be set off without taking into account all aspects of the learning process, the interests of all stakeholders and the creation of positive attitudes. By-passing these and going directly to the actual amendments to the examination system has poor chances of success.

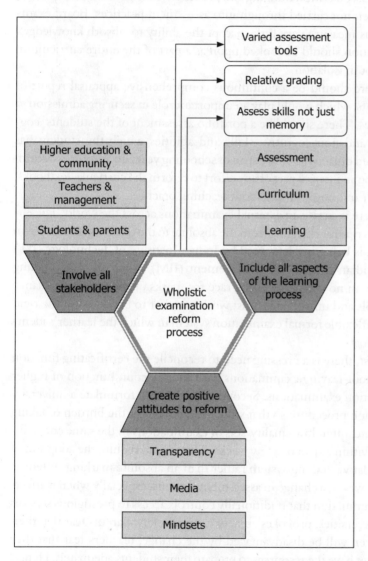

School principals can make a difference in their own institutions and improve the quality of education for students by designing their own curriculum, teaching/learning methods, in-service teacher training programme and comprehensive assessment and evaluation techniques.

Several reforms are required to bring about the necessary change; however, unconnected reforms made to isolated elements of the education system serve no purpose.

Even if there are positive changes in school curricula through an emphasis on critical thinking and problem-solving skills, these changes are often not carried through into assessment practices. Board examinations measure very little, except the ability to 'absorb knowledge'. Evaluation should be looked upon as a part of the entire curriculum, and not in isolation.

There should be a continuous comprehensive appraisal report of students, which would play an important role in securing admission to colleges. There should be a portfolio assessment of the students' cognitive and non-cognitive skills and abilities which the student has acquired during the entire span of schooling years. Examination reform must be an integral part of any effort to reform the curricula, textbooks, teacher training and classroom teaching practices.

There is a crisis in external examinations across the world. The climate is ripe for changing from the absolute to the relative grading system which is being implemented by Indian Institute of Technology (IIT) and Indian Institute of Management (IIM) as the absolute grading system in no way reduces the race for marks or the trauma of exams. Schools and universities must work together to break out of the rigid and inflexible formal examination system in which the learner's identity is lost.

First, there is a pressing need to reconcile the certificating function of school-leaving examinations with the selection function of higher education examinations. Second is the need to formulate a university selection procedure so that students are freed of the burden of taking separate, often low-quality, sets of examinations in the same core subjects within a span of a few weeks. This would require the adoption of the relative grading system rather than an absolute marking system.

However, a change in assessment systems, especially when it affects an examination that traditionally controls access to prestigious schools or universities, provokes anxiety in any society: parents fear that their children will be disadvantaged by the change, teachers fear that they will not have the resources to prepare their students adequately. Hence, it is very important to raise public awareness on these issues to bring about a change in the educational mindset.

Thus, a dialogue should be initiated with the universities to change the format of the entrance admission forms that today focus on cut-off percentages. One way could be for the universities to ask aspirants to write essays, which could also be a deciding factor for students seeking admission to other institutions of higher learning.

The four wheels of assessment

Examinations are not sufficient for student assessment. When structured effectively (not often the case in India), they can measure a student's conceptual knowledge, understanding and analytical abilities. However, this is only a small part of what needs to be assessed. If examinations are not assessment, then what is assessment? Is an alternative and viable assessment mechanism possible?

There are three steps to the answer of this question:

- to decide on the purpose of assessment
- to see what areas of student performance need to be assessed
- to define the method of setting benchmarks and the actions that are needed to follow up on the assessment

The purpose

If the purpose of schooling is to prepare students for life, obviously the purpose of assessment is to check if students are indeed prepared for life or have reached the trajectory (IEP) projected for them. Assessments give answers to questions relating to a student's needs and abilities. We have already seen that they are an intrinsic part of the learning process and are needed to boost the student's potential through a process of feedback.

Preparation for life has several dimensions—students, when they leave school, must be prepared for the requirements of higher education; they have to learn to face the competition for admissions to various colleges and later the competition for entry into various professions. Not only should they know how to get in, but also how to cope with and excel in new environments. Students should know how to take informed decisions and make choices that are true to their own personalities, aspirations and true to certain universal deep-rooted values. They need to know how to interact with the society and the community and cope with freedom, flexibility and change. These, very briefly, are some of the elements in preparation for life.

63

An assessment system that is able to check how well students meet these needs and give recommendations on reinforcement of strengths and remediation of weaknesses is what every great school needs. The assessment system ensures that students are able to build on the foundation laid by the school.

Assessment is a matrix. One axis of this matrix defines all of the dimensions of a student. The other axis defines the rubrics and set of instruments that give insight into each of these dimensions. The assessment is not just the sum of all the elements in the matrix. As our knowledge of quantum physics grows, we know more and more of smaller and smaller particles. As we approach the nano-world, assumptions and behaviours change from what we observe in the real world. There is a disconnect between the world we know and the world that exists at the quantum level. The whole is not equal to the sum of the parts—it is different from the sum of the parts.

Figure 4.6 To the right is the colour palette that has been used to create the picture of the girl on the left. While the palette is essential to create the girl, the colours have been conveniently sorted and arranged with no relationship to her. In the actual picture, each pixel of colour has been placed in a meaningful manner. A true assessment gives us an authentic picture of the student who is being assessed and not a set of meaningless statistics.

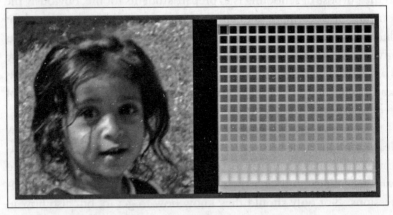

To give another analogy, this assessment is like a set of pixels in a picture. These pixels could be arranged either to give a summary of all colours used in the palette or added up to give a picture of the student. It is clear that the second option is more meaningful. Yet most of the time schools are content to present unrelated statistics on a student's performance in a manner that does not give us a true picture of the person. Often one or two assessments distort the entire picture of the student, because the entire picture is not part of the assessment process at all.

How do we achieve this wholistic picture of the student from the assessment grid? How do we work out the interconnectedness that exists between every element in the grid?

A large part of these interconnections is done almost subconsciously by most good teachers. Few teachers stop to think of how they have connected a certain grade, a certain type of behaviour or action to make some very shrewd judgements about a student. Not all teachers can make these connections, and not all make the same type of connections. A well-defined assessment system therefore is needed to help those who need to learn how to make these connections and to ensure a certain amount of consistency in the assessment made by different teachers.

Areas of assessment

A person needs to achieve various dimensions of fitness in order to survive. The assessment process needs to measure this achievement. For the purpose of assessment these dimensions can be grouped together to give 'four wheels' of assessment.

As one of the primary tasks of a school is to develop the intellect, fitness of the intellect can be split in two parts—academic fitness and fitness in various arts. Physical fitness is obviously the third wheel. The fourth wheel is the social and environmental fitness of the student. Linking all these four wheels together are the humane traits of the student—her emotional and spiritual development. This set of traits forms the axle that links all the four wheels together.

Academic ability assessment

Assessment of academic abilities has traditionally been the focus of assessment, and in fact in most cases is the only focus of assessment. Even where other aspects are evaluated, such as non-academic activities or physical fitness, these are done in a very cursory manner. Even under academic ability, it is often only memorisation and understanding abilities that are tested, though in recent times there has been an attempt to test application of knowledge too. The assessment of academic abilities needs to go far beyond this. While memory, understanding and application are necessary skills, they are not sufficient for academic excellence, let alone for preparation in life.

Assessment needs to measure:

- *Self-Development and Empowerment:* Is the student able to work on one's own? Can she define her own goals and achieve them independently? Does her work give her joy and self-worth and achievement?
- *Communication:* Can she communicate what she needs and what she has achieved effectively?
- *Analysis:* What is her depth of understanding and application of the concepts learnt?
- *Creativity:* Can she generate her creative inputs? Does she seek to enrich the work given to her?
- *Productivity:* Can she manage to meet varied requirements? And how quickly and effectively is she able to complete her tasks? Can she work to given time schedules? Are there some tasks in which she excels?

The measurement of memory, understanding and application are thus only parts of one of these skills—analysis.

Artistic ability assessment

It is clear to all that academic ability needs to be assessed. Yet, why do we need to assess artistic ability? It is common knowledge that arts have been used to enable people to express their ideas and communicate with others. Complex ideas can be best communicated through the arts—painting, sculpture, drama, song or poetry.

Development of artistic ability is linked to the development of analytical ability. Art helps us to create and visualise complex concepts easily. Art is an intrinsically creative activity and being able to perform and produce art develops and empowers the individual. Art is also closely related to joy—creating art gives joy not only to oneself, but also to all others with whom it is shared. Obviously, art develops all the skills that we need to measure under academic ability. It develops the intellect and is therefore a part of the total intellectual ability of an individual.

The measurement of artistic ability is however far more complex. It is easy to compare grades in physics with grades in history, but how does one compare the musical ability of one student with the painting ability of another?

Instead of developing very complex rubrics for measuring performance in arts, it will be better to make some very simple judgements on ability that will encompass all types of artistic ability. Here is an example of four types of ability that can measure achievements in all art forms:

- *Interpretation:* Ability to understand and explain art created by others
- *Replication:* The ability to replicate and perform art created by others
- *Creation:* The ability to create original art
- *Span:* The ability to create, re-create and understand many different types of art forms. This measures the extent of participation and involvement in artistic activities.

There are clearly different levels of achievement in each of these attributes. A sample report could read as follows, 'Not acceptable levels of interpretation, but excellence in original creation; span is limited to visual arts with low levels of performance and understanding of performing arts'.

Physical fitness assessment

This is the third wheel that is needed to move the student forward. Without physical health and fitness no one will be able to achieve anything—it is in fact the primary fitness and in fact the only fitness that is consistently required for each and every species. Scientific research has found that physically fit students perform better in all other activities, other things being equal. They are more alert, better emotionally balanced, more creative and definitely more productive. Physical activity releases inner tensions and gives a sense of joy and achievement.

There are many standard measures of physical fitness. One simple model is to measure basic skills through a series of well-defined tasks and application of these skills in performance in various sporting activities:

- *Basic Skills:* Flexibility, strength, muscular endurance, agility, balance, co-ordination and power
- *Application:* Level of understanding, participation and skill in a given sport such as soccer, tennis, basketball, athletics, swimming
- *Span:* Participation and level of excellence in a wide variety of sporting activities

Physical fitness encompasses the fitness of all students—according to their potential. Every human body is made in a different way—there is no absolute measure of physical fitness. Each student will have her own challenges—some students may have temporary health issues, others may be differently abled. The assessment ensures that every

67

student develops an awareness of the challenges she faces. It helps her to find the right path to maximise her physical potential.

Outreach: Social fitness

Whereas the first three wheels of assessment relate to the inner self, the fourth wheel refers to the manner in which the student relates to the world outside. A school needs to gradually lower fences and let students understand and experience the outside world. They need to understand the physical, social and economic world that they will need to live in when they leave school. How a student interacts with issues related to the physical environment, the norms of the society and community around them, and the economy need to be assessed. In fact, this is a truly crucial assessment, as it will have an impact on the direction and quality of the student's life.

How do we make this assessment?

- *Initiative:* Does the student take the initiative in determining the course of action in given programmes?
- *Follow-Through:* Does the student follow through on actions initiated by her or by others?
- *Participation Levels:* How deeply involved is the student in various outreach activities conducted by the school? Does she spend significant amount of time on these activities?
- *Span:* Is the level of participation widespread or limited to a few activities?

Assessments therefore become the core around which the entire learning process is built. An assessment is the starting point of the learning process and not the end.

One truth that becomes obvious, as we try to understand true assessment, is that the curriculum needs to be defined based on the assessment methods and not vice versa. It is clear that the above assessments would not be possible if there was no art curriculum, physical education curriculum or outreach curriculum. In fact, the content of the each of these also needs to develop from the needs of the assessment process.

So far, we have defined four separate wheels in the assessment process. Yet we know that for assessment to be valid, they need to move together. How do they move together? What is the binding force that connects all four to give the true picture of the student?

Humaneness—the axle

A student is not separate from the person's human qualities. The student may be a loner or a team worker; she may be truthful or loyal or both:

there are a myriad qualities that make her. These qualities will be reflected in each of the four wheels of learning. These qualities are what bind the assessment together. Any assessment of the student needs to look at certain basic qualities of students.

Most qualities and values that we can think of would fall within the core values listed in the following box. There are many other ways in which we can describe these core values; and of course, there are many other values that may be added to the list. However, almost any action that we take could be described in terms of one of these values, and they form the common thread that runs through all that students learn in school. Ultimately, if a school manages to strengthen these core values in every student, it would have more than justified its existence.

> - *Integrity:* The ability to recognise and follow truth; the strength to take the right decisions; self-respect
> - *Joy:* The ability to find happiness within oneself; to recognise and appreciate beauty; a sense of humour
> - *Peace:* The desire for peace and understanding of both the inner self and the outer world; the desire to bring about peace in all situations
> - *An Open Mind:* Constant search for new truths and better paths; an openness to new ideas; a positive approach that seeks solutions
> - *Love:* Love for all living beings, a desire to understand others, care for them; respect for life; love for one's country and for the earth we live in
> - *Leadership:* The ability to show others the right path, provide guidance, support, and the ability to follow the lead when required.

During the assessment process, teachers, parents and students need to connect the four wheels together with these values—they need to see if a student's helpfulness in the classroom extends to the playing field and if it is reflected in the outreach programme the person chooses. They need to see if her lack of joy is related to being taught in a style that does not suit her or whether it is a problem in her family or her inability to make friends.

By the very nature of its quality, the assessment of values in various fields needs to be subjective assessment. It will not be possible to define grades that assess the level of achievement in these values. Yet students need to be observed by teachers and parents and by themselves objectively. Actions need to be taken to ensure that they do inculcate each of these values in every aspect of their learning process.

69

Actions

Assessment without action is futile. The sequential cycle must be complete for the assessment to be of any use. Thus, results in the assessment cycle need to lead to defined learning inputs. The assessment can identify areas that the student is weak in and focus on those in the lesson. For instance, a low assessment in art and physical fitness, combined with high assessment in analytical achievements, is a child heading for a burnout. The assessment process then needs to take steps to remove this imbalance—to encourage the child to develop varied interests and to participate in activities in addition to academic study.

These actions on the assessment are the fuel that enables the student to move ahead at a faster, yet more balanced pace. The question remains how many teachers follow up on assessments? How many know how to proceed? This assessment model has a steep learning curve, and valid assessments will not be possible until teachers themselves are taught how to assess, the instruments to use, how to gather and collate data from these instruments, how to set benchmarks and the actions to take for different benchmarks.

This requires an entire curriculum for teachers consisting of guiding principles on how to assess work and use these data to move student learning ahead—this goes way beyond the test and examination correction guidelines. Teachers now have to assess not just the correctness of answers but also need to be able to grade students on various skills learnt in academic, art, physical education and outreach activities. They need to assess not just abilities but also attitudes. They need to be able to accept student and parent assessments objectively and without bias— more so, if these assessments vary from their own judgement.

Teachers also need to be given well-defined parameters for measurement. Academic input measurements are easily available and similar parameters need to be created for Arts, Physical Fitness and Outreach.

These parameters would be measured and collated through a wide variety of instruments such as examinations, projects, forms that collect teachers' perceptions about the student as well as student self-assessment.

These instruments would therefore have objective components and subjective components. Similarly, a system for evaluation of the humaneness aspects of students' needs to be available, for example, in forms designed to collect pastoral comments about the student. All these instruments need to be designed in a manner that can be put together to create a single big picture.

Figure 4.7 The assessment development cycle answers questions on the design of the different elements of assessment

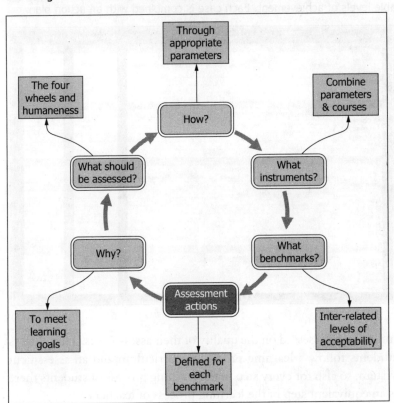

The next step will be to check whether the grades allotted are acceptable—and these benchmarks cannot be applied to an isolated 'wheel' in the assessment system. They must integrate all the wheels through the axle of humaneness. A student who excels in soccer, but not in academics cannot be rewarded by a place in the school team, if his poor academic scores stem from low effort.

Thus, benchmarks need to be developed in a transparent manner so that teachers know which combinations of scores are not acceptable, which are acceptable and which are excellent. For each of these they should also know what actions to take for each of the levels of performance. A student with excellent scores must be given enrichment exercises in the next learning cycle and the student with less than acceptable scores must equally be given remedial learning inputs.

For such an assessment to be effectively followed by teachers, not only must they be taught how to make these assessments, but they

71

Figure 4.8 This format gives some guidelines for combining benchmarks in the four wheels with personality traits to define acceptable and not acceptable levels of achievement. Each case is combined with an action plan.

Wheel	Parameters					Achievements	Values
Academics							
	Analysis	Creativity	Communication	Productivity	Self Empowerment		
Course 1							
Course 2							
Course 3							
Arts							
	Interpretation	Replication	Creation				
Art Course 1							
Art Course 2							
Art Course 3							
Span							
Physical Fitness							
	Flexibility	Strength	Muscular Endurance	Agility	Balance		
Basic Skills							
	Understanding	Participation	Skill				
Applications							
Sport 1							
Sport 2							
Sport 3							
Span							
Outreach							
	Initiative	Follow Through	Involvement				
Activity 1							
Activity 2							
Activity 3							
Span							

must also be assessed on the quality of their assessments. Thus, just as students follow a learning process, a curriculum and an assessment system, so also for every step in the learning process of students there is an equivalent step in the learning process of teachers.

Figure 4.9 The four wheels of assessment each have different parameters for measurement. An instrument such as this is an example of a highly simplified way of putting all the wheels together along with subjective comments on individual achievements and value assessments.

Combination Benchmarks	Individual Benchmarks					Actions
	Academics	Arts	Physical Fitness	Outreach	Value Traits	Rewards & Remedies
Not acceptable						
Case 1						
Case 2						
Case 3						
Acceptable						
Case 1						
Case 2						
Case 3						
Excellence						
Case 1						
Case 2						
Case 3						

While the details may be different for teachers and students, the steps remain the same and for learning to be effective in any school, the curriculum for teachers needs to be developed and implemented with the same rigour as the curriculum for students.

Summary

- Examinations are not a measure of student success and student success is not the purpose of assessment.
- The purpose of assessment is to increase the dynamic potential of a student by putting her through a learning process that is appropriate for her needs.
- To ensure accuracy, assessments are multidimensional and based on a wide variety of instruments and perspectives of teachers, students and parents.
- The instrument that has been given maximum importance is examinations.
- The purpose of examination could be either an assessment-certification function or a higher-education-filtration purpose.
- In India, board examinations do not serve either purpose due to a fragmented approach to education and a separation of the individual from the process of learning.
- Reforms to examination system are therefore necessary, but need to be approached in a wholistic manner.
- An alternative to the 'examinations as assessment' is required. The purpose of this model is to create an intricate and interconnected grid of nano-assessments that will join to form a true picture of the student being assessed.
- This model measures performance in the four wheels of learning: Academics, Arts, Physical Fitness and Outreach.
- The four wheels are joined together by the axle of humaneness.
- Assessment does not end with determination of levels of achievement of student—it is meaningless without actions that use this assessment to give an upward boost to the student's learning and abilities.
- Such an assessment model cannot serve its purpose without the total involvement and understanding of teachers.

5   Wholistic Learning

Great schools develop curriculum for critical thinking

In the earlier chapters, we noted that the curricula prescribed by various school boards in India have many gaps. A great school fills these gaps by creating courses for its students that develop the skills that do not find a place in the school boards curricula. The most important skills that students need to develop are critical thinking skills. Students, therefore, need a course that will specifically take them through a critical thinking learning process that will teach them how to learn.

Figure 5.1   The learning process consists of steps leading to the creation of new knowledge and its application in different environments. Teachers use their assessment of students to create the environment for such learning to blossom. They give students knowledge and skills to filter knowledge, and lead them through a process that helps them to reflect, understand and create new knowledge.

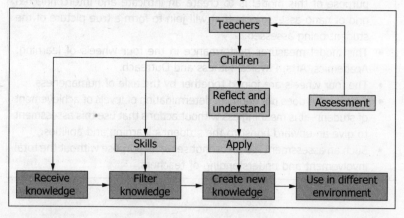

The first step in this process is to acquire knowledge. Often, teaching does not even reach this step. Students are accustomed to being spoon-fed with knowledge. They sit in classrooms and listen to the teacher.

They take notes and memorise these notes. At the most, they may read prescribed textbooks—and memorise the content. Few would know how to use resources in the library or even the Internet to search for knowledge that is pertinent to the problem at hand. They need to be taught to read widely and listen carefully. They need to be taught to seek a wide variety of resources—both verbal and written—in order to find the right clues that will lead them to gather the most relevant facts.

The second step is to filter knowledge. Students may reach the first step of gathering knowledge on their own. Internet search engines generate vast amounts of information on every conceivable topic. There is no need to read books any more. Most students believe that filtration means 'copy and paste at random from the first two search results'!

Obviously, the ability to filter knowledge requires more skill than this. It needs the ability to understand not only what is relevant, but also how much is required for the task. They need to know how to choose from a vast hoard of knowledge exactly what is needed and how to discard what is irrelevant. This in addition requires the ability to categorise and organise the filtered content in a manner that will be meaningful to others and to the student.

The third step is to create new knowledge. The aim of learning is not just to collect and rearrange the existing knowledge. Many millenniums ago both animals and humans had the same level of knowledge with respect to fire. If the gap between humans and animals has widened since then, it is because humans have used their knowledge of fire to create new knowledge. This constant creation of new knowledge over thousands of years has created the civilised society we live in today.

The existing curriculum leaves out this ability to question and take risks needed to create new knowledge to chance. It leaves it to those few people who have the inner drive to do something creative and new. The curriculum needs to encourage every student to develop this very basic human ability. It should actively pose challenges to them that will make them acquire knowledge, reflect on that knowledge and apply their knowledge to create new knowledge.

When the pre-historic humans learnt that food cooked in fire tasted well than raw food, they were gathering knowledge. When they used the fire to cook food of their choice, they were creating new knowledge. When they realised that they could use the same fire to temper metals, they were using this new knowledge in a different environment. This was a quantum shift to a higher level of understanding.

The fourth step in the process of learning, therefore, is to enable students to 'take off' to a higher plane. Steps that humans take to reach higher levels of understanding are not necessarily gradual steps. Sometimes these steps are great leaps upwards. A good learning programme will provide all the ingredients and the environment needed to help students take this leap. In this last step, the teacher is no longer holding the student's hand. She now flies on her own. For example, a colleague once shared with me that a remark by her in the biology class acted as a catalyst for one of her students to research on the medicinal properties of the guava plant. This research paper was adjudged the best in the state and the student went on to represent her state at the Inter-Zonal Science Fair at Hyderabad.

Truth, beauty and values: A course for critical thinking

Every great school would like to design a course to take students through the learning process in a manner that would teach them how to fly on their own. This course would seek to develop all the dimensions of knowledge that a student needs to succeed in life. Such a course would

Figure 5.2 Academic curriculum usually concentrates on truth. Wholism implies inclusion of all aspects of life including Beauty and Ethics.

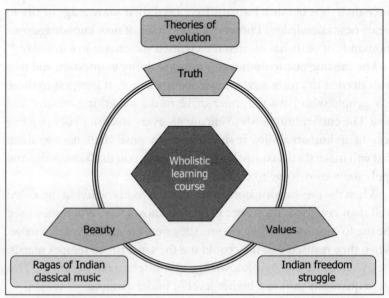

also need to develop skills that could be assessed by the four wheels of assessment—academics, arts, outreach and physical fitness. The inner thread of humaneness would run through all these. Such a course would be wholistic in many different ways.

If we take the triad of *Truth*, *Beauty* and *Values*,[1] these between them cover all the dimensions needed to succeed in life. In *Truth*, we have the ability to think with clarity, the ability to seek precision. In *Beauty*, we have the ability to find joy and a sense of wonder. In *Values*, we find answers to right action. A course built around this triad will take the student through the learning process. The four wheels of assessment would be used to keep the course focused on its goals.

The goals

This course will have goals in several layers.

- The first layer is that of the stated scholastic goals.
- The second layer is that of the learning process.
- The third layer is that of the assessment process.

The scholastic goals of the course are:

- To understand Truth through the theories of evolution
- To appreciate Beauty through the study of Ragas in Hindustani classical music
- To develop values through the study of the Indian Freedom Struggle

The learning process goals are:

The core learning process
Students will first receive and learn to filter information. Next, they will create new knowledge; and finally, they will apply this in different environments.

Horizontal integration
Students learn about Truth, Beauty and Values from each of the three issues to be studied (the theories of evolution, the ragas and the Indian freedom struggle).

[1] The idea is taken from Howard Gardener's curriculum on *Truth—evolution, beauty—Mozart and goodness—holocaust* and contextualised to the Indian setting.

Figure 5.3 It is not just the scholastic content of the course that is designed wholistically, but all the learning outcomes and the goals. The scholastic goals are integrated with the learning process goals. These are in turn integrated with the assessment process.

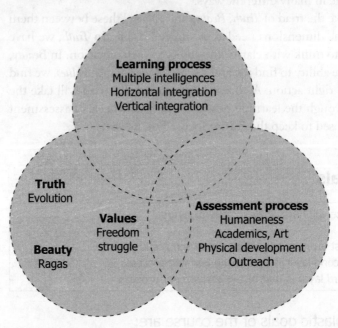

Vertical integration

This process of creating links will be spread over three years—moving from simple relationships to inter-relationships that are more complex.

The assessment process goals

These Learning Outcomes will be measured at the end of the course to ensure that students have achieved their goals.

Academic knowledge

Students will learn about the theories of evolution, ragas and the Indian Freedom Struggle.

Artistic skills

They will be able to appreciate the beauty in each of these and will create original art around these themes—either as music, or as a performance or as some form of visual art.

Physical development

Students will be involved in physical activities that will help them to understand these issues and concepts.

Outreach

Students will be involved in interactions, discussions and performances along with students from diverse backgrounds.

Humaneness

The notions of joy, beauty, truth and other values will form a common thread that runs through all the activities in this course.

The activities in this course will be designed to meet these goals. Some examples of activities that are possible are:

Year 1:

Academic activities

Truth

Students will be taught basic theories of evolution. They will compare and analyse how various theories differ.

Beauty

They will learn how the ragas are constructed. They will learn how each raga is associated with different emotions, different aspects of beauty ('Shringar' or 'rasa' associated with each raga). They will research stories and anecdotes related to the ragas.

Values

They will study the basic facts on the Indian Freedom Struggle. They will research stories of heroism from the struggle. These will be two different types of stories. One of the stories will be based on the life of a militant freedom fighter, and the other based on a story of a freedom fighter who believed in 'ahimsa'.

Art activities

Create an exhibition of models and drawings that depict the evolution of species.

Students will attend concerts where they will listen to ragas. They will be taught to listen with appreciation and will learn how to recognise a few basic ragas. They will also learn to sing at least one raga.

Write the script for a play based on an incident from the Indian Freedom Struggle and enact this play.

Physical development

Learn breathing exercises to improve singing. Practice various *yogasanas*, including sitting in *padmasana* and learn the correct posture for singing.

Outreach

The stage performance on the freedom struggle will be an inter-school effort that includes students from other schools.

Students will learn to sing the ragas along with students who have disabilities.

Figure 5.4 The chief characteristics of the first year of the course. At this stage the wholistic elements are concerned more with ensuring variety of activities than with integration.

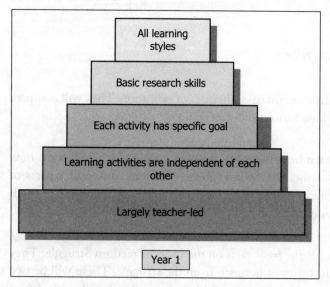

All learning styles

Basic research skills

Each activity has specific goal

Learning activities are independent of each other

Largely teacher-led

Year 1

The learning process in the first year of the course

Students learn how to gather knowledge and understand simple filtration of ideas. They use this to make written and verbal presentations on theories of evolution.

Students also learn how to translate concepts from one form to another. They learn how to translate verbal ideas on evolution into visual pictures and models. They learn how music can be used to describe and interpret emotions and ideas. The various activities through which they learn reinforce different intelligences and learning styles. In the first year, they do not specialise in any single type of intelligence or learning style.

Horizontal integration

In the first year, these linkages will be very basic. The stage perform-ance uses songs sung in the ragas that students have just learnt. Just as people evolve, so do ideas evolve. The concept of evolution is linked to the idea of evolution of ideas in the freedom struggle.

Vertical integration

Students in the first year start with accepting ideas given to them by teachers. By the end of the year, students will begin to compare differ-ent theories and question the flaws in each. They will use this attitude of questioning in the second year of the course.

In the first year, most of the learning is teacher-led. Teachers decide the activities, the syllabus and all the outcomes. In this year, the role that students play is that of receivers of knowledge.

Year 2:

The second-year content will be very different. The activities will not have distinct goals in the manner that the first-year activities did. It will no longer be able to separate which activity meets which goal. Now, each activity will integrate multiple goals.

Students will study the controversies in the theories of evolution. They will be given examples from the US experience where there has been a controversy in several states about the teaching of the Darwinian theory as it is in conflict with traditional Christian doctrine. Students will try to understand both points of view through debates.

Students will also learn how current theories of evolution explain the characteristics of the human body as it is today. They will learn how civilisation has changed the way we live. This change in civilisation has been much faster than evolutionary change in our bodies. Therefore, the human body is not always able to adapt immediately to these changes.

One example of this is the need for physical exercise. Civilisation has reduced physical exertion. Yet, the history of evolution tells us that physical fitness was necessary for survival once, and continues to remain necessary for survival today. Therefore, we must continue to remain physically fit, despite the fact that civilisation has reduced the need for physical activity.

The theory of evolution will also be related to the importance of speech in the development of human intelligence. Students will understand the relationship between speech and logical thought—both characteristics of human beings—to music.

They will further develop their understanding of music and the ragas. They will learn how to convert musical knowledge into the logical structures of a raga. They will attempt to explain why people find music beautiful—through both an appreciation of logical structure of the raga as well as an understanding of the biology of the human brain.

They will also study the patriotic songs that were used to arouse people during the Freedom Struggle. They will research to find out if particular songs become more effective when set in a particular raga. They will look for answers to why these ragas are effective and study how they affect the mind.

Other questions that students will seek to answer are:

What were the other triggers that the leaders of the freedom struggle used? How do different leaders create mass movements? Is a mass movement always 'right'?

The second-year activities are again art exhibitions, debates, plays and oral and written presentations that deal with these issues. Students this year have greater flexibility in choosing the type of activities they would like to use to explore and express these ideas.

Figure 5.5 Year 2 sees greater inter-dependence between activities and greater independence for students. Development of higher order skills is another feature of this year.

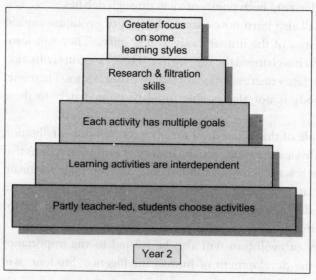

The role of the teacher is to keep students on track in terms of the stated goals of the syllabus for the year. Teachers will ensure that students answer the various questions posed to them. They will help them to locate the information required to answer these questions. However, they will give students a choice in the type of activity they will use to answer these questions. They will ensure that there is proper spread of these activities.

Year 3:

In the third year, students decide both the content as well as the activities. Teachers will give students various questions that are examples of the type of research they can do. These are to ensure that students remain within the framework of Truth, Beauty and Values on the one hand and the theories of evolution, ragas and the Freedom Struggle on the other.

Students will have to develop a research project based on this framework. They will present the finding of this research project through a medium of their choice—multimedia presentation, a formal research paper, songs, plays, sculpture, paintings or even a martial arts display. Students may work alone or in groups.

This ensures that students having been exposed to different learning styles and different learning processes now choose the style and process that appeal to them.

Some of the questions that students could work on are:

Is truth absolute? Is there only one perception of beauty? Is there always a morally right answer? These could be based on:

- The controversies in the theories of evolution—can we consider any particular theory to be true?
- Fusion music—does a raga need to remain 'pure' and absolute or can it be modified and merged with other forms of music?
- Was ahimsa the best path to freedom or would some other method have led to better results?

Students will be encouraged to choose their own topics based on the learning of the past two years. They will be encouraged to choose controversial topics and will be instructed to use logical, emotional and ethical arguments to prove the premise they have chosen to support.

Figure 5.6 The third year is the year of the student. This year the student learns to work independently to create new knowledge. She learns to apply higher order learning skills within the given framework.

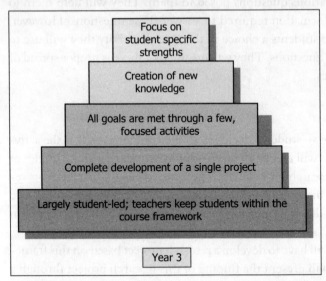

Focus on student specific strengths

Creation of new knowledge

All goals are met through a few, focused activities

Complete development of a single project

Largely student-led; teachers keep students within the course framework

Year 3

In this year, teachers play the role of resource persons and referees. They will interact closely with each child and each group of children and ensure that each comes up with a meaningful presentation.

A course such as this will be conducted independently of the syllabus prescribed by a board. Yet there are many elements that are common—all students study the theories of evolution as part of their science syllabus and the freedom struggle as part of the history syllabus. Therefore, this course will also help them to link different disciplines in their formal curriculum.

A generation ago, students who studied science went on to lifelong career in a science-based profession. Today, this is no longer true. People in every profession are crossing over to different disciplines. Even if they do not cross over, job assignments within every profession require people to have broad-based knowledge and the ability to filter and correlate very diverse types of information. This course on Truth, Beauty and Values teaches students how to gather knowledge and apply it to any situation. It teaches them how to ask the right questions, how to find the right answers and finally, how to present these answers effectively.

Summary

- Great schools fill gaps in a board curriculum by developing their own courses.
- These courses develop learning skills.
- The four steps of the learning process are: Receive knowledge, Filter knowledge, Create new knowledge, Apply knowledge in a different environment.
- A course that will develop these learning skills needs to include skills that will enable students to succeed in life.
- A wholistic course that enables students to learn about Truth, Beauty and Values will meet these goals.
- Students can learn about truth through the theories of evolution, beauty through Indian music ragas and values through the study of the Indian Freedom Struggle. These are the scholastic goals.
- The learning process goals are development of multiple intelligences and higher-order critical thinking skills, horizontal and vertical integration.
- The assessment process goals are to build up academic knowledge, artistic ability, and physical development and outreach involvement along with the inner core of humaneness in all these.
- The course is conducted over three academic years.
- In the first year, the course is largely teacher-led. There are a large number of activities, each with specific goals. The level of inter-dependence between these is relatively little.
- In the second year, there is greater student involvement in learning. There is greater inter-dependence between activities and goals. Higher-order learning skills are learnt.
- In the third year, the course is largely student-led. Within a given framework, they have the freedom to develop a research project of their choice in the manner they wish. This year, they create new knowledge.
- A course such as this prepares students for life in an unknown future. It gives them skills to cope with and stay ahead of change in an increasingly fluid world.

6

Technology

Great schools stay ahead of change

At no other time in the entire history of the human race has change happened as fast as it is happening today. Our domains of knowledge are changing in every direction and in every field. This is because, apart from other factors, access to the changes in knowledge is faster than it has ever been before, and therefore reaction times have shortened.

Why do schools need to keep up with change?

Technology has inundated us with information, which the human mind is being constantly challenged to convert into increasingly complex knowledge. Students will inherit this world tomorrow. Schools thus need to be in a state of dynamic change because their students are entering an economy that will require them to manage complexity, create ideas and use ever-evolving technologies.

This need to keep pace becomes critical for survival today—we either keep up with the changing times or become obsolete and fall off from the path of development and growth. In fact, it is not enough just to keep pace with the changing times. If students seek to become leaders, they need to keep ahead of the changes, to anticipate future changes and plot the course of their goals accordingly. Most important of all, they need to become the actual creators of this change. The constant change in this world is one of the reasons why all the stakeholders in the school need to be in a learning mode. It is not possible to have a static set of goals—the future is, after all, unforeseeable.

Great schools, therefore, keep themselves updated on changes in knowledge not only in the domains that are being taught—the sciences, the social sciences, the languages and so on—but also the science and art of learning and teaching and the science of how the human mind learns. They filter out the most effective among the emerging pedagogical methods and constantly integrate them into their curriculum.

> Goals and aspirations need to be dynamic and adaptive to these changes, and the human mind needs to develop an attitude that welcomes and makes productive use of the constantly emerging new knowledge. There is no place for inertia for the leaders of tomorrow.

Figure 6.1 Attitudes of an educational institution to change can be dynamic or static. Leaders are those who anticipate and create change. An organisation that ignores, or is unaware of, change cannot last in today's world.

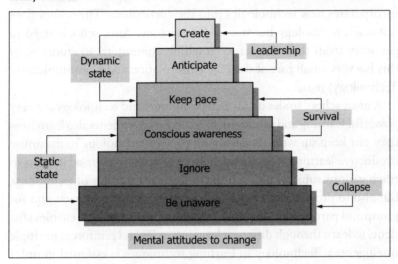

Figure 6.2 Changes are taking place in several domains that affect the learning process. These changes have an impact on the way people live by giving them greater freedom, flexibility and access to knowledge than has ever been seen in the history of humanity.

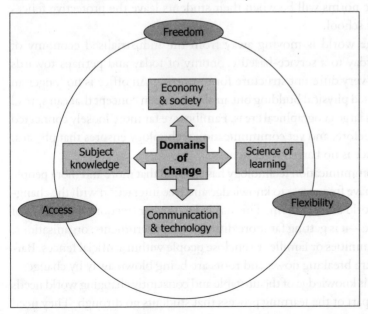

Schools need to use changing knowledge effectively

A great school keeps pace with technological changes in order to use this knowledge effectively in the teaching-learning process. It constantly incorporates new technologies into the curriculum. The school does not teach technology but uses it for teaching. Also, schools need to get away from the mindset of 'teaching computers' to students, as this is a very small part of the ICT (Information and Communication Technology) issue.

A great school understands that computers and technology are very powerful learning and productivity tools. Here, students also learn how they can keep up with the changing pace of technology to maximise productive learning right through life. Computers are used not just to teach various subjects through the multimedia features of technology, but also to provide the tools for cross-integration of subjects and for group and participative learning. Technology is a tool that enables students to learn through different learning styles and reinforces multiple intelligences. Technology in learning techniques is essential in order to keep in touch with change.

Advances in knowledge have changed not just the science and technology of various subject domains, including the domain of the science of learning, but in the process changed the very structure of society itself. Schools need to anticipate and prepare for what social and economic norms will be when their students leave the protective fences of the school.

The world is moving away from the industrialised economy of yesterday to a service-based economy of today and perhaps towards some very different structure for tomorrow. An office is no longer an enclosed physical building but an abstract open concept that can spread across large geographical areas. Families are far more loosely connected than before, and yet communication technology ensures that physical distance is no barrier to closeness.

Communication technology has ensured that more and more people now have free access to knowledge and free interaction with the changing world around them. This has led to greater freedom in the lives of people—it is getting far more difficult for governments, organisations, communities or families to enclose people within artificial fences. Barriers are breaking down and roots are being blown away by change.

This knowledge of the unstable and constantly changing world needs to be part of the learning process that students go through. They need to know how to deal with change, where to be flexible and where to stay rooted.

Learning and ICT as an agent of change

While changes are taking place in every aspect of our lives, one change that has had a truly great impact on the way learning happens is in the fast-paced advances in information and communication technology. Much has been said and written on using technology in education and which has, in a sense, become synonymous with using computers in education. ICT is increasingly becoming a dominant part of the technological aspect of education. It is now a common thread in every knowledge system and every field of specialisation. Familiarising all students (and teachers) with technology needs to be an integral part of every curriculum. Every industry and vocation today uses technology in its own way and each requires knowledge of computer sciences and applications that is specific to its needs.

Computers are emerging as an important pedagogical tool. By making students work on computer themselves, they enable participatory learning in controlled environments. Under normal circumstances, it is not possible for a teacher to watch every student in a class who is engaged in some activity and keep some control to ensure that they are moving towards the required learning outcomes. Computers can remove part of the effort of this guidance by giving students some of the more mechanical instructions required for the activity and ensure that they remain on track.

Thus, the learning experience has now become decentralised; every student is hooked on to a computer and does not need to be receiving instructions from a single teacher. The student could be anywhere in the school, or even at home, and yet complete the required activity with effective technological supervision.

Participatory learning implies interactive learning. Students are no longer passive listeners in the classroom, they can each interact with the programme according to their own pace, needs and interests. Learning is no longer being forced upon them—they are the ones who are proactively moving towards the required goals of that lesson.

The multimedia capabilities of a computer make it a very powerful medium for making learning an enriched experience. This is the aspect of computers that has most appealed to teachers and students alike.

Figure 6.3 Learning through technology impacts the quality, style and reach of the learning process

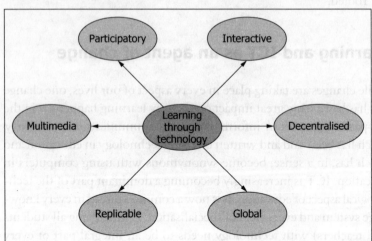

Colour, sound, movement are all magnets that grab the attention of children everywhere.

Easy replication of educational programmes makes it possible to reach very large numbers of students and to provide all with high-quality learning experiences. It is not possible for a teacher to be everywhere all at once, and so a teacher can reach a limited number of students. Teachers, too, vary in quality from classroom to classroom even in the same school. Replication of computer programmes ensures that all teachers are supported by material that is consistent in quality and gives similar learning experiences to all.

Finally, the Internet ensures a large geographical reach; even remote areas are no longer cut off from the latest advances in spheres of learning. This globalisation of education is possible through the Internet. Knowledge, even in these isolated areas, is always up-to-date and universally spread.

The power of information technology has very few limits, removes many of the roadblocks to effective learning, and empowers teachers.

This is perhaps the simplest possible example and it covers several types of intelligences, several learning styles and all parts of the brain. A teacher who has this resource is able to give a much higher level of individualised and newer learning experience to her students without needing any extra time and very little extra preparation. It gives a teacher the time to build in other activities that are personalised for each student thus making the learning experience richer for her and her students.

ICT not only personalises education, but also makes distant worlds accessible, provides access to every kind of information that a student or a teacher may require, can be used to deliver instructions in both active and passive forms, thereby appealing to different intelligences in a wide variety of learning styles.

> **Example 1**
> Every student has access to educational programmes on a computer. She can work on this programme at the pace that suits her; many programmes have the ability to customise the learning environment so she can choose the environment that suits her. The student can also choose the types of activity that appeal to her most—read the text or listen to it, look at the pictures, animations and movies or work on the interactive problems. In due course, she will do all the things that reinforce her learning in many different ways.

Referring back to the section on theories of learning, we need ICT to:

- Reinforce multiple intelligences
- Provide balanced learning techniques to learners of all kinds
- To create learning environments to suit all types of the brain

All intelligences need to be used in instruction and all need to be reinforced. Visual, aural, linguistic and logical intelligences are reinforced with computer-based lessons that use multimedia—sound, movement, music, language and interactive problem solving.

Technology as a communication tool leads to cooperative learning by enabling students from different locations to work and learn jointly. This facilitates group learning: students work together and communicate ideas through e-communication tools—e-mail, chat, discussion boards and virtual classrooms—to work on common goals with peers within and outside the school. Students participate in joint projects and discussions of global issues with students worldwide. Therefore, ICT develops both interpersonal skills and intra-personal awareness. Interacting with different cultures through the Internet and e-friendships makes students ask themselves existentialist questions.

ICT is especially effective in providing instructional methods for learning any single concept that appeals to all the intelligences, including role playing, musical performance, cooperative learning, reflection, visualisation and story-telling. It is important to keep in mind that ICT is only a part of this exercise. The concept that is being studied is that other non-technology related exercises are also essential to the learning process and need to be integrated with the lesson.

Example 2
Young students studying about a festival can enact the festival and sing songs related to it, see movies and presentations and read stories based on the festival, create digital art and their own digital cartoon strips to summarise their perceptions of this festival. They can discuss this festival via discussion boards with students in other countries to compare how their peers elsewhere celebrate the same festival.

Teachers should ideally design their instruction methods to connect with all four learning styles—experience, reflection, conceptualisation and experimentation. While it is easy to design classroom lessons that require students to reflect and understand abstract concepts, it is often not easy to give direct exposure to experiential learning for those students who are concrete perceivers and active processors.

Example 3
Students integrate several disciplines and active experience by using digital camcorders to enact (drama, science) lessons, based on a script written by them (language, value inculcation), then edit and enhance the recording using appropriate software.

However, technology permits students to simulate chemistry and physics experiments in controlled and safe environments before they actually do these in the laboratory. These simulations are also used to simulate experiences that may not be safe enough for students to do in the laboratory under any circumstances.

Teachers can use technology to introduce a wide variety of experiential elements into the classroom, such as sound, music, visuals, movement, experience and speech. Students can create and experiment with their own digital music, visuals and animations in presentations.

Theories of learning based on an understanding of how the human brain functions hold that a curriculum be organised around real experiences, complex and integrated disciplines, or 'whole' ideas. In order for a student to gain insight into a problem, there must be intensive analysis of the different ways to approach it.

Because every brain is different, educators should allow learners to customise their own environments. This can be made possible through smart cards for students that keep a record of the customised requirements of a student. Though the entire class may be working on a common concept, each student works at the level, depth and environment appropriate for them.

> Example 4
> Students study geographical maps through 'whole-brained' methods: textbooks, computer presentations, physical mapping of their neighbourhood, drawing maps and converting the information collected into digital maps that give them an understanding of the different layers of information available in maps.

To foster a more whole-brained scholastic experience, teachers should use instruction techniques that connect right-brain learning activities (by incorporating more patterning, metaphors, analogies, role playing, visuals, and movement) into their left-brained activities (reading, calculation and analysis). Using all the techniques listed above will provide this 'whole-brained' experience to students. Information technology adapts itself easily to both right- and left-brained learning.

Technology is also a very effective tool for helping children with disabilities to learn. Many of these children have an affinity with computers. Children of all abilities feel computers are non-judgemental, infinitely patient and adapt immediately to their level of understanding and speed. They are far more confident and less hesitant to take risks when they work with a computer than with a human being.

Roadblocks in implementing technology-based instruction

If information technology is such a powerful tool, why is it not being used actively? Why is its potential not being fully exploited?

One factor is the *information overload* constraint. Those who are already not comfortable with technology find it difficult to sift through and assimilate the very vast amounts of information (lots of it irrelevant) that technology gives access to. This sifting of knowledge itself is a skill that needs to be learnt by educators and students alike.

The *excessive pace of change* is another constraint. Information technology is constantly evolving. Its half-life is shorter than any other field of knowledge. It is very difficult to keep pace with constantly changing technologies and their ever-emerging new applications in the

Figure 6.4 Behind every reason given as a drawback against the use of technology is a new skill that needs to be learnt. Those who have a positive attitude to new skill development accept technology as a challenge that must be taken up.

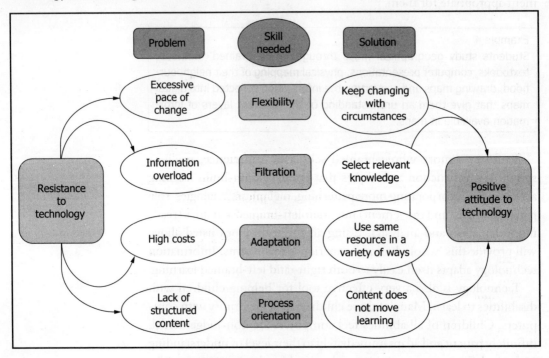

field of learning. This excessive pace of change also makes technology-based learning an expensive proposition—which is the *high-cost* constraint. Software and hardware are often obsolete by the time they reach the school, and require major and expensive upgrades every year.

Another important constraint is *lack of structured content*. Content takes time to develop, is expensive and is often outdated by the time it is ready. Many educators believe that technology is an important tool for unstructured and flexible learning and therefore structured digital content is irrelevant. The market for structured content is just not large enough to be economically viable.

The most important constraint, however, is the *attitudinal constraint*. While students adapt to technology-based learning without hesitation, adults struggle with steep learning curves. If the potential for information technology-based learning has not been realised it is due to educators' inability to develop the same level of comfort with using technology that students have. These are the people who believe that technology-based instruction is over-hyped. Hopefully, as children grow up and become the next generation of educators these negative perceptions will fade away.

Removing this attitudinal constraint will go a long way to removing all other constraints. However, educators must first become aware of the relation between improved cognitive skills and technology. They need to understand how they can use information technology to learn and grow and to achieve higher goals for themselves and their students.

IT can be an instrument for change

If we assume that the purpose of an educator is to enable optimal learning of students, then it is not enough for the student to be the only learner in the system. Theories of the brain tell us that it is important for the brain to be continuously in a learning mode, else it decays. Until educators practice this for themselves, they cannot inculcate proper learning culture in their students.

Once educators accept and open their minds to the potential of information technology, they will step out of the vicious, obsolete cycle of teaching-learning-teaching. The very pace of change in the field of IT, the variety and the breadth of knowledge available compels educators to keep learning and to keep up to date, and this has positive repercussions on themselves and their students. It is for this reason, more than anything else, we need to use information technology for learning. For, in the process we open our minds, change our attitudes, and learn that the only constant in this world is change. As soon as we lose our fear of change, we actually empower our students and ourselves.

ICT and skill development in the curriculum

Even among those who agree that computers and the related information technology should be used in education, no one seems to have any single workable model on *how* it should be used. This is a field that is changing in unpredictable ways and its potential is only constrained by human imagination. There is probably already a technology available for almost any use we can visualise. There are distance education techniques, there are multimedia content models, there are online assessment programmes, and there are videoconferencing lectures, virtual classrooms, scientific simulations and so on. The list is endless and so are the vendors trying to sell different versions of each of these.

What we have, therefore, is an embarrassment of wealth of information and excess of confusion. ICT can do too much for us to comprehend where to start.

How does a school tackle this bewildering variety? Do they expose their students to all or only some selected technologies? What are the resources needed? How do they keep pace with the very rapid changes in this field? Will it really help the student in the end?

One reason why so many questions arise is that most schools approach the entire issue in a piecemeal manner. 'Let us do multimedia content, word processing, presentations, Internet and animations....' Few stop to ask themselves, 'Why are we using technology at all?' And those who do, would probably answer, 'Because it is there'.

To find a more appropriate answer to these questions, we need a re-look at the purpose of information technology in education—or in fact the purpose of anything in education. Once we know what ICT is trying to achieve, the rest of the questions become a little easier to answer. Thus, it becomes necessary to turn the picture around and look not at what ICT can do, but at what the learning process needs to achieve and use what ICT has to offer in order to achieve this. In the process, we may have to ruthlessly discard many exciting features of technology if it does not serve any pedagogical purpose.

Let us go back to the question, 'What is the purpose of a curriculum?' The answer, as we discussed in Chapter 3, is: to prepare students for life, to give them the skills that they will need in order to succeed in life. The chapter describes the process by which a curriculum can be designed so that these skills are inculcated. But what are these skills? They have not yet been clearly defined. As the premise has already been made that content is not as important as process, the present chapter could have used examples from history or physics in the curriculum to describe the skills students need to develop. However, the present chapter tries to answer the question, 'What are the skills that a student needs to develop' by using information technology in education as an example. There are many advantages to this: We are then not confined to any single field of learning; technology is, after all, only a tool and can be used in any discipline. It is also a tool that that can be effectively used to implement the four components of the learning-teaching process:

- Individualisation
- Vertical integration
- Horizontal integration
- Constant innovation and creation of new knowledge

Finally, in the process, we also answer many questions and problems that are specific to using technology. However, we need to constantly keep in mind that technology is only one of many tools that edu-cationists can use.

Wholistic skills

Let us start with the five basic skills that technology (or any learning process or any subject) must impart to all students. *All these are components of what we had earlier called 'critical thinking'.* None of these skills exists independently and each is affected by the others. Nor are these five all-inclusive or the only skills a student needs to acquire; yet all have paths that lead to any skill that may be missing from this list.

Self-development and empowerment

The core skill that any student needs to have is the ability to develop herself, to grow and therefore to be self-empowered. Each student needs to choose her own path, to develop her strengths and overcome her weaknesses. She needs to inculcate value systems that will guide her actions and social responsibility and good citizenship that will enable her towards self-actualisation.

Communication

A student is not an island—she lives in and is a part of the society around her, and therefore needs to communicate her views and ideas and also receive ideas. She needs to construct these ideas with clarity in her mind and communicate them effectively—either through lan-guage, visuals, sound, movement, to as large an audience as she needs.

Analysis

To be able to think and communicate with clarity, she needs to develop her analytical ability, her ability to search, collect, sort and filter inform-ation; to think linearly and in complex webs in order to create something new or to bring new perspectives to what is already known.

Creativity

The purpose of education is futile if it does not create students who create new knowledge. Human beings cannot empower themselves if they are not creative. Their imagination drives them—whether it is in the invention of a new sound, word, picture or thought process, they are continuously creating something new.

97

Productivity

She cannot be creative unless she is also productive. Her learning must be productive—she needs to use learning techniques that will help her to reach her goals in the most fruitful manner possible. She also needs to manage information productively and without wasting time and energy on fruitless tasks.

Figure 6.5 gives a web of some of the ways information technology tools can be used to reinforce these skills. It reveals only the tip of the iceberg in terms of the potential of information technology as a skill development tool.

Figure 6.5 Every course in the curriculum must link these skills together in the learning process

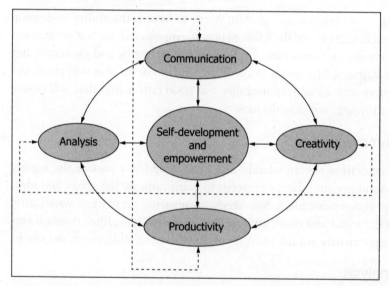

Curriculum design for ICT: Some answers

Schools use information technology to develop students' learning skills.

This model answers many of the questions we had posed earlier, the core question being: How should schools use information technology?

From this statement follow the rest of the answers. A school that has invested in the basics of connectivity and in some standard software can use technology very effectively to develop learning skills.

The standard software familiarises students with software that they will be expected to use later in life in most professions—word processing, presentations, spreadsheets, graphics and so on. All, or any, of these applications can be used by a creative teacher to design assignments that can help develop different types of skills in the students.

Thus, even on a small budget, schools can use ICT very effectively. A school that uses simple animation software and lets students create their own animations of concepts they are learning, is probably doing much more for its students than a school that invests huge amounts in buying subject software with professional animations. In the former, the students are active creators while in the latter, students are passive observers (using software that may become obsolete next year). In the former, students may not be able to 'cover' the physics syllabus by making all the required animations, nor will their animations be as sophisticated as the professional ones.

However, they would have learnt how to research what experts have said about a concept, filter out what is not required now, analyse this concept in order to depict verbal descriptions in a visual manner and to sequence these visuals logically. They would have also added their own notions of aesthetics to the art, layout and colours they use in the animations they create. They would be able to work in groups, with each group member contributing according to her strengths, and learning how others approach the same task.

Ultimately, the sense of achievement and fulfilment will be far greater, and this knowledge and these skills will never become obsolete. Even software with some limited interactivity built in cannot match the power of the open-ended projects that students can do, using ICT. Students should be using ICT to create new things—art, literature or robots. That is the first priority and if, after this, schools have funds and students have time to spare they can watch animations of physics concepts and answer multiple-choice questions online.

Thus, when budgets are limited, as is generally the case, schools have to be very careful about the kinds of choices they make. Other conventional techniques for 'covering' the syllabus are as effective as technology and are far less expensive. As long as technology remains expensive, it must be used effectively and productively for skill development rather than for filling students with information.

Content is a function of skills and not vice versa

While Figure 6.6 focuses on information technology examples to show how different skills can be reinforced, we could have used an example from the study of history to reinforce these skills. Students study history

99

Figure 6.6 A web of possibilities using ICT to develop fundamental learning skills

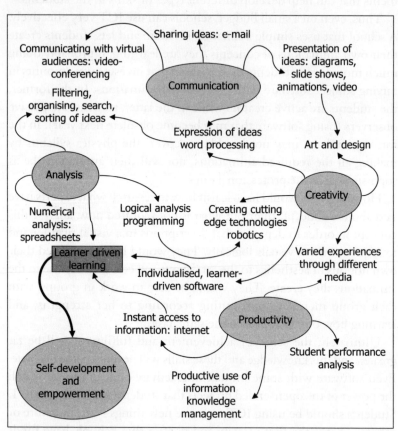

not to memorise the names of kings and queens and the dates of battles they have fought. Students learn history to know how the world was in the past and to learn wisdom from the actions of people who lived before.

They can use this knowledge to increase their productivity; they do not constantly need to re-invent the wheel as they build upon the accumulated wisdom of years gone by. Students also study history to appreciate the many beautiful artefacts that people have left behind and to learn that those who create beauty are immortal. Students also learn history for the sheer joy and challenge of solving the puzzles left behind—to deduce the lives of people in ages gone by from stray stones they have left behind.

Examples such as these can be found in every field of knowledge. When the goal of any system of learning is the process of learning and the development of skills, it does not really matter which subject is used to impart these skills. This is particularly relevant today, when we live in a world of exploding knowledge and it is not humanly possible for a student to master every subject fully. Students need to know a little about everything and should have the ability to learn in depth about anything. ICT is one of the most important tools that make this kind of learning happen, but it must never be forgotten that it is merely one of the many tools available to educators.

Summary

- Positive and dynamic attitudes to change have become crucial today. Leaders are those who create change.
- The chief domains of change that are relevant to schools:

  - expanding knowledge of various subject areas
  - advances in the science of learning
  - information and communication technology
  - society and economy

- Information and communication technology is an important agent that enables change in schools.
- It is an effective and productive tool to ensure learners learn through multiple intelligences, multiple learning styles and whole-brain experiences.
- Through ICT learning becomes participatory, interactive, decentralised, replicable, global and incorporates multimedia.
- As this type of learning is new, there is considerable resistance to using technology but most of the problems can be resolved through positive attitudes to the development of new skills and new solutions.
- ICT is intrinsically well suited to develop positive attitudes toward change, as it is one of the fastest-changing fields of knowledge.
- A major problem faced by even those who have positive attitude is to devise a working curriculum model for technology.
- This problem is solved if ICT is used not to learn content but to develop learning skills.
- Five fundamental learning skills that are part of 'critical thinking' are

  - self-development and empowerment
  - communication
  - analysis

- creativity
- productivity

- Once these become the goals of ICT, even with limited resources, technology can become a powerful tool for learning.
- It must always be noted that ICT is merely a tool; any subject and any field of knowledge can be used by a school to enable the development of the required skills.

Teachers

7

A great school has great teachers

The success or failure of a school rests with the teachers who actually turn its vision into reality. Without the right kind of guidance from good teachers, no student will reach her goals. If we were to ask a cross-section of people who have succeeded in different occupations, to name one person who set them on the path to success, most would name a teacher. Most of us will have memories of at least one teacher who inspired us and made us believe in ourselves.

Whatever else it may have—the greatest curriculum, the best management, impressive infrastructure or the brightest children, a school cannot call itself a great school if it does not have great teachers.

If you were one of the lucky ones, you may also remember a teacher who everyone in the class listened to in enthralled silence, including the rowdiest backbencher. No one ever fooled around in her class; yet this was also the class where every student took part in truly lively, humorous and passionate discussions. The subject she taught does not matter—the discussion may have been an analysis of the reasons for the mysterious disappearance of the Indus Valley civilisation or it may have been on the beauty of the process by which nerve impulses travel in the body. Yet, you developed a love for the subject that remains with you today.

You always knew where you stood in your assignments because your homework came back promptly with incisive comments. If you had done well (which was often, because you enjoyed working and research-ing the interesting projects she gave), she would never fail to praise you. She was a teacher who was known to be fair to all and no one was afraid to go up to her for help. She would find time to listen and yet al-ways seemed to know which excuses were genuine and which were not. She was the one who helped you realise that you were a lot smarter than you thought you were. When you left school, even though you had not seen her for years, she was the one who set you on the path that ultimately led to your success today.

This is the view of a teacher as seen through the eyes of a student. Yet, a student sees only some facets of a great teacher. She may instinctively know that there is probably much more to her as a human being and a professional than can be seen through a student's eyes. What then are the qualities that make a great teacher?

The six fundamental qualities of a teacher

There are six important qualities that a teacher has:

- excellence in domain knowledge
- knowledge about theories of cognition
- an attitude that life is an adventure and requires courage
- ability to communicate this knowledge and this attitude to those around her
- character and integrity
- passion and humour

Domain knowledge

A person becomes a teacher because she has some knowledge that she wishes to communicate to her students. This is her domain knowledge. Her knowledge of her subject is not just accurate and up-to-date but also interpretative—she analyses this subject in depth—from

Figure 7.1 Each of the six fundamental qualities of a teacher has a different type of impact on her ability to be effective

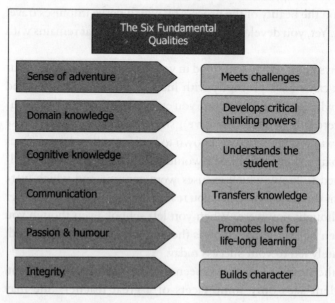

the simplest to the most complex levels—and links these to her aware-ness of other domains and other fields of thought. It is this sense of exploration of her own domain that she offers to her students, not just facts and definitions. She has so much joy in her knowledge of her specialisation that she cannot keep it to herself. She thus transmits not just the knowledge but also her enthusiasm for the subject.

Knowledge about theories of cognition

The second skill is her cognitive knowledge or knowledge of how a student learns. A teacher knows how to deal with students; she can always find the right triggers that will make them focus on the tasks given to them. She helps students to learn in an interesting and joyful manner. She is familiar with the relevant theories of cognitive science and implements these in her teaching. She knows how to deal with different age groups and with students of different abilities and learning styles. She is also sensitive to their cultural, social and economic back-ground, and uses examples and language to which they can relate.

This teacher also knows that students need to be exposed to rich and varied experiences if she has to capture their interest and attention. Therefore, she builds these strategies into the learning experiences that she is using to teach and students in her class will listen to her and to each other.

They will get the opportunity to talk and express their opinions and be given assignments that they need to work on their own as well as in groups. The students will use different means to communicate their work—through writing, through art or through technology. They will learn in different environments—in the classroom, through technology and multimedia, on the playfield, in the laboratory and through visits and interactions with people and places in the real world.

Yet despite these diverse activities, the teacher will ensure that each activity moves the student closer to her goals. The student will be con-stantly given inputs and feedback that will make sure that she does not lose focus. Therefore, the teacher uses her cognitive knowledge to en-hance her understanding of how students learn and then use this under-standing to make learning as effective as possible for her students.

Sense of adventure and courage

The teacher's awareness that life as a teacher is an adventure is the third skill she requires. Without this, no amount of paper qualifications will help her students. Every teacher needs to have joy in her work as well as in being with students. She looks at her task of ensuring her students (with diverse abilities and needs) meet their goals as an exciting challenge.

She does not expect that the path to effective learning will be easy, nor does she take the easy way out in the work assigned for her. When faced with difficult situations, she does not seek escape but seeks solutions; nor does she take recourse to complaint. For her, the objective of being a teacher is important and she is focused on her goal of moulding the intellect and character of each of her students, however much effort that may take. Therefore, she is constantly searching for new paths that will lead her and her students to explore new territories.

Because she has this sense of adventure, she is excited every time a student finds joy in learning something new. She is energised every time a student moves to a higher point of self-realisation. In this process, she finds her own self-fulfilment and satisfaction of her inner desire for achievement. This enthusiasm and energy is what ultimately translates all her domain and cognitive knowledge into a successful learning programme for her students.

Along with a sense of adventure, she has the strength to act in accordance with her own values and the greater good despite pressures pushing her in other directions. It is her courage that gives her the ability to take chances, to take risks, to put the cause before the desire to be popular.

She gives her students opportunities and challenges that will build their confidence and stretch their courage. She motivates them to take risks and take bold stands for their convictions and principles and prepares her students to step fearlessly into the world—ready to take the risks that will ultimately define their lives. She is an example of making courageous decisions such that her students remember her as a role model when they face challenges of their own.

Communication

The chief task of all education is communication. Communication in education becomes important because education is the communication of not just ideas, but of abilities as well. While going through the learning process, it is not enough for the student to listen and understand; the student must translate all that she has heard, into action. She must be able to apply this education in real-life situations.

A great teacher, therefore, is a great communicator. She puts in a lot of effort in using correct, precise and appropriate language to communicate. She also uses non-verbal cues, visuals and technology to communicate. She knows that she has to make every word and every gesture count. She is aware that in a class each student hears the same words differently and interprets them in diverse ways. She also knows that different students absorb knowledge differently and in accordance with their learning styles.

Therefore, she communicates the same ideas in many different ways, not just to embed that idea in the student's mind, but also to ensure that whatever her learning style, the concept has been communicated to the student through the medium that she finds most comfortable.

While other professions focus on a single type of communication, such as a dramatic performance or a newspaper article to communicate ideas, a teacher uses many different types of media to communicate. She is constantly searching for better ways to communicate because she knows her students are constantly distracted by the instant gratification of popular media. She has to compete with and communicate better than slickly packaged popular media programmes.

A teacher knows that communication is not a one-way road; therefore, she listens to her students, their words and their body language. Whatever the subject she may be teaching, she works on the language and communication skills of her students. She knows that this is not just for the English, Hindi or French classroom. In today's increasingly competitive world the only edge a student may have over another is her ability to communicate well.

Character and Integrity

A good teacher is a person of great character, integrity and strong conviction. She is honest and authentic in working with others. She consistently lives up to commitments to the students and others. She works with them in an open and forthright manner. She involves her students in sports, where they can build character as part of a team. She appreciates and corrects students on the basis of character and allows them to experience the consequences of poor choices. The teacher talks to them about heroes and positive values, is sensitive to community values and is a model for her students by being a person of absolute integrity. As a role model, she sets high standards for herself and her students.

107

Passion and humour

The most important quality a good teacher possesses is passion—a heartfelt, deep and authentic excitement about her work. She enjoys what she does. She cares for each student and has true interest in them. There is a quote from an unknown author that says: 'You cannot kindle a fire in any other heart until it is burning in your own.' She loves to learn and grow and is enthusiastic and eager about her students doing the same.

In my over two decades of being an educator, I have come across many great teachers who have made a crucial difference in the lives of their students. These are teachers who encourage, enlighten, inspire, raise the bar and challenge their students to reach for it. The methods of a great teacher are as varied and distinctive as the teachers themselves, but the result—inspired teaching—is a gift enjoyed for a lifetime. Here I am sharing a few compelling stories of few such teachers.

- This year while doing prepositions, I came across an exercise based on Anne Frank. It was a short passage that ended with a brief resume about her. I have been fascinated about the Second World War since I was eleven and voraciously read, or rather devoured, books about it. So, the urge to share a part of the forgotten history got over me and I decided to go ahead with it, hoping that it would arouse curiosity in my students to know more about the Second World War. I gave the exercise and as they wrote it down, I waited for them to ask questions. As soon as they were finished, the questions poured out. I crossed my fingers and then set about telling them in brief about the war and the Jews and then the little girl. They were enthralled, and though it was a story about hardship, which was alien to most of them at that age, they connected with it. As it was the story of a child, some of them ended up misty-eyed.

  I was overwhelmed when the next day four students came up to me proudly holding brand-new books, *The Diary of Anne Frank*—in their hands. There were two more who had rummaged through their parents' collection to read it. Tears welled up in my eyes, for it had worked out better than I had thought. Hopefully, they will go on to read more about it.

  Abha Hundal

- Every day Mohua was seen in school with a bag over her shoulders, her small pink plastic lunchbox in her hands and an indistinguishable expression of determination on her face. I had always known her to feel out-of-place in the special section, to believe her presence there was all a big mistake. But Mohua suffered from epileptic fits for which she was under medication. Every day after lunch, I ensured that she went to the Sick Room to take her medicines. Besides, she was a slow learner and had difficulty in coping with the normal curriculum. As I had done for all my students, I explained Mohua's condition to the class. Some teachers took keen interest in knowing more about Mohua's disability. I did not want the students to be surprised by her behaviour.

From classification of plants and animals in science to realms of the earth in social science, Mohua was a keen listener. But she faced the problem of not being able to pen all that she heard. Sometimes this even forced her to look towards her neighbouring students for help, which was always a risky prospect. I decided that to help her, I must provide her the notes so that she could freely concentrate in the class without being bothered about making her own notes. So I photocopied all the class notes for her. But for her favourite subject, science, the notes were never enough. Long discussions and explanations in class were almost impossible to be converted to ink. After a long meeting with the science teacher, we decided to record all the lessons on an audiotape. So for every class, I used to keep a tape recorder on the teacher's table and switch it on as soon as the teacher began the class.

Mohua had many friends. They were always 'chit-chatting' around the corridors. Many were invited to her birthday and many invited her to theirs. Among these she had a special friend called Payal whom she called every day to learn the homework, even though I had specified it to her and written it in her diary.

As I sat at the back of an English class one day, Mohua suddenly burst into laughter. This outburst was instigated by the story being read out in class, although the entire class was silent. At this all eyes turned to stare at her. When this started happening more frequently I tried to control her but she resented this and showed signs of disgust.

Twice a week, I took Mohua for computer classes. I was surprised to see her struggling to type her thoughts on the keyboard. Her disability brought along with it some visual motor problems. This is one of the reasons why she was also slow in writing what she heard in class. Even in the art classes where she was required to express herself creatively, she was slower than the rest of the students.

Physical education is compulsory for all students, including the students of the special section. But Mohua somehow never desired to be on the field, to hold a ball, to shoot a basket or even run on the grounds. Invariably she would slyly sneak back into class and come to me with some excuse. We would then sit together in the class and I would take out my big book of short stories and read them out to her. Instead of being there out in the sun, there was just a small stream of sunlight creeping in through the window panels as we used to sit together reading the stories of Nikolai Gogul.

Rochana Ghosh, Special Educator

- Alka, a four-year-old child, had been adopted only six months before she began attending school. She was just about getting used to her new family and new environment when she had to take the next big step in her life—going to school. Although, she came willingly and did not show any visible signs of pangs of separation from her mother while at school; her need to feel secure, wanted and loved made her behave in a peculiar manner. Her behaviour in school made her stand apart from her peers. She talked incessantly repeating every word said to her in class and craved for some physical reassurance. Aware of her background, the teachers interacting with her used to give her hugs. It reached a point where she wanted to be hugged at all times. So much so that it started coming in her way of participating in class. She would cling to adults, stay close to her peers. She also had a glazed look in her eyes.

  If denied, she would throw tantrums. The process we devised took time but worked. We talked to her regularly and explained logically that her tantrums disturb the class. Responding to her, listening to her alone gave her the confidence that we were genuinely interested in what she wanted to share. At the same time we made it clear to her that we would share the same listening time with others. Regular meetings with her mother, keeping her engaged and using similar strategies at home began to show results.

  We also settled on one big hug in the morning and one in the afternoon. We acknowledged her need for physical reassurance and addressed it by getting her a life-sized doll that she would carry and hug whenever she desired. Over the months, she grew out of it. She has now made friends and has begun participating in all activities.

  Rekha Bakshi, Vasant Valley School

The four foundations: What a teacher does

These six qualities of a great teacher are what are visible on the surface. A great teacher is not just born with these six qualities; she first builds a foundation on which these qualities stand.

This foundation consists of
- extensive planning for her lessons
- creation of an environment conducive to learning

- an in-depth assessment of students (both academic and pastoral)
- the pursuit of professional self-development

Planning

A great teacher knows that mere inspiration will not get her very far in her work. Therefore, she plans extensively in order to make the most efficient use of all her strengths. She plans for her students; she sets goals for each student according to her needs and abilities. She plans enrichment activities for high achievers and remedial activities for those who are lagging behind. She plans for herself.

She keeps track of the curriculum given to her and ensures that it is spread out evenly over the year. She makes sure that every element in the curriculum is delivered to her students in the right sequence and at the right pace. She also makes sure that students learn from a wide

Figure 7.2 The teacher ensures that assessments are a cycle of continuous feedback and all her actions related to student learning are based on this feedback

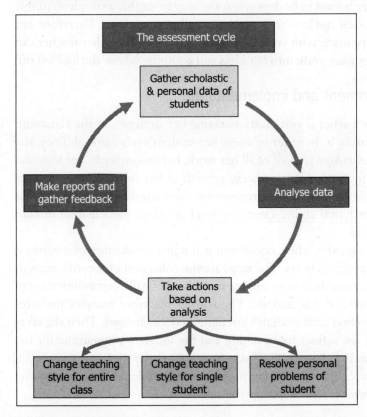

variety of experiences—through projects, discussions, visits outside school and technology. Her well thought-out planning and foresight ensures that all these activities are conducted efficiently and with focus on the right goals.

The teacher is not bound by the curriculum and textbooks prescribed by the board. She plans for a curriculum in a much larger sense: one that develops skills and values in addition to factual knowledge and critical thinking. Therefore, she plans for horizontal and vertical continuity. Her plans integrate her subject domain with other subjects and fields of knowledge.

She makes sure that students understand the relations between different fields of knowledge. Her plans link students' past knowledge to what they will be learning later to ensure continuity in the level of detail that students are exposed to in the classroom. This planning ensures that students get both the big picture and the little details without ambiguity.

In order to achieve all this, she makes both long-term and short-term plans. A teacher also knows that however much she may plan, there are bound to be days when she may be unable to implement this plan herself and have to depend on a colleague to do so. Therefore, her plans are made with such detail and clarity that any other teacher can read her plan, walk into her class and continue where she had left off.

Assessment and implementation

A great teacher is constantly assessing her student—in the classroom and outside it. In order to assess her student's scholastic abilities, she keeps extensive records of all her work: her assignments, her tests and her homework. She also keeps records of her subjective perceptions about the student and comments on their scholastic abilities such as their analytical ability, creativity, level of effort, participation in class and so on.

For a good teacher, assessment is not just a collection of records; it is a four-step process. The steps are the collection of records, analysis of these records, actions on this analysis and finally, communication of the results of this analysis. The teacher therefore analyses these records to find each student's strengths and weaknesses. Then she takes action; she refines her teaching and the learning programme for her students based on the feedback she gets from the students' assessment. She also communicates her findings to her students, their parents and other teachers in an appropriate manner.

Student assessment is not just related to their academic and scholastic abilities. The teacher also assesses their personal attributes. She is constantly observing her students in different environments—their behaviour, personal traits and changes in these. Due to these observations, she is aware of differing personal needs of her students and deals with these needs accordingly.

A teacher's interactions with her student are based on her assessment of the student's character and personality. She knows when a student needs firm handling and when she needs to be given space. She knows what interests the student and how to use these interests to promote effective learning. She gives constant feedback to students (and their parents) to foster their self-belief and confidence.

Assessment for a teacher is also self-assessment. As part of her analysis, she also analyses her effectiveness as a teacher. If a student does not understand a concept, she does not assume that the problem is with the student, she first checks if she has done all that is possible to make the student understand this concept. This self-appraisal is an in-built part of her daily routine. In addition, at least once or twice every academic year, she conducts a very exhaustive self-evaluation and review of the months gone by and checks whether her performance during this period is meeting the benchmarks of a good teacher.

The following case studies illustrate the point that assessments are used by the teacher to gather continuous feedback on which all her actions related to student-learning are based.

Case Study 1

Gather scholastic and personal data of the students
Teaching mechanics to a group of bright and questioning minds made my lessons a very interactive and satisfying experience until I started teaching three-dimensional geometry. Initially, adding a third dimension and doing the computations came very naturally to my students who had the concept of co-ordinate geometry in place.

The problem began when I started taking an arbitrary point in space and assigning coordinates (XYZ) and locating its exact point in the space.

Analyse data
A brief interaction with the students led me to their difficulty of not being able to visualise the third co-ordinate, which was something very new to them.

113

Take actions based on the feedback

I took help of the immediate surrounding, i.e. my classroom and identi-fied the three co-ordinates in the corner of the wall for them to be able to see it—X and Y along the floor and Z along the height of the wall. I approximately located the position of the fan in the class with X, Y and Z co-ordinates.

Next, I took an example of a book kept on the table directly under the fan and asked the students to locate the three axes. At this stage, they were able to identify that the X and Y co-ordinates remain unchanged and only the Z co-ordinate changes.

Change teaching style for all students

To further drive home the concept, I designed an activity wherein the students actually developed a cuboid from a rectangle by folding and pasting (simple) it to a hexagonal prism (advanced).

The activity not only broke the monotony of the class, it also generated new enthusiasm as the practical application of the learned concept was there for them to see and understand.

Later I made reports and gathered feedback from every student and ensured that they had understood the concept before moving ahead.

Rajshree Sood

Case Study 2

Objective

To assess Class XI history students who were given a research project on Medieval World in Europe and worked in partnership with another student.

Process of evaluation

1. Goal: *Gather data of students' scholastic focus*
   Research Diary: Each student had made a research diary for making notes from library material and Internet.
   I looked at the following:

   - How systematic the student was in maintaining a day's output
   - Whether the sources of books and Web sites, links from the Internet had been logged
   - Were there any interesting and new aspects that they had discovered during the research process?

2. Goal: *Gather Feedback on Students' Group Work*
   Team Work: The areas I evaluated were:

   - How did they divide the research tasks in their group?

- How did they complement each other's strength and weakness?
- Did both partners play an equal role during the presentation?

3. Goal: *Analyse the Data of both their Scholastic and Personal Attributes as Presenters*
   PowerPoint Presentation: I graded for content and process:

   - They had to keep to the stipulated time of 15 minutes.
   - Were the handouts of their presentations precise and informative?
   - Had they established a clear hypothesis for their research theme?
   - Were they able to defend their findings with quotations from primary and secondary sources?
   - What was the quality of the visuals and presentation and teamwork?
   - How well were they able to elaborate on any aspect when questioned by me or a peer?

4. Goal: *Actions based on Analysis of Students' Scholastic and Personal Needs*
   Student self-evaluation was in the form of a project evaluation; they had to answer the following:

   - Cite sources that you found most appropriate to your research.
   - How did you make use of this search strategy to structure your presentation?
   - Explain three or four novel insights or ideas of research inputs of your team member.
   - Which issues or concerns did you address?
   - How was your presentation different from others?
   - Give a brief and candid feedback on my inputs to you both in the project outline and in the research process.

Teacher evaluation:

- This assessment process was a novelty for the class—they worked cohesively as a group and were eager to come forward with many independent insights.
- As a teacher I was able to gauge each student's personal and scholastic ability.
- The student feedback has been a learning process for me because for the next similar assignment, I will fine-tune my methods and incorporate individual and group needs of the class to become more effective.

Sreela Mitra

115

Case Study 3: The Story of Abhimanyu

Section A

Earlier students had a problem in coming to grips with this particular episode of the *Mahabharata*:

We tackled this problem in the following ways:

- Read from story books/comics to trace the background of the Battle of Kurukshetra and create an interest among the students.
- The teacher highlighted all the important characters and drew the family tree of the Pandavas and the Kauravas.
- Screened the episode of Abhimanyu from the TV serial on the *Mahabharata*.
- Engaged the students in discussion of what was fair and unfair in the battle.
- Using the TV serial, drew up the code of war as it existed in those times and highlighted the traits of the chief protagonists of the episode and their actions that portrayed them in good and bad light.
- Got the children to draw up a list of just and unjust characters of the epic and what constituted fair and unfair behaviour.
- Role-play based on the episode of Abhimanyu was used to further clarify the story and the personification of characters.

Section B

The students had a problem with the pronunciation of certain words and their spellings:

- We re-read the story, based on individual reading of the epic by each student, to help get the modulation, intonation and pronunciation correct.
- Drew up a list of difficult words and constant repetition in the class enabled the students to pick up the words.
- Students were grouped in pairs and asked to orally construct sentences in front of the class, with the list of words learnt from the text.
- Exercises on vocabulary and sentence construction, homophones, synonyms and antonyms were given a lot of importance to enable students to use words with ease in oral and written expression.
- Literal comprehension was handled with relative ease so we used just three questions for students to draw out facts from the story.
- It has been observed with earlier batches that drawing inferences and framing answers correctly has been a weak area. Simple questions, like explaining and giving reasons, were discussed first as an oral assignment and then reinforced through written work.

Section C

Creative development
Students were asked to research real-life episodes of exceptional bravery and write a story about it.

Research work
Students were encouraged to relate the epic of the *Mahabharata* to the actual site of the battle: in which state of India did it take place? Does the battlefield still exist? Are there any historical remains dating from that period?

Compare this epic with another great epic of India and with epics from other countries.

Language development
Extend the story to a study of similes.
Draw up a list of similes that suit the story

- as bold as brass
- as tough as leather
- as hard as a rock
- as brave as a lion

Lead the study further to other comparisons and more similes.
Follow it up with exercises on similes in the text and as separate work sheet.

Mohini Marya

Creating the right environment

There are many dimensions to the environment—the scholastic environment, the pastoral environment, the physical environment and the collegial environment. All these are needed to create the right kind of environment for learning.

The scholastic environment is chiefly created by her interactions with the student within the classroom and during the formal teaching-learning process; the pastoral environment is her interaction with students inside and outside the classroom. The physical environment is created by her interaction with the administration of the school and her effective utilisation of the physical resources within the school. The collegial environment is not just her interaction with her colleagues, but also includes her own behaviour and actions in different situations that serve as a role model for other teachers.

117

The *scholastic environment* is the one in which most of the learning and curriculum of the school happens. Here, the teacher maintains disciplined behaviour of the student through close but unobtrusive control. Yet, she is flexible and responds promptly to different types of classroom situations.

She knows when to enforce strict discipline and when to let students unwind. She creates the right amount of tension that will stretch the children to their true potential. She encourages students to interact with her and with each other for constructive discussions. She encourages students to take up responsibilities and makes sure that administrative matters are dealt with efficiently and in a manner that will not disrupt the smooth flow of her learning programme.

The *pastoral environment* inside and outside the classroom is as important as the academic environment within the classroom. The teacher ensures that student interaction with each other is friendly and cooperative both within and outside the classroom. The interaction between student and teacher is one of mutual respect and understanding.

The teacher deals with indiscipline or misbehaviour promptly and with tact and fairness. She uses her assessment of personal attributes of her students to know each one as an individual and when needed, gives parental care. She communicates closely with parents to understand the effect of the environment at home on her students and makes sure that this does not hamper the student's learning.

The *physical environment* of the students is equally crucial to learning. No student can work efficiently in aesthetically displeasing surroundings. The teacher therefore ensures that the classrooms and other learning areas are clean and well maintained. She encourages students to display their work in different learning areas in an artistic and visually appealing manner. She creates excitement and interest in the physical environment by constantly changing the environment of the learning areas by changing the displays frequently and changing furniture arrangements.

The *collegial environment* is one aspect of the learning environment that a student does not experience directly. It is the relationship of the teacher with her colleagues. The great teacher knows that a relationship of respect, warmth and friendship among colleagues is as important for the students learning as is the relation between students and between students and teachers. The teacher thus ensures she has a positive relationship with all the staff in the school.

She is approachable and ready to help her colleagues when required. She is equally comfortable about approaching her colleagues to seek help and learn from them. She is not threatened by the success of others but on the contrary, genuinely proud of their achievements. When faced with conflict, she seeks solutions and deals with each situation with tact. She does not accept dereliction of duty by her colleagues and takes steps to ensure that students do not suffer.

Figure 7.3 A great teacher is not a passive acceptor of a given environment—she actively contributes to different types of environments in the school

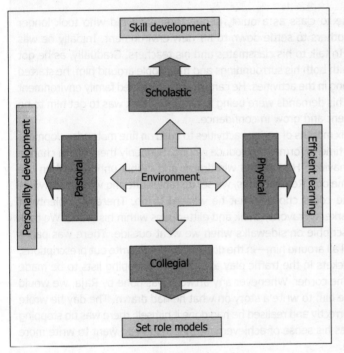

She is also aware that teachers as a group are dependent on each other—no one can function in isolation, or effectively, if colleagues do not co-operate. Therefore, she makes sure that her own behaviour and attitude towards work are above reproach. She sets an example for her colleagues by being punctual to school and class, by not missing classes and by completing assigned tasks on schedule. She is known for her positive attitude to additional responsibilities and her ability to manage multiple tasks efficiently and without causing stress to herself or to her colleagues.

She does all this for many reasons—she knows that an environment where teachers bond well with each other, with friendship, helpfulness

119

and responsibility, is good for the students both in terms of their learning and character development. She knows that after their parents, teachers are the role models for children. Students observe teachers closely and try to emulate the example that they set.

Here I would like to share some stories where teachers have contributed to the creation of a positive learning environment.

Story 1

Raja came to class as a quiet, gentle three-year old who took longer than the others to settle down to his new environment. Initially he was reluctant to talk to his classmates and his teachers. Gradually, as he got familiar with both his surroundings and the people around him, he started participating in the activities. He came from a protected family environment where all his demands were being fulfilled. Our task was to get him to be independent and grow in confidence.

After six months of various activities to build on fine motor development came the time to formally introduce writing. Suddenly there was a change in his behaviour. He seemed withdrawn and visibly unhappy when the books came out. Realising this, we set up tables offering various activities so that he could choose what he wanted to do. There was plenty of paper, markers, crayons, chalk and glitter pens within his reach. We took chalk to scribble on sidewalks when we went outside. There was paper and pencil all around him—in the doctor's corner to write out prescriptions, parking tickets in the traffic play area and for shopping lists to be made in the home corner. Whenever any artwork was done by Raja, we would encourage him to write a story on what he had drawn. The day he wrote a letter correctly and realised he had done it himself, there was no stopping him. It was his sense of achievement that made him want to write more and more.

Surprisingly, now a time has come when he is among the first to finish his written work. He has grown in confidence, has many friends and is enthusiastic about what he does.

Story 2

I can relate this back to the time of the Kargil War when I was in Akhnoor, a small border town in Jammu and Kashmir. Due to heavy shelling, people living in the border areas had to be evacuated and shifted to safer places. They were put up in tents, and schools had to be closed down to provide shelter to people.

No one knew how long this would continue. After a few weeks more tents were pitched near the campsites to hold classes. Some classes were held under the trees and in open fields.

However it was realised that sustaining the interest of students for long in such an environment is difficult. Many schools continued operating as a mere formality, but one particular camp school stood out due to the effort of a few teachers like Ms Raina.

The uniqueness of her teaching was that she made her own syllabus keeping the present environment in mind. She taught the children about the different kinds of trees in that area and their uses, the terrain and the different kinds of soil. She encouraged them to conduct experiments on biodegradable and non-biodegradable materials and their role in the environment. For mathematics, she would teach profit and loss and then give projects or call someone from the camp who had set up a shop, to discuss how she ran her business. A bank employee would come and discuss about interest—simple and compound. Grandparents would be called to talk about the freedom struggle and the status of Jammu and Kashmir then and now.

A lot of other teachers too were soon following Ms Raina's teaching style. With the return of normalcy, schools reopened and children went back to their regular routine. What stood out was that the students could internalise what they learnt as they could relate it to their surroundings.

A great teacher gives so much of herself to her profession because she is a loyal member of the school family and is proud to be a part of a great school. She has taken the time and made the effort to understand the vision of the school and is, in fact, actively involved in the enrichment of this vision. She uses every opportunity to communicate this vision and sense of pride in the school to her students, colleagues, parents and others.

Pursuit of self-development

A great teacher will always keep moving forward—she will never allow herself to stagnate. She knows that she cannot make her students into learners unless she herself is one. She is aware that the knowledge she has is not a fixed constant but is a growing process. Therefore, she actively seeks out a variety of professional growth opportunities.

She participates in seminars and conferences that will broaden both her domain knowledge and her cognitive knowledge. She also conducts events within and outside school where she and her colleagues share

Figure 7.4 The edifice of the complex learning structure that is required for a student rests on the actions of teachers. These actions are planning, assessment (including implementation), creation of the right environment and self-development. When this foundation is firmly in place then learning becomes a (w)holistic experience.

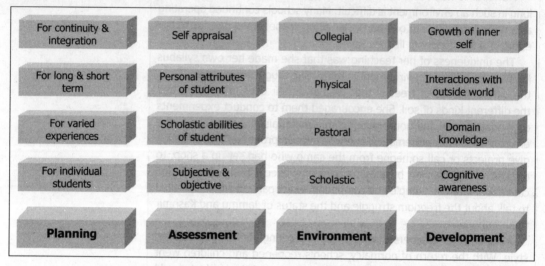

Planning	Assessment	Environment	Development
For continuity & integration	Self appraisal	Collegial	Growth of inner self
For long & short term	Personal attributes of student	Physical	Interactions with outside world
For varied experiences	Scholastic abilities of student	Pastoral	Domain knowledge
For individual students	Subjective & objective	Scholastic	Cognitive awareness

their learning. Her collaborations are not limited to schools, but include the academic world outside the school—in institutions of higher learning, universities, etc. She also keeps in touch with the community and emerging professions that her students will move on to later in life, so that she can prepare her students for life in these. She is aware of the changes in the society, economy and world around her. She moves with the times and is one of the first to adopt new technologies and new methods of learning and teaching.

She is also constantly growing as a person, learning more about herself through continuous self-assessment. Though she is constantly changing as she learns and grows, yet she is firmly rooted to her values. She is known for her honesty and integrity and commitment to the uplift of society and community around her. She has her own life and interests outside the school that help her to become a complete person and she successfully balances her personal and professional lives.

A Day in the Life of a Teacher

The alarm goes off at the crack of dawn. Can I steal a few more minutes of slumber? Oh no! Certainly not! In a flash, I realise it's another action-packed day and the action begins from the moment I rub the sleep out of my eyes. In a trice, I am up and about. I plunge headlong into the morning household chores of packing both the breakfast and lunch for myself and the family and grooming myself down to those much talked-about diamond earrings. All along, I issue a volley of instructions to everyone around to stir the rest of the household into action. I go through all this in a blur of heightened activity before I step out and cruise my way to school. The frantic pace of the early morning routine has set the adrenaline coursing through my veins and got me completely charged and ready for the many roles I will be expected to play in the course of the day.

I dump my bag in the Staff Room and hurry to my class to get my students ready for the morning assembly at 7:30 a.m. Classes follow one after the other and the piles of correction on my table begin to assume the contours of a mountain range. A quick bite downed with a cup of hot steaming coffee and I use my free period to correct notebooks with the hope of reducing that range to rubble. I often wonder who ever coined the term 'free period'! Then it is back to more classes with activities planned to make the learning process more interesting and meaningful. After such an absorbing session, I can scarcely believe that it is already lunch time Students come to have their doubts cleared and problems attended to and I don the hat of a tutor and counsellor to sort out the issues and problems that vex their troubled souls.

Lunch is downed in a hurry as I fleetingly catch up with my colleagues and their lives before rushing off to a meeting in the Head's office to discuss important issues of students and their problems or perhaps systems and their implementation. I emerge resolutely from the meeting and head for Private Study where I set more work for students to tackle on their own though I am around all the time to clear their doubts and check their assignments.

An hour later, after the last lesson when I was on substitution, thanks to a dear colleague who has taken the day off for a valid reason of course, I rush to my designated duty area to disperse the children at the end of the school day at 3:00 p.m. I had hoped to get back to the Staff Room and get down to the task of entering the students' grades into the computer, something that had been at the back of my mind all day long. But once parents spot you at the dispersal area, they want the latest update on their child's performance. It is not in the teacher's nature to turn them away so, after a prolonged exchange on the physical, emotional, social and intellectual development of their ward, both teacher and parents part ways amicably. I then attack the computer and punch away till all the grades are entered and hopefully saved!! I then pack my bag and pick up the most urgently required piles of correction and head homewards. A quick cup of tea and a snack and I am ready once again to correct the pile of notebooks and prepare for the next day's classes before the family comes in and demands my time and attention. Dinner is round the corner but there are a couple of calls I have to make while I get the meal organised. Some parents have to be congratulated on their child's performance and some have to be solemnly told that their's are not exploiting their potential to the fullest.

Finally, our family congregates around the dinner table—the only meal when we are all together and catching up with each other. The telephone rings and it is the Head politely inquiring if it was the right time to call and gives me a fresh set of duties for the next day! I digest that along with dinner and when the family has finally called it a day, I settle down to correct the last few notebooks. It has been a long and busy day and sleep is heavy on my lids. I put the ubiquitous pen away and descend into slumber.

Harried may be I certainly am, but happy! For a schoolteacher, that indeed is the way to be!

Vidya Surendaran

The teacher as a learner

Great teachers are as much learners as students are. They are constantly growing, rediscovering the world and themselves. More than 'teachers', they are the creators of fruitful learning environments for their students and are their mentor and role model. They understand the learning styles of each student and teach accordingly. They do not live in enclosed ivory towers; they are dynamic members of the academic community. They do not indulge in parallel play or adversarial behaviour but work in co-operative teams towards a common understanding of the school's vision.

Probably there are not many such teachers in the real world, but those who come close to these qualities can change the lives of their students and of the world. No one will dispute the enormous influence of teachers in all parts of the development and growth of nations.

Teacher quality issues

Most people believe that the teacher profiled in the earlier sections belongs to a species that is facing extinction. Teaching in schools is becoming the last choice in professions. Those who fail to get a job elsewhere offer their services to schools, and often leave at a moment's notice (or even without notice) when they can get a 'better' job. There-fore, schools are forced to take on teachers who do not meet even minimal standards. The timetable cannot wait for that great teacher—classes have to be held —so the first applicant usually gets the job.

Most schools would blame this on governmental control over schools. Schools do not have freedom in almost any financial matter—fees are regulated by the government, the way the school resources can be used are also regulated, as are the minimum salaries that can be paid to teachers. This creates a vicious cycle. Competent people do not become teachers as they can earn much more in some other profession. As there are few competent teachers in the school system, schools do not have the incentive to try to raise salaries for teachers.

Even if schools find competent teachers, they cannot raise their salaries. Due to the limitations on students' fees, they do not have the funds to pay teachers competitive salaries. This leads to the parallel problem of schools collecting fees that may not be quite legitimate—in the form of donations, annual charges or payments made separately for events and activities held in the school. These charges in any case are rarely for the benefit of teachers!

The lack of opportunities to rise in the organisation is another aspect of the teaching profession that daunts prospective entrants. Intellectually gifted people will not be content to remain in an organisation that offers little or no scope for promotion or self-development. As an employee grows in the organisation, she expects to move onto positions of leadership[1] and greater responsibilities. The only promotion available is that of school principal, and when there are 100–200 teachers in the school, chances of becoming a principal are remote. When a teacher enters the profession, she knows that there will be little or no change in her job description 20 years ahead.

Some teachers will get the opportunity to become heads of departments or co-ordinators of various activities that take place in the school. Though these are leadership roles, most of them have a limited tenure and once this ends, the teacher goes back to her normal teaching activities. In fact, most of these posts run concurrently with normal teaching activities.

[1] I am of the opinion that all teachers are leaders in a classroom setting. They play a vital role in providing instructional leadership in classrooms. They constantly make decisions in the classroom and also encourage students to take decisions. They possess many qualities of a leader such as knowledge of children and subject matter, empathy, commitment, sensitive to communities and families, readiness to help, team spirit, ability to communicate and many more.

Figure 7.5 The poor quality of teachers is a consequence of the working conditions—low pay, few promotions, stress and tedium. The poor quality of teachers worsens the perception of teaching as a profession, and these poor-quality teachers are unfortunately not competent enough to ensure better conditions for themselves.

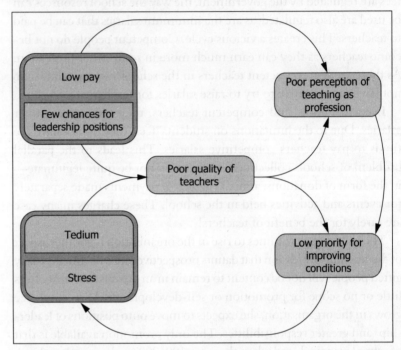

This brings us to the tedium of the job. A large part of the school-teacher's job is repetitive. There are any number of routine tasks such as corrections, reports and keeping of records. She has to teach the same concepts to the same class year after year, and often to different batches of students in the same year. The stories about teachers teaching several generations of students from the same yellowing notes are a reflection of this fact. There is also often no freedom for creativity. It is not easy to find different ways of communicating the same facts every time. There is, therefore, a tendency for a teacher to use the same techniques that have worked well in the past.

The teacher works with a given curriculum that she has to complete within given time limits and has little or no freedom to make changes. Often this curriculum is heavy and factual and there is not much scope for creative inputs. Even if the teacher could think of creative ways of imparting this knowledge, and even if she was given the freedom to do so, she would not have the time. Most syllabi have to be completed within very rigid time lines. In such circumstances, teaching can become extremely monotonous.

The other problem is stress—both physical and mental. A school teacher is on her feet for most of the day, she moves from class to class, often running out of time, and during the periods when she has no classes she has to finish her corrections, her reports, organise activities and make plans for forthcoming lessons. Most teachers end up taking their corrections home; often there is just no time to complete all the work in school.

At the same time, a large part of the stress is in having to deal with students and their individual identities that pull them in different directions, yet the teacher has to take them all down the same path, often against their will or interest. She has to deal with several sets of such children, each with their own, unique problems.

In this sense, teaching in a school is far more stressful than teaching at the college or university level—where the students have achieved some maturity, are generally self-motivated and studying courses of their interest and choice. In a school, there are either very young children with limited communication abilities or teenagers going through the turmoil of adolescence.

Complex challenges

Despite the poor perceptions that many have about the teaching profession, it is not a profession for the intellectually weak. A teacher interacts constantly with the brightest minds and has to keep ahead of her students in order to be able to guide them. Today this is far more difficult than it has ever been because the teacher is no longer the student's sole access to information.

Media and communication technology have ensured that students have easy access to any kind of information. The role of the teacher has therefore changed from an instructor to a facilitator. Her role is no longer to give information but instead to give students the ability to analyse and apply knowledge. She cannot just teach students that Delhi is the capital of India; instead, she has to give them the tools to understand the reasons and influences of Delhi being the capital of India.

While defining the qualities of a great teacher we have seen how complex the role of a teacher is. Although it pays only as much as a blue-collar job—or less—the content and intellectual requirements of the job are as complex, and sometimes far more, than well-paid white-collar jobs.

The kind of teachers that these low salaries attract cannot do justice to the job. Often they are not even aware of the challenges of the job. Many believe that it requires no great skill or preparation to read out to a class from a textbook. In fact, this has become the general public perception of school teaching—that it is a job that requires neither much skill nor ability. The consequence is poor quality teaching and chaos in the classroom, gives the teaching profession a bad name and deters even those who would like to take on the challenge. Better teachers are also discouraged by the quality of their colleagues—they would prefer to join a profession where colleagues are people with better abilities.

Schools that aspire to greatness therefore have to tackle this challenge. It is perhaps a greater challenge than the creation of a learning process-based curriculum. If teachers cannot understand the philosophy behind this curriculum, they will not be able to implement it. The challenge is twofold: one, to find and groom teachers who meet the ideal; and two, to create an environment within the school that will induce teachers to stay on despite the low salaries; an environment that will reduce the tedium and stress but increase the creative opportunities and sense of adventure.

Summary

- A school is great only if it has great teachers.
- The six fundamental qualities of a great teacher are domain knowledge, cognitive knowledge, a sense of adventure and courage, the ability to communicate, character and integrity and passion and humour.
- These qualities stand on four foundations:
- Planning: Long- and short-term plans for individual needs of students, for variety in the learning experience and for horizontal and vertical integration.
- Assessment: Both subjective and objective assessments of the students' scholastic and personal needs as well as self-appraisal.
- Environment Creation: Creating an environment that fosters learning, character and personality development, efficiency in the physical surroundings and a collegial environment that provides students with role models.

- Development of Teachers: Continuous learning and keeping touch with advances in domain knowledge and cognitive awareness; keeping in touch with all that is happening in the outside world; development of the inner self.
- It is becoming increasingly difficult to find teachers with such qualities.
- Low pay, few opportunities for promotions, the tedium and stress in the job deter the best minds.
- The poor quality of teachers reinforces a vicious cycle—the poor perception of the teaching profession worsens, leading to less incentive to improve working conditions and this again leads to poor quality of teachers.
- Teaching is an intellectually demanding job; it is not for the weak minded. The task of creating great teachers given these conditions is the most challenging task that great schools face.

8 Teacher Curriculum

A great school attracts great teachers

A great school believes that all students possess unique abilities and immense potential. It also believes that all teachers possess abilities and potential and that this potential only needs to be developed to make them into great teachers.

School teaching is a neglected profession. Any bright young person would put it down as one of the last choices for a profession. The pay, the working conditions and the quality of professional courses for teacher education deter even those who are interested. Finding great teachers for a great school therefore becomes a daunting task. The solution to this problem lies not just in finding the great teacher, but also in making the existing teachers into great teachers.

The school therefore creates an environment in which teachers will thrive—an environment that will give them the freedom to follow their creative instincts. They provide the encouragement to teachers to take on new challenges and provide the resources needed to accomplish the goals that they set for themselves.

As teachers in a great school are always in the learning mode, they are constantly trying out new techniques of teaching and motivating students. Most of these experiments are successful because the school provides teachers with well-defined systems which will help them to plan and work out the smallest details of their innovations.

The school also provides all the required resources to make the experiment a success. However, while teachers put in every effort to make their experiments work, they are not afraid of the consequences of failure. In this school, a failed experiment is also counted as a positive learning experience and is shared with students. Teachers, therefore, have both an outlet for their sense of adventure as well as a security net.

This school does many other things to make a teacher's life in school satisfying and productive. These are the standard practices found in every good organisation to develop its human resources. The remuneration will be the best that this profession offers, the teachers are provided with as many benefits as is possible, given the regulations set down by the government. The school ensures that there is an atmosphere of mutual respect and camaraderie. Teachers are treated as individuals with different needs and aspirations, and their personal requirements are accommodated as far as possible. Teachers respond to this environment by giving as much as they can, they are highly motivated and enthusiastic.

By creating such an environment, the school attracts the very best teachers and specially those who enjoy challenges. Those looking for an easy tenure and a comfortable routine stay away.

A great school creates great teachers

Few schools have programmes for teachers to induct them into the school philosophy and vision. More often than not, teachers learn about these through informal interactions that come up in an unplanned manner. Schools do hold seminars and workshops for teachers—but these are not part of some larger plan. Often these are held to fill a vacant slot in a staff meeting or are the result of an offer from an outside agency that is conducting this workshop.

Great schools do not leave this kind of training to chance. They are not content with just attracting the best in the available pool. They take many proactive steps to ensure that their teachers remain in the learning mode. A systematic process of needs assessment is used to acquire an accurate and thorough picture of the strengths, needs and areas of interest of each teacher. Based on the information gathered from this comprehensive assessment (through questionnaires, focus groups, classroom observations and teacher's self-assessment), great schools formulate an Individualised Education Plan (IEP) for each teacher. Reflecting the needs assessment, they have a curriculum for teachers that will take them through well-defined steps to higher levels of professional competence.

> - The first step is the development of core teaching skills
> - The second step develops leaders within the school
> - The third step develops visionaries—those who will be leaders in global fields of school education.

Curriculum for core teaching skills

Usually, when a teacher joins a school after completing a degree in education, it is assumed that given a syllabus, she will be able to handle

Thus in a great school, just as students are not 'handed down' a syllabus to memorise, but are involved in a student led learning programme, so also teachers are not handed down a given curriculum for students, but are participating creators of this curriculum.

her students and teach her class. However, given the poor quality of most degree programmes in education, this would often be a false premise.

Even if the teacher went through a good teacher development programme, there is a lot that she needs to learn about the school she has joined. Each school has its own philosophy and traditions, the methods of functioning will vary from school to school. This will be much more so in a great school. Here, a lot of thought has gone into the development of learning systems for students, so the learning programme is likely to be unique in many ways. No new teacher can intuitively grasp these and it would be extremely inefficient for the school to expect that she will do so in due course through observation and experience.

Therefore, the school puts in place proactive programmes for the orientation of new teachers to teach them the most basic teaching skills—this time in a context that is specific to the school. The idea is to familiarise the teacher with the mission, values and the vision of the school. The aim is to cultivate a sense of ownership among the teachers for the school without which it would be impossible to implement the school's vision.

This orientation is also useful for teachers who have been in the school for a while as a refresher course. For the older teachers, this orientation is an opportunity not only to refresh what they already know about the school's vision and philosophy, but also an opportunity to pick up the latest advances in the science of learning and teaching and in their domain subject. Apart from these orientations, there are whole series of well-defined programmes spread over every academic year aimed at cultivating a variety of qualities in teachers and ensuring that they remain in a learning mode.

What does this training consist of? This training or orientation spans different types of skills. The basic skills that every teacher needs to have are:

- Domain knowledge
- Awareness of cognitive theory and its implementation
- Management of students
- Management of time and resources
- Productivity and efficiency

All these are part of the self-development of the teachers. In each, the underlying motive is not just to develop knowledge and awareness but also to increase motivation and generate enthusiasm.

Development of domain knowledge

As has been said earlier, domains are constantly expanding—we live in a world of change, and teachers need to help students to cope with this constant change. They need to be able to use this ability to deal with change to initiate further growth and leadership. It follows then that teachers too should be able to surmount the challenges that change brings. A teacher needs to be always up to date. The school therefore has programmes and resources that will help teachers to hone their knowledge of their domain. These would help teachers stay abreast of the research happening in their field of specialisation and be aware of not only the current wisdom, but of likely future trends.

Figure 8.1 Training ensures that teachers develop wider perspectives and awareness of their subject specialisation in perspective

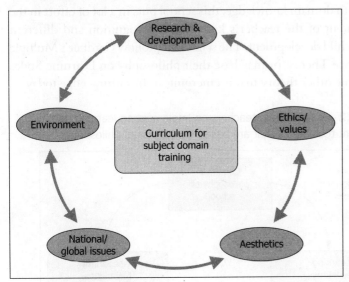

Domain knowledge is not limited only to an understanding of the subject in question. Every teacher needs to be able to integrate discussions on values and ethics as a part of their subject.

These schools therefore develop an awareness of these issues in teachers first. Only then can the teacher pass this on to their students. They conduct courses in humanities for all teachers—for example, a history course would be conducted from the perspective of enabling teachers to think on issues related to tolerance, respect for diversity, need for objectivity and lack of bias. It would help them to integrate these values and other ethical issues into their classes.

Also linked to such courses would be training on issues that confront the society. Through seminars and conferences, teachers would learn and gain a perspective and insight into the complex issues facing the country. This will be in addition to their participation in discussions on environmental awareness and social responsibility.

A neglected part of a teacher's domain knowledge is the awareness of aesthetics. There is no field of study that lacks beauty, nor is there any science so dry that it lacks art. The awareness that science and arts are two sides of the same coin is one that great schools instil in their teachers. Not just the arts teachers, but also every teacher in the school participates in courses on art appreciation and learns to link this to her subject or specialisation.

Development of cognitive skills

Along with domain knowledge, this school puts in a lot of effort in the development of the teacher's knowledge of cognition and different stages of child development. The school may follow Gardner's Multiple Intelligence Theory, or may base their philosophy on Learning Styles or on some other theory that is emerging at the cutting edge today.

Figure 8.2 Schools train teachers on implementing learning and assessment techniques that are based on the school philosophy

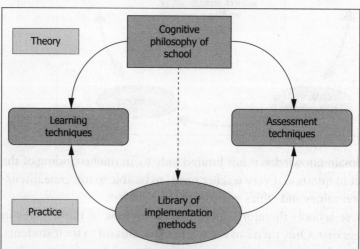

They make sure that the teacher understands both the theory and how to apply this theory in her day-to-day interactions with her students. Therefore, teachers are given inputs on how to incorporate

different types of learning styles in their lesson plans, how to integrate lessons across different disciplines, and so on. Teachers also learn about various activities that they can use in the classroom, in the laboratory or outside the school.

The cognitive domain is very large. While it is important for teachers to know the theories of cognition, small details in the implementation of these theories are also critical. These small details of a lesson range from ideas on basic teaching techniques to the use of teaching aids. Included in these are the development of assignments, worksheets and setting of examination questions. The thread of the learning philosophy needs to run through all these. Thus, if the philosophy is multiple intelligences, a lesson in physics will incorporate not just logical/mathe-matical reasoning, but will also include activities for the creation of models that develop spatial/visual intelligence. If the topic is sound, then students will learn about sound by listening to music. While learn-ing mathematics, they may go around the school campus and onto the play field to calculate areas and dimensions.

Teachers do not get such examples about various activities in isola-tion. Their training helps them to understand the rationale for each of these activities. In this manner, the cognitive programme for the stu-dents gains a very specific focus. It is very clear to the teacher that the aim is to develop different types of intelligences while acquiring subject knowledge.

The school also gives teachers the resources to make effective and accurate assessments of their students. They are given inputs on methods of correcting assignments and other work submitted to the teacher. The teacher learns how to develop the rubrics for this assess-ment, so that she can be objective and ensure that every student is measured against the same standard. She is also given inputs on follow-up actions she can take. Thus, the rubrics not only define the marking scheme. They also define whether this student needs further enrich-ment activities or whether she needs remedial action.

Student management skills

The next skill that the teacher needs to develop is her ability to manage her work. The most important part of this is managing her students. She needs to know how to deal with different situations in the class-room, how to deal with students as a group and as individuals.

The school thus ensures that teachers have a basic knowledge of child psychology and different stages of the student's intellectual, social and emotional development that will enable them to manage students. This knowledge enables them to understand their students better, to use the right triggers to motivate learning. With a better understanding of the psychology of children of different ages, teachers can intervene and interact in a manner that is appropriate to the age of the student. This helps in giving better quality pastoral care to all students—including those who may have problems either in school or at home.

Teachers understand how social interactions and peer influence help learning. They learn how to manage diversity in their students. They develop skills to deal with students from different social, economic, cultural and religious backgrounds with sensitivity and awareness.

A part of managing students is managing the parents. Each parent has different aspirations and different ways of bringing up their child. They come from different backgrounds and have different value systems. The school therefore trains teachers on its parent interaction policies. These are well defined and laid out without ambiguity. Teachers learn how to deal with different types of situations that may arise. They know which issues they can deal with alone and which issues require the intervention of other teachers or heads of school. This ensures that teachers speak in one voice to the students, to the parents and to the outside world.

Figure 8.3 Teachers are trained to understand both social interactions and child psychology that affect the behaviour of individual children as well as groups of students

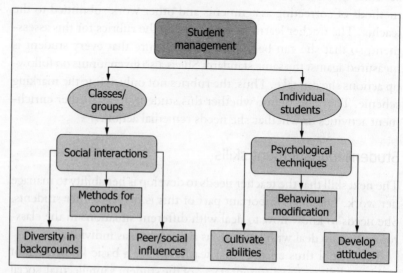

Work management skills

Teachers work with limited time—they often have a curriculum given externally by a school board which is only a subset of the larger curriculum of the school. They also have limited resources—no organisation has unlimited resources and schools suffer in this respect more than most.

Teachers are trained to manage their time effectively—this often means doing multiple tasks at the same time or making a single task meet multiple purposes. The setting of assessment rubrics is an example of this. A teacher who has learnt to create well-defined rubrics before she begins to correct assignments or tests will be able to work much faster. She knows exactly what qualities she is looking for in every answer to every question. The rubrics will also simultaneously help her to assign different types of follow-up action for each individual child.

Given the limited resources, teachers make their own resources and are encouraged to use their innovative ideas to create resources in-house. They use the animations on landforms made by students in higher classes to explain these concepts to students in lower classes. This requires the co-ordination of the technology department with the social science department, of the higher-class teacher with the lower-class teacher. The school provides forums where teachers of different classes and departments can get together specifically to brainstorm on such ideas and thus ensure that resources that one teacher has developed can be shared with others across the school.

Productivity and efficiency skills

The most important productivity tool that teachers have is their lesson plans. If these lesson plans are made with the correct degree of detail and depth, then most of the teacher's work is done. However, making proper lesson plans for the week, the term and the year is a skill that needs to be learnt.

The school provides teachers with this training. Teachers get ready-made formats that help them to understand all the elements of a good lesson plan. Teachers also have access to lesson plans made by other teachers so that they can learn and adapt these to their own needs. A centralised database helps in sharing ideas and in monitoring the plans of teachers to ensure that students get well-prepared and well-planned learning experiences.

137

Figure 8.4 Schools enhance teacher productivity by training them to manage knowledge and to communicate effectively. Familiarity with technology is needed to create, manage and use information resources effectively for planning.

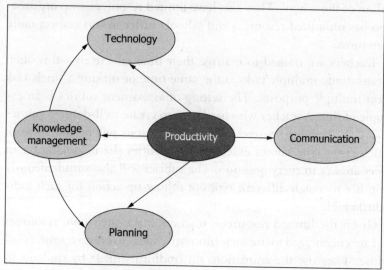

Great schools go to great lengths to provide productivity tools to their teachers—apart from the centralised lesson plan database; teachers would also have access to online reports on student performance. Each teacher would be trained to use these resources effectively. Training on the use of various ICT productivity tools—ranging from simple e-mail and word processing to more complex spreadsheets and databases—would be an essential part of every teacher's curriculum.

Other than the planning of the lessons, there is the planning for the calendar of the school. Teachers are involved in this planning and therefore get to know the larger picture. If they are involved in the development of the school calendar, the science teacher can co-ordinate her lesson on the phases of the moon to coincide with the social science department's viewing of the moon by telescope at night. The language department could create a brochure on the Taj Mahal just after the history department's visit to the monument. Thus, one way of increasing productivity and quality of the teaching programme is by involving teachers in areas outside their immediate teaching domains and helping them to understand their role in the overall scheme of the school.

Another crucial way of boosting productivity is through efficient and accurate communication. All teachers need to convey ideas, concepts and assessments to their students. No two brains interpret the same words in exactly the same manner; so often the same statement made by a teacher is understood differently by different students.

Teachers therefore need to become excellent communicators to ensure that every student understands clearly and accurately all that has been said and explained. They need to use many different techniques to explain a single concept; they need to know how often to repeat instructions and how to rephrase these in different ways.

The school helps teachers to develop these language skills. They are given several opportunities to write; they write reports for student assessment and for assessment of activities that have been held as part of the curriculum. They express their opinions on a variety of issues that are related to life in school.

Teachers are also given opportunities to speak at different forums— during staff meetings, while making presentations to members of their department and to the rest of the school on work that is happening in school. They are given opportunities to listen and learn from teachers who have established themselves as excellent communicators. This is apart from formal workshops on developing good language and communication skills.

Methods used by the school for teacher development

This school makes sure that teachers have the resources to learn and refresh their learning constantly through access to a well-stocked library and to the Internet. The school also finds many other ways to make the teacher remain in the learning mode—by having a regular programme for teachers to interact with experts in the field—either within the school or outside.

It encourages teachers to become members of communities of like-minded teachers who meet and discuss domain-related issues at regular intervals, either in person or in virtual meetings. Apart from these workshops, conferences and e-conferences, schools conduct formal training programmes that are targeted at very specific skills— development of lesson plans, using online databases or creating rubrics for evaluating student work.

They assign mentors within the school for teachers. These mentors are group leaders, co-ordinators and heads of department who are available to give advice and clarifications to newer teachers. These mentors actively seek out other teachers and ensure that there is sharing of ideas and development of new ideas.

By exposing teachers constantly to new ideas, schools ensure that teachers know how much is possible. Yet, these are only ideas. Teachers have to follow a basic framework of essential rules, functions and methods. This ensures that order is maintained and that the quality of the school's programme is not diluted. It ensures that teachers do not deviate from the school's philosophy. Once this framework is in place, teachers are given a lot of freedom to adopt new ideas and create their own new techniques—which then go on to add to the library of knowledge that the school maintains and which can be shared with other colleagues.

Thus the training programme or the curriculum for teachers deals with both issues—of ensuring that they are aware of the framework within which they must work and also ensuring that they are aware of where they have the freedom to innovate and how to use this freedom effectively. The school's curriculum for teachers thus creates a pool of highly motivated teachers by showing them how much they can do and then by giving them the support to go ahead.

Leadership curriculum

Teachers are not a homogenous entity—every teacher has different skills and different potential. In each group, certain teachers will stand out as leaders. Some may be leaders due to the quality of learning experience that they give their students. Some others may have excellent pastoral relationships with their students. Yet others may be efficient programme developers and implementers. A great school recognises these leaders. It does not just encourage them, but also develops a curriculum for them so that they can develop their leadership skills.

The skills that great schools develop in these teachers are:

- Communication skills
- Organisational ability
- Interpersonal skills
- Awareness of the big picture

Communication

Good teachers are always good communicators, but for a leader, communication is much more than being able to convey ideas accurately. Leader-teachers learn to go beyond mere clarity of speech and writing. Teachers who have shown that they have good communication skills in the classroom are given specific opportunities to present complex ideas to colleagues, parents or the management.

These may be verbal presentations or written reports describing different systems in the school. They will be selected to conduct work-shops for other teachers explaining the techniques they use in the classroom. These teachers are given responsibilities in school that tap their communication skills. They are appointed to write the letters that go to parents informing them about different activities held in school. They are assigned to help other teachers to write good reports. Apart from this informal training, they also receive formal inputs in workshops and discussions on the verbal and non-verbal language they can use to express their views.

Figure 8.5 Leaders in communication skills get different levels of responsibility depending on their ability

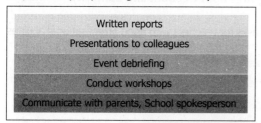

Communication is also about listening to others and gathering perceptions from a variety of points of view. Good communicators are given the responsibilities that require them to listen and gather inform-ation from different sources. For example, they may be responsible for the debriefing that takes place after an event. For this purpose, they collect views from teachers, students and parents on the success or problems faced by the event. They gather and present ideas on how to make this event a greater success in future.

Finally, communication is the ability to accept negative feedback with grace. A leader makes sure that others are not afraid to give her their honest opinions. The school encourages all teachers to voice opinions without fear of victimisation. However, those who listen to criticism—and use it for self-improvement or for finding solutions to problems—are encouraged to become leaders.

Organisational ability

Different types of activities are constantly taking place in a school. These are related to learning within the classroom, in areas of the school out-side the classroom or outside the school. Apart from taking classes, the next most important task of a teacher is to plan and organise these

141

activities. Some teachers show an aptitude for this—any programme conducted by them is planned to the last-minute detail; emergency backup plans are always in place and the programme runs smoothly both before the audience and behind the scenes.

Mere efficiency is not sufficient for leadership. Equally important is the ability to take tough decisions under pressure and the ability to delegate responsibility. Teachers who are good organisers are given teams of teachers to work with and are expected to distribute and delegate tasks. They are also given the freedom to take risks and the authority to take decisions. Many schools function under an authoritarian regime where decisions are handed down by the head of the school, but not in a great school. Here, teachers actively participate in decision making, and decision making requires both freedom and authority.

Figure 8.6   Examples of tasks for teachers with good organisational abilities

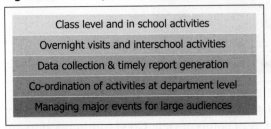

Class level and in school activities

Overnight visits and interschool activities

Data collection & timely report generation

Co-ordination of activities at department level

Managing major events for large audiences

Some examples of the tasks that these teachers are responsible for are: organising student visits outside the school and events such as competitions within the school. Others manage critical functions such as ensuring that data on student performance are collected from various teachers on schedule and timely reports are generated for parents. Those with the ability to manage teams and the ability to delegate responsibility effectively, organise major events such as the school's annual showcase for parents or academic conferences for teachers from across the world.

Schools train teachers to conduct these events efficiently. They are taught the means by which they can give freedom to their team members. They receive training on how to appraise rather than direct the work done by the team members. They learn to ensure that tasks are completed with efficiency but without intrusive control.

Inter-personal skills

Some teachers are excellent at handling classes. They rarely face problems of inattentiveness or lack of discipline. These teachers know more about their students than most other teachers do—they are aware of not just the students' abilities but also their aspirations and desires.

They have the ability to interact with their students on a personal basis and encourage them to confide their innermost thoughts and problems. These teachers show the same interpersonal skills with their colleagues. They not only get along well with others but also ensure that there is an atmosphere of friendship amongst all teachers. They take the initiative to smoothen out the inevitable tensions that arise in any organisation. Other teachers tend to follow their lead.

Teachers with such strong inter-personal skills are given long-term responsibilities—they lead departments of teachers with varied personalities. Departmental heads receive training in teacher psychology and methods of developing the right kind of attitudes in others. They also involve them in frequent discussions on ethics and value inculcation. They are additionally trained to act as role models, to act and behave in a manner that will set an example to other teachers. They learn to give their department members a sense of ownership and pride in their work and in their department.

Figure 8.7 Teachers with good inter-personal skills can have a strong influence on the behaviour of other teachers. Therefore, they receive training in teacher psychology and value inculcation.

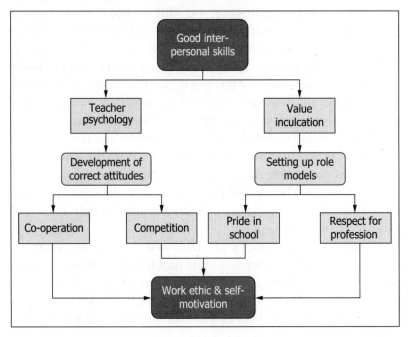

Yet, leadership is not limited to smoothening of tensions—often it requires the creation of the right kind of tensions. These leaders learn that teachers in their department must be made to put in the effort that will stretch them to their potential limits. They learn to create the right balance between both the competitive and the cooperative spirit.

Awareness of the big picture

The awareness of the big picture is both at a micro and at a macro level. At the micro level, a leader needs to understand all the details of her responsibilities. At the macro level, she needs to understand her role in the context of the school in its entirety.

While many teachers are sensitive to the fact that they are a significant part of the larger picture that makes the school, there are very few who take the initiative to understand all the rest of the parts that make up the school. Therefore, great schools actively cultivate this attribute in those teachers who show leadership qualities and have been selected to lead.

At the micro level, the head of a department needs to understand the role of every teacher in her department. She needs to have an overall awareness of their subject domains and of the cognitive understanding that each needs to possess for the age group she teaches. She should be able to make her teachers interact with each other in order to draw on each other's strengths. Beyond the scholastic domain, the head of the department should also have certain administrative awareness of the various tasks that need to be done to ensure the success of various activities as well as an overall picture of the resources required for these.

At the macro level, she needs to understand how her department networks with other departments and what she needs to do to ensure greater and smoother interaction between departments. She should not let her loyalty to her own department get in the way of her appreciation of the role of others. Sometimes she will need to accept a lower priority for her department if this is in the overall interest of the school. Good leaders are dedicated to their responsibilities and often this dispassionate worldview is very difficult for them to cultivate.

Leaders learn to understand this big picture by ensuring that all of them meet regularly to discuss the issues that affect the school. They take part in discussions related to all the functions of the school at a managerial level. These could be discussions on the schools budget, on student admission policies or the development or restructuring of various systems in the school.

Planning for the school's timetable and calendar of events are examples of collective exercises. Activities for the academic year are arrived at through deliberations and brainstorming sessions involving all the teachers. It is the first stage of planning that helps to focus on the key issues, the objectives of learning, the process of learning, the outcomes and the impact. The calendar (see pp. 146–51) contains a list of 15 school events in an academic year along with the process that was used to finalise them.

The heads of department are also given responsibilities that go beyond their department. They may be assigned the task of co-ordinating certain inter-departmental activities. The school consciously tries to integrate all the various systems in the school and makes sure that school leaders are the active creators of this integration.

A Curriculum for vision—creating giants

A great school nurtures its teachers—it takes them systematically to higher levels of responsibility and gives them greater challenges at each step. A teacher rises from being a great teacher to being a great leader within the school. Just as many more of its students become leaders, as compared to other schools, so also there are many more leaders among the teachers of this school. Among these leaders, some stand out. These teachers combine the qualities of great teachers with all the qualities of great leaders. There is a special curriculum for these outstanding teachers that will take them to a higher level of leadership.

The most important lesson that these teachers learn is vision—they learn to look ahead, to dream about how they can transform their world. Their view is no longer limited to the school, but to a worldview that may relate to innovative research in some aspect of education, management of educational institutions or the development of educational reforms for the future. Every teacher's dream will be different, but the dream will go beyond the boundaries of the school. Great schools encourage these visionaries. They give them the time and the resources to pursue their vision, they send them across the world to interact and learn from experts in their field of interest. These teachers receive encouragement, even if their area of interest will not directly benefit the school or its students, either now or in the near future.

While most schools will encourage teachers to become good teachers and effective leaders, there are very few that will encourage great teachers within the system to grow larger than the school itself. This is not true in a great school. This school takes pride in many great leaders in various organisations across the world, because these were once teachers in their school. It is not afraid to lose them, because the school itself has a larger vision of its role in the world of education. Teachers never leave this school because they have found a better school to work in, but move ahead because the school has given them a greater dream to achieve.

145

Calendar 2006

Gain to the people (core, peripheral witnesses)			
Core	Secondary	Peripheral	Loss if the activity did not happen
Activity: Trips to Sultan Garhi			
People responsible for carrying out:			
Students: Participation in preserving heritage/ need to preserve heritage, a sense of belonging and oneness with our environment and appreciation for our heritage; students get an understanding of history, culture, conservation, intermingling of cultures; a sense of responsibility; good experience to understand history, students learn about the heritage of our country and learn how to preserve old monuments; awareness amongst teachers and parents as directly or indirectly they are also a part of this; learn about our heritage and what can one do to preserve it	Teachers: an opportunity to observe students in the real world, the same as the core; lead by example, set standards, its historical heritage, same as core	Parents and the public: this will make them aware of the environment too, hope that the new generation is concerned and is being led in the right direction; public will also take greater interest in maintaining cultural heritage	Children will not gain an understanding of the importance of preserving our heritage. An opportunity for MS & SS to work together in the community. We will miss out on a very important learning experience, children might become philistines in case they do not get exposure from home as well, no cultural awareness, sense of responsibility, student do not get a very important learning experience, will not get an insight into the preservation of old monuments and learn about our heritage
Activity: Assessments and discussion			
People responsible for carrying out:			
Learning curve of students, the teachers and children will know the strengths and weaknesses; helps us to look at children individually, create plans for each one of them to overcome specific difficulties that they face. Identify areas that need to be strengthened; teachers can understand lacunae in teaching methods, from the assessment and discussion we help the student understand where she/he stands and where she/he needs to work, will help in identifying the strengths and weaknesses of students and their overall performance, way of 360 degree assessment	Teachers: able to establish baseline and modify strategies, the parents will know their children's progress, feedback on the child's learning, make plans together, teachers can make individual plans for students and identify learning styles	Parents: Monitor child's progress, the heads will know the progress of the children and how well the teachers know them, helps me to understand how children are performing in other areas of school, understand their strengths or difficulties; parents can assess their child's performance	Progress of child will not be monitored to establish standards, we would get complacent and not be able to make the children into lifelong learners; poor learning, incomplete learning, ignorance about difficulties that children face in understanding, feedback on the teaching methods; are our objectives being met? we do not help the student where she/he stands and where she/he needs to work; will not get an idea on the level of understanding

Gain to the people (core, peripheral witnesses)			
Core	**Secondary**	**Peripheral**	**Loss if the activity did not happen**

Activity: Book Week

People responsible for carrying out:

Core	Secondary	Peripheral	Loss if the activity did not happen
Enrichment & interaction with authors and sharing and listening to different perspectives/ buddy reading; will encourage the students to get excited about books and realise the value of reading, encourages children to read, write and explore the world of literature; a great opportunity for non-readers to improve reading habit and value of reading; students get an incentive to read and understand the value of literature, encourage more and more students to read by creating an exciting environment	Will be encouraged to update themselves by reading too; by a process of osmosis the larger community learns and grows; will also gain awareness on current literature available	Will be encouraged to buy more books for their children; increase knowledge of books and literature; understand the strengths of individual students outside the classroom; will buy books for children and thus motivate them to read	Specially for SS: Opportunity to be sensitised (MS). SS ch. Lose out on being read to; exposure to literature/bonding opportunity, the children will only be fixed to the TV and computer; no reading, no celebration, no enhanced awareness about literature; non-readers will never get a chance of getting to know the joy of reading and writing, we did not improve reading habits and value of reading; there will be no exposure to literature and thus lose out on enhancing their awareness

Activity: Socio Quiz

People responsible for carrying out:

Core	Secondary	Peripheral	Loss if the activity did not happen
To showcase their knowledge, compete and have fun while learning; a great learning experience and interaction with other school students; great learning experience for everyone, learning is fun!!!	Generates excitement about school; strengthens school spirit; thrill of organisation and playing host to other school students	Awareness; a sense of pride and ownership; learning experience	Learning from each other; excitement about new learning and competing with other schools; enrichment and knowing your standard vis-à-vis other schools

Activity: Laissez Faire

People responsible for carrying out:

Core	Secondary	Peripheral	Loss if the activity did not happen
To showcase their knowledge, compete and have fun while learning, enhance interpersonal skills and public speaking skills; to apply taught concepts in the field of creativity; learning with fun and interaction with others, a great learning experience and	Generates excitement about school, strengthens school spirit, builds up a sense of belongingness, helps children to learn positive things from other	Awareness, a sense of pride and ownership; opportunity to interact with an important economist and build up the spirit of enquiry; learning experience	Increased awareness about economic issues; learning to question, challenge, present, work as a team, learning from each other; excitement about new learning and competing with other schools; remain restricted to the four walls of the classroom

Gain to the people (core, peripheral witnesses)			
Core	**Secondary**	**Peripheral**	**Loss if the activity did not happen**
interaction with other school students; exposure and interaction with students from other schools and also with eminent personalities from the concerned areas	schools; enhances their creativity, helps them to think beyond the given; thrill of organisation and playing host to other school students		and not be able to appreciate other's point of view; reduced interaction with other schools; organisational skills, time management, ability to handle success and deal with failure; we cannot give learning with fun and interaction with others; enrichment and knowing your standard vis-à-vis other schools

Activity: Outreach Activities

People responsible for carrying out:

Children: Understanding of needs of community and the disadvantaged/ tolerance/ sensitising; will give them oneness with their environment and make them give back to society; helps children to understand the connection to the larger world that they live in and how we all can help in the overall progress of the society; sensitivity, sensitisation towards weaker members of society and sense of responsibility to society; helps children understand their responsibility towards the community and in the larger sense, the country	Teachers: relating real life situations to curriculum/ gauging of social skills, the same as the core; sensitivity, setting standards, empathy, awareness; setting standards for students and help in making them good human beings	Parents: reassuring for them that their child is participating in a selfless activity, the same as the core; through osmosis a larger cross-section of people become socially responsible; social awareness amongst parents will also be enhanced by helping their children in such activities	Children will not have an opportunity to connect with the real world. Tolerance, sensitivity to the community; we will grow to be selfish and non-compassionate individuals; lack of sensitivity to the larger society that we live in; will learn to take responsibility and be involved in the process of improving things around them, lack of sensitivity and responsibility; not being able to connect with all sections of society. Feeling of 'I CARE' for the environment

Activity: Essentials

People responsible for carrying out:

Make them into sensitive and compassionate individuals with values that will help them	Same as the core; awareness, building up a	Same as the core; a more sensitive and empathetic	We will grow without our basic values and beliefs; hollow human beings with no sense

Gain to the people (core, peripheral witnesses)

Core	Secondary	Peripheral	Loss if the activity did not happen
stand out and learn in any situation; children understand that the most important thing about learning is to be a good human being and not only to be a good scholar; in the classroom children learn to look at issues from so many different perspectives, to become good citizens of tomorrow; inculcate a sense of values and become good humans; it makes them realise that it is the most important ingredient of one's life	solid foundation which does not crumble under pressure	community of students and teachers; compassionate individuals who work towards long-term goals; a sense of empathy amongst the society in general and learning of values	of right and wrong; will open their eyes and mind to a host of issues outside their purview, will lead to self indulgent individuals who lack inner strength. No conscience; susceptibility to crime and easy way of life, insensitive society with no values; an individual can also make the difference

Activity: Hobby Exhibition

People responsible for carrying out:

Core	Secondary	Peripheral	Loss if the activity did not happen
Children: sense of achievement and an opportunity to show off the grades coming in their way. Deciding factor, a chance to learn and develop an area of interest as a hobby; to showcase the work done by the children in the hobby classes; enhances self image; useful utilisation of leisure and has a cathartic effect; learning new skills other than academics	Teachers: interaction with a range of students; learning about other hobbies; will see the talents other teachers and kids have; appreciate other people's work; conducive environment for creativity and aptitude to blossom; motivates children to express their creativity; interaction of teachers with students outside the classroom and learning new skills	Parents: sharing the achievement and supporting the school; will get to see the talent of the teachers and students; learn to appreciate creativity among the children; sense of pride; share in the joy of their children's creativity	Motivation and sense of pride and desire to pursue other interests; it would be boring to only do academics; an opportunity to showcase their work; lack of creativity, monotony and boredom in one's life; no means to channelise energy in positive direction; pursue their hobby and not learn new skills; 'My first exhibition' is a great feeling

Activity: Inter-House Western Music Competition

People responsible for carrying out:

Core	Secondary	Peripheral	Loss if the activity did not happen
To showcase the musical sense and talents of the children; aesthetic abilities; the joy of participation and achievement; show their musical talents	Enjoy listening to good music sung and played by our students; generates excitement	Same as the previous, *joie de vivre*, enhanced musical appreciation abilities	The role this plays in boosting the children's morale will not be there; inability to showcase their talent;

Gain to the people (core, peripheral witnesses)			
Core	Secondary	Peripheral	Loss if the activity did not happen
	about school, strengthens school spirit, awareness about school; seeing the students showcase their talent and listen to good music		learn about music, work as a team, compete, lead; house spirit; lack of competition not able to show their musical ability; its also an opportunity for those children who are not very bright in academics

Activity: Western Music Competition

People responsible for carrying out:

Children: Acknowledgement of talent for SS: talents show no barriers	Music department	Students/parents: sharing in the achievement/supporting peers/supporting school music department	Children will be denied the opportunity to pursue their talents. Achievement in the non-academic areas will be non-existent

Activity: Musical Evening

People responsible for carrying out:

Same as above; to showcase the talent of the children, aesthetic abilities, a musical sense; this will help to show there talent in music	Same as above; generates excitement about school, strengthens school spirit, awareness about school	Will get an opportunity to hear their children and appreciate them	Same as above; inability to showcase their talent, learn about music, work as a team, compete, lead; school spirit

Activity: Annual Play

People responsible for carrying out:

Same as above in all categories; to showcase the talent of the children, to learn team work; to learn about literature, production processes; this will help student to learn about literature and perform	Generates excitement about school; strengthens school spirit; awareness about school		Loss of an opportunity to learn the nuances of theatre; work as a team; missing out on production and acting aspects of theatre specially when drama is a major component of the course work; makes the studying of drama wholistic

Gain to the people (core, peripheral witnesses)			
Core	Secondary	Peripheral	Loss if the activity did not happen
Activity: Class XII Sleepover			
People responsible for carrying out:			
An opportunity to bond with each other and their teachers along with a feeling of patriotism; helps children to bond with each other, understand the privilege of living in a democratic nation, celebrate the spirit of independence, realisation of their identity	The teachers will be able to bond in a different way with the kids, set a precedent; something that they can look forward to	The parents will see the function in the morning	The children will miss out on the fun of being together in safe surroundings; the great bonding that happens; some important memories about school, it is a lifetime experience one can have
Activity: Parents vs Students matches basketball, cricket, table tennis, tennis, squash			
People responsible for carrying out:			
This will give them a chance to bond with each other and show off their talents in the field of sports; bonding between the parents and school, acts like an adhesive for the team members; learn about the spirit of competition, hone game skills, team spirit	The physical education teachers will get an opportunity to organise a different kind of game; school spirit	The viewers will see their parents in a different light	For parents, the feeling of being one with the school will not be there; spirit of competition, sportsmanship, competition, team work; students will learn to play with much more control and respect
Activity: Debates of other schools that we participate in every year like Doon, Mayo, Scindia, Shri Ram, etc.			
People responsible for carrying out:			
This gives our students the opportunity to understand the competition they face outside and also to rise above the others; build oral skills, creativity, presence of mind, ask questions, build school spirit, learn to compete, to learn from others; understand our shortcomings and strengths; learn to compete; build awareness on current issues; develop oratory skills	The teachers will be able to teach a very important skill to the kids, hear good speaking skills, good language; how to put forward an argument, enhance vocabulary, school spirit; will be able to mould good orators; teach students to be competitive	Our students' talent will be showcased to them	An important skill will not be learnt; it is a lost opportunity in impromptu speaking skills, learning to think creatively and on the spot; understand to look at things from a variety of perspectives; children with good public speaking skills and a questioning mind will lose out on such a great opportunity to be among other school children with equally passionate thoughts about major issues; the art of dialectics and choosing to disagree, healthy criticism and being ignited by the charged atmosphere, lack of awareness; will not learn an important skill which will be required later in life; great opportunity to visit and know new people, places, school systems

Summary

- Teaching is a low-priority profession, so great schools need to put in proactive measures to attract and retain the best teachers.
- Schools attract good teachers by creating a satisfying and challenging environment for teachers.
- They constantly develop the potential and abilities of good teachers through a three-step process—development of core teaching skills, development of leaders and creation of visionaries.
- A curriculum is needed for teachers to help them understand the school vision and to ensure that they always remain in the learning mode.
- The Core Teaching Skills Programme consists of the development of:

  - Domain knowledge—this consists of advances in the field of specialisation as well as the ways in which the subject links to discussions on ethics, values, issues, the environment and aesthetics.
  - Cognitive skills—here teachers learn both the theories of cognition as well as the techniques of implementing the theories that the school follows.
  - Student management skills—teachers learn to manage students in groups by understanding social interactions. They learn about individual students through exposure to child psychology.
  - Work management skills—teachers are trained to manage time and resources.
  - Productivity and efficiency skills—schools provide productivity tools to their teachers through technology, through knowledge management and through instruments for planning.
  - Schools use a variety of methods for implementing this curriculum—these range from formal training sessions to informal interactions with teacher-mentors.

- The Leadership curriculum comprises:

  - Communication skills—leaders are trained in higher-level communication skills and given responsibilities that exploit their strengths.
  - Organisational ability—teachers with leadership skills receive training in organisation of more complex activities as well as in team management
  - Inter-personal skills—teachers are trained to become role models and motivators through a better understanding of teacher psychology and value inculcation.
  - Awareness of the big picture—training in developing an understanding of responsibilities at the micro and macro level.

- Training for Vision:

  - All great leaders have vision. Great schools are not content to make competent leaders within the school, but create giants with a world view who will some day become leaders at a global level.

Lesson Planning

Need for planning

One of the consequences of living in a world of constant change is that we have less time to focus on any one activity—whether it is reading a book, going on vacation or working on an assignment at work. A generation ago, most children read *Ivanhoe* by Walter Scott. This is a great novel but dense by today's standards with about 200 pages of introduction to the story. Then, teachers taught the same wisdom year after year from the same yellowing notes pages that they had used (and probably borrowed from a teacher before them!)

Today we live in a world where commercials tell an entire story in less than 60 seconds. Students have a very short attention span, accustomed as they are to instant gratification from the media. In addition, they also often know more about technology than their parents and teachers.

Every teacher is not very familiar with technology, yet they have to help students make sense of an ever-widening and ever-changing world of knowledge. Teachers have to put across stories far more complex than *Ivanhoe* to students with an attention span of maybe 60 seconds. They can no longer walk into a classroom with a general idea of what they want to teach and expect to do full justice to the subject, to their role as teachers; nor can they expect to hold the attention of their students.

A teacher today, therefore, needs to design lessons that meet multiple purposes. The lesson must grip the students' attention. It needs to overcome the problem of her short attention span. At the same time, the lesson must be up to date and also a little ahead of the students' awareness level. Finally, and most important, the lesson needs to guide students to achieve their learning outcomes.

The purpose of these lessons is not just conceptual understanding, but also to help students to apply their knowledge in diverse situations. The lesson must focus on the learning process and develop the ability of the student to learn how to learn in a manner that engages her total attention and involvement.

Such lessons do not just happen by chance. They require both research and planning. This is the basic reason why the science of lesson planning needs to be given far more attention than it has received so far. Despite this pressing need to be able to plan for effectiveness, teachers are rarely taught how to make a good lesson plan. Training teachers to plan lessons becomes an important part of the curriculum for teachers.

The goals of a lesson plan

There are two main aspects to a lesson plan. One is conceptual understanding. On the surface, this is the sole purpose of the lesson—to teach students about the properties of light, the reasons for Indian freedom struggle or the application of the Pythagoras' theorem. Certainly, it is very important that the students learn these concepts at the required depth and detail, but beneath this is a deeper purpose: that is to teach students to think, to analyse and to create new knowledge.

The second component of the lesson plan is therefore the learning process. The teacher uses these techniques to engage the total involvement and attention of the student in order to achieve the purpose of her lesson.

Figure 9.1 Lesson plans need to capture both conceptual understanding as well as the learning process

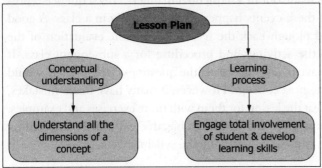

A conventional lesson plan

For many teachers, a lesson plan is a chapter in a textbook—Chapter 6, pages 127 to 132! Teachers may take this as the easy way out despite the fact that those who go through a good teacher training have learnt how to make lesson plans. The correct, conventional method of lesson plan defines a series of steps that the teacher must follow:

First step: To define the curriculum topic—(in this example): An explanation of the Pythagoras' theorem.

Second step: The learning objective—to understand the relationships between the sides of the right-angled triangle.

Third step: Students prior knowledge: Students know the various basic properties of triangles. They know how to square a number and find square roots.

Fourth step: Procedure and activities: The teacher draws the relevant diagram and works out the proof on the blackboard. Students may be asked to draw these diagrams and write out the proof themselves.

Fifth step: Space and material requirements: The teacher requires a blackboard and chalk. Students require geometry equipment to draw accurate right-angled triangles.

Sixth step: Review exercises: Students are given dimensions of two of the sides of the right-angled triangle and are required to calculate the length of the third side.

Last step: Evaluation: The teacher corrects the exercises given to the students.

The plan is made out in a sequential manner. This sequence represents the way these events happen chronologically in a class. A good teacher would plough back the feedback from the evaluation of the students into the activities and procedure for a subsequent class. If the students have overall answered the questions correctly, she would move on to the next concept. However, if many have made mistakes, she would repeat the lesson for them with more exercises and examples. The curriculum topic and learning objective will not be affected by the evaluation, since it is 'given' by the syllabus.

Gaps in the conventional lesson plan

This process pays no attention whatsoever to the entire range of skills that must be incorporated into the lesson. As it is a mere vertical

Figure 9.2 The conventional lesson plan sequence. A good teacher would modify her procedure and activities based on the student evaluation.

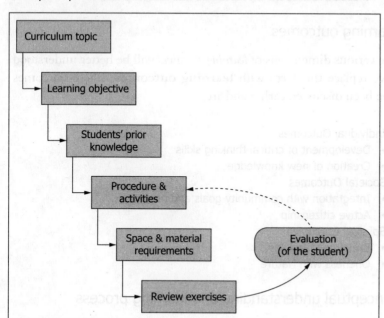

sequencing, it leaves out the horizontal range of conceptual inter-relationships as well as the range of learning skills that students need to develop. It does not speak about the learning process at all as it is, after all, just a list of activities that happen in class. The entire sequence can be made with no reference to either the learning process or to conceptual understanding. The evaluation in this plan at most evaluates the students' understanding—it does not evaluate if they have reached their learning outcomes and it has no feedback loop to evaluate itself.

Thus, this plan suffers from two major flaws. First, that it is merely a chronological sequence of what happens in the classroom, and second, three important elements of this plan are one-dimensional. These three elements are—*lesson objective, lesson activities* and *evaluation*.

Removing the gaps—creating an optimal lesson plan

Great schools therefore train teachers to make lesson plans that incorporate the learning process into the plan. Teachers learn to make multi-dimensional plans, each of which incorporates not only the conceptual

157

understanding of the subject, but also the learning philosophy of the school. What then is the structure of this lesson plan?

Learning outcomes

The various dimensions of *learning objectives* will be better understood if we replace this term with **learning outcomes**. These outcomes have been discussed earlier and are:

- Individual Outcomes
  - Development of critical thinking skills
  - Creation of new knowledge
- Societal Outcomes
  - Integration with community goals and needs
  - Active citizenship
- Spiritual Outcomes
  - Excitement and Joy
  - Oneness with Nature

Conceptual understanding and learning process

Lesson activities need to be replaced by the integration of two factors—conceptual understanding and learning process. The concept in all its dimensions and the process of learning must come out in every lesson plan. The process of conceptual understanding does not just describe a concept and how it works. It is integrated with the learning process, the four cornerstones of which, as we have already discussed are:

- Cohesion between different disciplines through *horizontal integration*
- Continuity through *vertical integration* or continuity over time
- *Cutting edge* learning technology—using processes as discovered by research in the science of learning
- *Individualisation* in learning and teaching styles

Horizontal integration is when the learning of a concept happens with answers to questions such as: How does this concept link to other fields of study? What is the history of this concept? What is its past and expected future? What is its current relevance? What are the real-life applications of this concept? For the above-mentioned example, all these answers will be found with relation to the Pythagoras' theorem. The Pythagorean theory has an interesting history that ranges from Greece to India, China and Babylon. It is applied in a variety of situations such as finding the height of unknown objects or in making building corners into perfect right angles.

Vertical integration takes place when students learn about the various levels of complexity of this concept, the simpler levels that the students are already familiar with and the more complex applications of this concept that students can expect to know in the future. The teacher may mention in passing that they will need to use their understanding of this theorem when they study trigonometry.

Cutting edge learning technology is the 'activity' aspect of the lesson plan. What are the activities that will make learning exciting for students? What are the techniques that will grip their attention? This is where teachers use different teaching styles and learning styles that teach to different types of intelligences and to different types of experiences for students. This is where teachers apply their understanding of human cognition in the teaching-learning process.

The intelligences reinforced in the conventional lesson plan that we described earlier were linguistic and mathematical. Teachers can use visual spatial methods by making students cut out triangles from a square and rearrange these to prove the theorem. They could use kinaesthetic methods by taking students out to the play field and make them drive in stakes of wood into the ground using string and measuring tape to create perfectly right-angled corners.

Individualisation deals not only with the teaching to learning styles of a particular student and the pace at which the student will learn: The core philosophy behind this is that all learning should be learner-centred and learner-driven, and that the learner should have a greater say in how she will learn. The role of the teacher is to guide her to realise her true potential.

Individualisation thus deals with the learning outcomes for each individual student. Every student needs to create new knowledge, but each student will do so in her own unique way. Each will contribute to society in a different way, and each has different value systems and different paths to joy. A teacher, therefore, needs to understand each student and plan a menu of learning processes or different paths to the learning outcomes that are flexible enough to reach out to every student.

Thus every lesson plan will have activities for students with different requirements—students with high potential who understand the concept faster than their classmates will be given progressively tougher problems to solve, and may be asked to design some of the activities for their fellow students. Those who have trouble understanding the concepts may get simpler problems that will help them to understand the concept at the pace with which they are comfortable. The teacher may set aside time for one-on-one discussions with these students.

Following are examples of lesson plans that could make learning meaningful and purposive while at the same time challenging the students to build upon their capacities and develop new skills.

Lesson Plan: Class XI

Concept
Essentials of History

Resources
1. *What is History?* by E.H.Carr
2. *The Routledge Companion to Historical Studies* by Alan Munslow
3. *History and Beyond* by Romila Thapar

Objective
a) To enable students understand the tools of history and historiography and its application at a more complex level
b) As a teacher
   • Identifying complex level thinking strategy; facilitate students to make inferences independently and increase their past knowledge of tools of history (vertical integration).
   • Ask open-ended and extension questions to develop students' independent thinking; emphasise that they should use precise words, not 'stuff', 'you know'; that there can be many answers to one issue (horizontal integration).
   • Not give value judgments; train students to listen to each other and reflect on their thinking; ask students the process by which they obtained their answer; -respect their ideas.
   • Communicate to students that lively exchange of ideas makes thinking enjoyable.

Duration of teaching concept
Between 4 and 5 classes

Method
1. Introductory class: Elicit student response on what has been their perception about defining history. Taking cues from their answers, explain how at this learning level the subject becomes multi-dimensional. Illustrate by discussing E.H.Carr's (after explaining how

---

he brought about new perceptions about the study of history) common sense view of history: **what distinguishes historical facts from other facts; the significance of evidence in history;** arriving at a definition: **what differentiates historical facts from opinions;** read out a value statement and a fact from the day's newspaper to highlight the difference; conclude class by asking students what they think are the **skills developed by history;** write their answers and formulate what is commonly accepted as tools of history.

2. Begin class by recapitulating the definition/difference between fact and opinion and the skills acquired in this subject. In this class, explain how location of towns/kingdoms is linked to physical features of a country; give examples from ancient Indian history (Indus Valley civilisation, the concentration of urban centres in the Indo-Gangetic plains, ports in peninsular India) and ask students to give instances (India or other countries) from contemporary times; from these examples ask them to arrive at an inference: **link of history with geography; relevance of past to present.**

3. Move the concept forward by asking students to chart out the history of their lives with documented evidence to back their past: they could cite photographs, school reports, or any other; from this exercise explain that their **evidence is called sources of history;** explain **difference between primary** (a monument, Taj Mahal) and **secondary source** (article in a magazine about Taj Mahal requiring restoration); take this to a more complex level by examining the **different kinds of sources: archaeological** (monuments, coins, inscriptions) and **literary** (religious, secular, foreign accounts) through a flow chart on the blackboard.

4. Discuss a completely new tool of subject: **historiography**—explain its meaning, and with help of a previous concept known to them, highlight the different schools of historiography that exist in the writing of Indian history.

    Example—Events in India in 1857
    Sepoy Mutiny (Imperialist historiography)
    Revolt of 1857 (Rationalist)
    First War of Independence (Nationalist)
             OR
    History of Kings and Rulers (Nationalist)
    Role of the Common People (Subaltern or Marxist approach)

Ask students what kind of historiography will examine events of 9/11 in the USA or election results of 2004 in India; ask a student to write the varied responses on the blackboard—and **infer from these how history can be reconstructed.**

5. Wind up the concept by a **visit to the National Museum and National Archives:** give them a pre-visit note on what they should be looking for in the (*a*) Museum: the different kinds of sources they will view, like the Harappan gallery section which has coins and the gallery on the Silk Route which has manuscripts; (*b*) National Archives: state letters, documents of land deeds, etc.; here not only will they identify the primary and secondary sources, but also write a report as a post-visit exercise.

Activity
Visit to the National Museum and National Archives

Assessment
Worksheet (attached)

Expected learning goals or evaluation
1. Individual Outcomes: Emphasis on complex level of thinking and enhancing existing domain knowledge will be achieved through horizontal and vertical integration in the course of teaching as per this plan.
2. The hands-on activity of actually getting first-hand exposure to sources will make the students internalise their learning as both the content and process of learning has been focused on (activity aspect).
3. Spiritual Outcomes: New experiences both in theoretical and practical aspects provide excitement and interest.
4. Societal Outcomes: Application to real-life situations will enhance skills as world citizens.

Worksheet

Class: XI

Conceptl: Essentials of History Worksheet

Time: 20 minutes

Marks: 15

1. Read the following excerpt from the novel *Those Days* and answer the questions given.

   On a fine April morning, John Bethune set foot on Indian soil. He had been interested in India since the time that, as practicing lawyer in London, he had been invited to participate in a lawsuit regarding *sati*—the Indian practice of burning widows on the funeral pyres of their husbands. The invitation had come from a group of Indian traditionalists who had appealed to the Privy Council to revoke the ban on *sati* if it ever came to be passed by the British government in India. On making enquiries, Bethune discovered that such a ban was under serious consideration, following appeals made by several enlightened Indians who considered *sati* to be a blot on their religion and culture. The discovery left him thunderstruck.

    a) Identify and write **one fact** and **one opinion** statement. **2**
    b) What is the difference between fact and opinion?   **2**

2. The city of London faces a new threat after the incidents on 7 July 2005. Identify one primary source and one secondary source that you, as a student of history, could use to write a factual account of the day.   **2**

3. What conclusions can you draw as a student of history from the following primary sources: **2 × 2 = 4**

    a) Account of Megasthenes, the ambassador of Seleucus in the court of Chandragupta Maurya
       'The greater part of the soil is under irrigation and consequently bears two crops in the course of the year.'
    b) Inscription on an Ashokan rock edict:
       'There should not be honour to one's or condemnation to another sect; on the contrary, other sects should be honoured. By doing so one promotes one's own sect and benefits another sect.'

4. Who was Mrs Roy? (Reconstructing history from given evidence or sources)   **5**
To many in the neighbourhood, Mrs Roy was a mystery. She died three days ago. The postmortem report said that the cause of death was old age. She lived alone, had a maid who looked after her, and only went out for a walk. Mrs Roy has no surviving relatives. She had left no will behind, but a neighbour who had met her occasionally found the following in her cupboard:

• Two Vir Chakra medals
• A jar of coins from around the world

- A plastic box containing letters, many of them signed 'from your loving Bubbu', dated in the early 1971s, postmarked Dhaka
- Three photographs:
  - one of a young couple: the women in a bridal sari, the man in a suit dated January 1962 (written on the back)
  - the second, an old black-and-white photograph fading a bit, also a studio wedding photograph
  - the third photograph is of an Indian General, a Pakistani General signing a document and a young officer in the middle offering a pen
- Newspaper clipping in Bengali

1. From this information, construct a brief history of the life of Mrs. Roy.
2. What would be the primary and secondary sources you could use?
3. What conclusions would you draw about Mrs. Roy from the evidence presented to you?

Subject Teacher	Class 3	Date from	Date to
Concept	Energy		
Objective	To understand what is energy and classifying the different types of energy.		

Day 1

Method of instruction	Discussion on what is energy. Children need to understand the fact that when a force is used to do work, it is called energy. Energy is the ability or capacity to do work which can be further explained with the help of a slide show. Different types of energy are: 1. Potential and kinetic energy 2. Heat energy 3. Solar energy 4. Light energy 5. Energy from wind

	6. Energy from water 7. Sound energy 8. Electrical energy
Resource	Discussion, slide show
Homework	
Evaluation	
Attachment	

Day 2	
Method of instruction	A trip to the field in the afternoon class: Children carry their pinwheels made with different materials and of various sizes and make a comparative study to find out which pinwheel spins the best and the reasons for it. Next, they are made to use their muscular energy to kick and stop a soccer ball, and in this context they are introduced to the concepts of potential and kinetic energy. After that, they are made to touch the water coming out of a hosepipe exposed to the sun for sometime. On the basis of this they are asked such questions as: Where does the energy to heat the water come from? Would the water get as hot as it is if the hose were in the shade? Some hoses are black and others are green. Which one heats water the most? As a follow-up activity, children in the next class are shown brochures on solar heaters and the functioning of solar cookers was demonstrated in the science lab. This can then be continued with a debate on the benefits of solar heating. Finally, out of pages of old newspapers, they are encouraged to make voice amplifiers which would help them to call their friends from the other end of the field. As they get ready to return to their classes, they touch their head to approximately verify if the temperature has increased compared to the initial one before they walked out of their class.

Resource	Field, pinwheel, soccer ball, hosepipe with water, voice amplifier.
Homework	
Evaluation	
Attachment	

Day 3

Method of instruction	A trip to the kitchen: Take potatoes and let the children peel them. Now put these potatoes in the pressure cooker with water. The pressure is enough to lift the weight on the pressure cooker. This can be explained to the students in the context of the steam engine where the energy from the steam make the piston go up and down which in turn moves the shaft and then the wheels. On boiling, the potatoes become soft. Similarly children may be shown the difference between cooked and uncooked rice and spaghetti.
Resource	Kitchen, pressure cooker, potatoes, rice and spaghetti.
Homework	
Evaluation	
Attachment	

Day 4

Method of instruction	A trip to the science laboratory: Holding a spoon with the thumb and the index finger under a tap of running water. The energy of the water flow exerts a pressure on the fingers. In this context, it can be explained to the children how the flow of water in dams turns the turbines which help in the generation of electricity. The movie 'Swades' can be mentioned, for example. Insulated copper wires, batteries and small bulbs to be kept in a work station. Children need to learn to remove the insulation and connect the wires properly to the bulb and the battery so that the bulb glows.

	In another work station, pebbles, sand and iron fillings are mixed together and in the last work station, salt, sand and iron fillings are mixed together. What kind of energy should the children use to separate all the components?
Resource	Science lab, spoon, insulated copper wires, battery, bulb, pebbles, sand, iron fillings and salt.
Homework	
Evaluation	Based on the worksheet
Attachment	

Day 5

Method of instruction	
Resource	
Homework	
Evaluation	
Attachment	

Activity outside the classroom (Game, experiment, groupwork etc.)	Review/Assessment carried out
Slide show and trips to the field, science lab, and the kitchen.	Based on the worksheet
Essential	Integrating with other subjects
Time management and hunger for knowledge	Physical education and visual arts.

Private study	Skill	Resource

Remarks by Head of the department	Remarks by Head of senior/ junior school

167

Worksheet

1. These girls have no hat, and it is very sunny outside.

a) Design and make a hat that will protect the girls from the sun.

b) Would you design the same hat for a boy? Why? ....

c) What materials would you use to make the hat?
....

d) What colours would you use?
....

e) What sort of things could happen to you if you do not wear a hat in the sun?
....

2. Have you ever seen your city at night?

a) Make a picture of your city at night.

b) What sort of lights will you see at night? (natural or artificial)
....
....

c) What are the lights used for?
....
....

d) What is the source of this light?

....

....

e) Where do you see the brightest lights in your locality?

....

....

f) Do you think streetlights are necessary? Why?

....

....

g) How do you feel about advertisement signs that are left on all night?

....

....

3. Use some string and plasticine to make a pendulum.

a) How many times does it swing in a minute?

....

....

b) What happens if you put a really big blob of plasticine on the string and let it go?

....

....

c) Make the string shorter and let it go. What happens?

....

....

d) What happens when you make the string longer?

....

....

e) In the Jhula Bari, can you make the swing go faster?

....

....

f) Do the swings go faster when you swing harder or does it simply go higher?

....

....

g) What are the different types of energy that come into play both in the pendulum and the swing?

....

....

169

Ecology and Environment
India's Suez—Is it Ecocide?

Subject: Biology ⠀⠀⠀⠀⠀⠀⠀⠀⠀**Duration: 40 min.**
Class: XII ⠀⠀⠀⠀⠀⠀⠀⠀⠀⠀⠀**Marks:—30**

I.⠀Read the passage below and answer the questions that follow:

A canal linking the east and west coast was first suggested in 1860 by A. D. Taylor, a British commander of the Indian Marines. Today, every Tamil Nadu politician is upbeat about it. Billed as India's Suez Canal, it is projected to reduce the navigable distance between India's east and west coast by 400 nautical miles. Ships will save 21 hours each way and will not have to circumnavigate Sri Lanka. The economic benefits would be immense. It is for this reason that the *Sethusamudram* Ship Canal Project (SSCP) was envisaged. It entails excavating the shallow sea between the Palk Bay and Gulf of Mannar (44.9 nautical miles of it) and creating a canal linking India's east and west coasts.

No one seems concerned about the disastrous environmental costs involved and the virtual wiping out of India's biologically richest coastal region. In human terms, the livelihood of five lakh fisherfolk spread across 138 fishing stations along five coastal districts, will be severely hit.

The 10,500 sq km Gulf of Mannar (GoM) area, along which the canal is proposed, was notified as a Marine National Park in 1986. It is home to over 3,600 species of plants and animals, including 117 species of corals and conches, endangered mammals like dugong and all five varieties of sea turtles. In 1989, it was declared a Marine Biosphere Reserve. In 2002, the Global Environmental Facility (GEF) of the UNDP established a trust for it at Ramanathapuram. The GoM is home to 21 islands which harbour fringing reefs that has representatives of every animal phylum known (except amphibians).

All this now stands threatened! According to the Nagpur-based National Environmental Research Institute's (NEERI) Environment Impact Assessment (EIA) report, there is hard strata under the soft sediment and may require blasting if the strata encountered during the dredging were to be hard rock. Scientists of the Centre for Marine Fisheries Research Institute (CMFRI), Mandapam, have warned that marine animals are extremely sensitive to sound; using explosives will spell mass marine death. The EIA has also warned that construction will increase marine turbidity leading to toxicity in the water column, reducing sunlight penetration and available oxygen, resulting in the smothering of biota and deposition of silt on free swimming and benthic animals.

1. What does the *Sethusamudram* Project entail?   3
2. The dredged canal may get filled back. Besides, the area is prone to tsunamis. What ecological disasters are forecast because of such a project?   4
3. Expand the abbreviations and where are they located?   2

   a) NEERI

   b) CMFRI

4. As a student of environment and based on the EIA, what measures would you suggest to ensure sustainable development?   4

5. Enlist the conditions that are ideal for coral reefs. What is coral bleaching?   2

6. Mention the flora and fauna that one would encounter in the free swimming and benthic regions of the ocean.   2

II. The concept of Biosphere Reserve (BR) was launched in 1975 as part of UNESCO's Man and Biosphere programme. Biodiversity reserves are a special category of protected areas of land and/or coastal environments, wherein people form an integral component of the system.

a) How many biosphere reserves are found in India?   1

b) Draw a diagram to show the different zones of a terrestrial BR.   3

c) Enlist 3 important functions of BRs.   3

III. Biodiversity is not uniformly distributed across the geographical regions of the earth. Certain regions of the world are mega-diversity zones where a very large number of species are found. For example, India accounts for 2.4% of the land area of the world but contributes 8% of species to the global diversity.

    Norman Myers developed the hot spot concept in 1988 to designate priority areas for *in situ* conservation. The hot spots are the richest and most threatened reservoirs of plant and animal life on earth.

1. What are endemic species?   1

2. What is an IUCN Red List?   1

3. How would you differentiate between an endangered species and a vulnerable species?   2

4. Explain what is *in situ* and *ex situ* conservation. Give an example each to elucidate your answer.   2

Lesson Plan: Class XII

Subject
Biology

Resources
a) Web sites:
www.reefrelief.org
www.sciencenetlinks.com/lessons
www.wsws.org/articles/2005/dec2005/inda-d14.shtml
www.enviropedia.org.uk/contents.php

b) Bibliography:
   (i) *Widening Perspectives on Biodiversity*/edited by Anatole F. Krattiger, Jeffrey A. McNeely, William H. Lesser, Kenton R. Miller
   (ii) *Biodiversity: Conservation and Management*/B.K. Singh
   (iii) *Biodiversity Conservation: Whose Resource? Whose Knowledge?* edited by Vandana Shiva
   (iv) *Aquatic Biodiversity in India: The Present Scenario*/edited by D.R. Khanna, A.K. Chopra and G. Prasad
   (v) *Biodiversity and Environment*/Arvind Kumar

Objectives
1. To enable students to understand the intricacies of Nature and repercussion of anthropological activities on it.
2. To develop higher order thinking and develop values regarding environment conservation.

Duration of teaching concept
3–4 lessons

Method
1. In the first lesson, introduce the concept by a recapitulation of various natural resources and their conservation (usually done at the secondary level in Social Studies). Concept of biodiversity is introduced with a slide show to show the huge variety of flora and fauna that exists in Nature. Also, show snapshots of species that are threatened and some that are already extinct. Discuss the magnitude of bio-diversity at the genetic, species, community and ecosystem levels. The effect of latitude and altitude on biological diversity and various gradients that exist in nature.
2. In the second lesson, highlight the importance of biodiversity: ask the students on what is their opinion on the matter. Quiz the students

on their perceptions on various sources of threat posed to biodiversity and, thereafter, what conservation measures should be adopted in different scenarios.

3. In the third lesson, make the students prepare 5-minute presentations on different aspects of the topic. Another discussion point could be the various biodiversity conservation measures undertaken at:

- The national level by declaration of national parks, sanctuaries and biosphere reserves by the Ministry of Environment and Forests; various projects undertaken by government and non-government organisations.
- The global level, e.g. the Earth Summit held in 1992, the Rio +10 Summit held in Johannesburg on 2002.

4. An educational trip is organised to the National Bureau of Plant Genetic Resources (NBPGR) as an out-of-class activity to learn about the conservation measures being undertaken.

Assessment
Worksheet (attached)

Expected learning outcomes
1. Individual Outcomes: Students are sensitised about environmental issues and concerns that would enable them to adopt a systems approach towards the conservation process.
2. Spiritual Outcome: Students appreciate the fact that they are a part of the larger whole; an effect on one would definitely impact the others.
3. Societal Outcome: Students would become tomorrow's planners, administrators and decision makers. It is therefore crucial that they make informed decisions keeping all stakeholders on the context.

Feedback and update

Evaluation needs to be replaced by *Feedback and Update*. Any system and any process needs to be reviewed continually. As in the case of the curriculum, this review is not only to check if students are achieving their learning outcomes, but also to check if the system is the best possible one for helping students to reach their learning outcomes.

The teacher therefore designs certain rubrics by which she will evaluate both the students and the plan. For students, she defines certain performance standards. Those who exceed these standards will be given enrichment activities; those who do not meet these standards will be given remedial reinforcement.

For the plan itself, she has a separate benchmark—if student performance for most of the class is within a certain normal range, she will consider the plan successful. If the performance was below the range, she will analyse which aspect of the plan failed. Were the learning outcomes unrealistic? Was the procedure too complex, too simple or too disorganised for the students? Were the assessment exercises formulated at the correct level of difficulty?

If performance of the class as a whole was above the normal range, then she has to decide whether this was because her performance as a teacher in that class was brilliant or whether the plan was made too simple for this age group. Therefore, unlike in a conventional plan, it is not sufficient just to repeat the same plan with a class that has not understood the concept or the learning process.

The three processes therefore that any good lesson plan needs to integrate are:

- Defining outcomes
- Conceptual understanding and learning to learn
- Feedback and update

Implementation issues

For a teacher who would like to teach straight out of a textbook, even the conventional lesson plan is a lot of unnecessary work. For such a teacher, the Learning Process plan will appear very unreasonable. Even dedicated and sincere teachers have neither the time nor the resources to bring all these elements into their lessons. Yet, they will agree that if they did have the time and resources, they would certainly like to incorporate if not all, at least some of these elements into every lesson plan.

Further, even supposing that all teachers are willing to develop such a plan, do they know how to do it? This type of a plan is complex, its elements are not sequential, but form an intricate matrix. It would be very easy to lose track of the basic learning outcomes while making such a complex plan. One teacher, while she may not know all the answers to making such a plan, will definitely have some of the answers. If she could share her knowledge and insights with others, the entire community of students and teachers sharing their best practices could probably find all the answers.

Such sharing could happen through group discussions, workshops and one-on-one meetings. However, only those teachers who come in personal contact with each other can benefit through this kind of sharing.

175

Figure 9.3 A simplified, sample matrix that teachers can use

Subject	Mathematics	Class	VIII	Date from:			Date to:	
Name of teacher:								
Concept	Pythagoras' theorem							
Learning outcome:	Understand the proof of the theorem; learn to apply this knowledge to calculate missing lengths in triangles; real life applications of theorem							

Day	Method of instruction	Resources required	Exercises/class activities	Evaluation: remarks at the end of the day
Day 1	Discussion of brief history; examples of real life applications; description of proof; explanation of proof using diagrams	Blackboard; geometry equipment; scissors and coloured paper	Puzzles for which they need to cut out triangles from squares to verify theorem	Most students were able to work out the puzzles
Day 2	Sample problems will be solved in class and students will be given exercises	Blackboard	Worksheet of problems	Students A, B and C had problems, will need to solve a simpler worksheet first
Outside class activities:		Pegs, measuring tape, rope	Students will make rightangled corners using the materials	
Learning Skill:	Mathematical, logical, visual and kinaesthetic learning styles are developed			
Integration with values/issues:	National pride—Indians were one of the earliest to derive this theorem			
Integration with other subjects:	History of science in India			

Sharing a database of lesson plans

The solution to a much wider sharing is simple. This requires that a standardised format be made within which all the elements of the plan will fit. The format defines areas for description of not just the concept to be taught, but also of the various elements of the learning process that must be incorporated. Thus, the matrix of all elements is defined and given to the teachers.

Once the structure of the lesson plan is set, teachers can store all their ideas and techniques in a common searchable database. They can then refer to lesson plans made by other teachers. Technologies are widely available for such a scheme and each school can decide on the type of matrix that will suit their learning philosophy and the type of sharing that they believe will be most effective.

Some examples of how sharing ideas is possible:

Case 1: Teachers who are teaching a subject to a particular class can look up this database to get ideas from the plans of other teachers for the same subject and class. These could be ideas on different teaching styles, exercises, activities and resources (individualisation). No two teachers teach the same subject to the same level of children in exactly the same manner.

Figure 9.4 A teacher learns from other teachers of the same subject and discipline

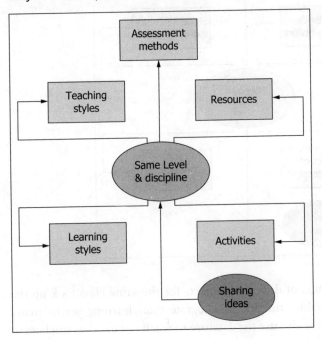

Therefore, teachers can gain exposure to new perspectives by this sharing of ideas. These could also be teachers who have taught this subject in previous years, or teachers from other schools.

Teachers tend to get stuck to a certain method or technique after a few years of teaching a particular subject. They need this exposure to get away from following the same beaten track year after year.

Case 2: Teachers also look up plans of teachers in lower or higher classes to understand how much the students already know and to prepare them for what is required in higher classes (vertical integration).

177

This ensures a smooth flow of learning. Students realise that the learning process is a continuous process that does not end every year. They are able to correlate their earlier learning with current concepts.

Figure 9.5 Teachers of different classes can co-ordinate the vertical integration of lessons

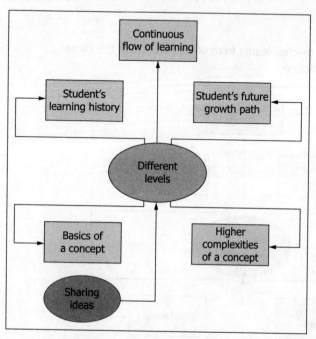

Case 3: Teachers of different subjects for the same class look up the database to enable students to integrate their learning across many disciplines. They also use the database to reach out to other teachers so that across disciplines many teachers can co-ordinate their lessons (horizontal integration).

Case 4: Teachers need not be bound to the lesson plans of only their discipline or their class level. They could look up plans of any subject and any class to see how teachers approach value integration, learning style integration in their classes (individual learning outcomes). By looking at plans made by leader teachers, they gain insights into the philosophy and the vision that is unique to every school. They learn from other teachers how to transmit this vision and philosophy to the students (societal learning outcomes).

Figure 9.6 A database is a powerful tool for (w)holistic learning. Teachers can co-ordinate lessons and ensure that each reinforces the concepts that her colleagues are teaching.

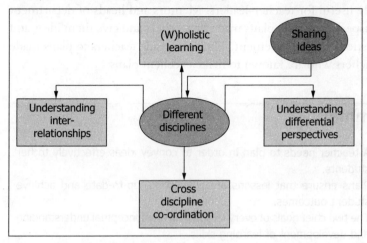

Figure 9.7 Sharing of ideas has no limits—teachers learn from others, irrespective of their discipline, specialisation or age of their students.

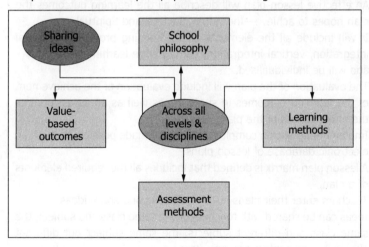

Once these ideas are incorporated into a lesson plan, a plan is no longer an isolated element in an island of the teacher's making, but is part of a larger picture. A resource such as this serves multiple purposes. Teachers learn how to make effective plans. They are guided on the school's learning philosophy.

The database increases their effectiveness—they now have easy access, many more ideas and teaching-learning methods. It increases

179

their productivity—they do not have to re-invent the wheel, but can build upon the ideas of others. It makes difficult tasks easier and ensures that teachers remain in the learning mode. A resource such as this is equally useful for teacher-leaders. Mentors and heads of department can inspect the lesson plans made by teachers and give them ideas and suggestions on improvement. They can guide teachers to plans made by teachers who are known to make excellent plans.

Summary

- A teacher needs to plan in order to convey ideas effectively to her students.
- Plans ensure that lessons are interesting, up-to-date and achieve student outcomes.
- The two chief goals of every lesson plan are conceptual understanding and development of learning skills.
- Conventional lesson plans are sequential and reflect the sequence in which learning place in class.
- These do not include all dimensions of the learning process.
- An effective lesson plan will describe all the learning outcomes the plan hopes to achieve—Individual, Societal and Spiritual.
- It will include all the elements of the learning process—horizontal integration, vertical integration, cutting edge learning techniques—and will be individualised.
- The evaluation of the plan will include evaluation of the achievement of the learning outcomes in students, as well as an assessment of the effectiveness of the plan.
- Implementing such a complex plan can be made possible through an electronic database of lesson plans.
- A lesson plan matrix is defined that includes all the required elements of a plan.
- Teachers enter their plans in this database and share ideas.
- Ideas can be shared with teachers of the same class and subject, the same class and different subjects, the same subject but different classes or any subject and any class.
- The database is thus a tool provided by a great school to help teachers to achieve their teaching outcomes.

Teaching for Diversity and Inclusion

10

Great schools celebrate diversity...

The first step towards encouraging diversity is the need to build up a student clientele with diverse abilities and diverse needs. A great school tries as far as possible to make sure that the profile of the students in the school reflects the profile of the community around the school. Therefore, students in the school should belong to every ethnic, social and economic class and of diverse learning abilities that is to be found within the vicinity of the school.

Figure 10.1 Individualised learning in great schools leads to recognition of diversity. The learning environment in the school then creates a positive cycle that affects not just the school, but also the entire community.

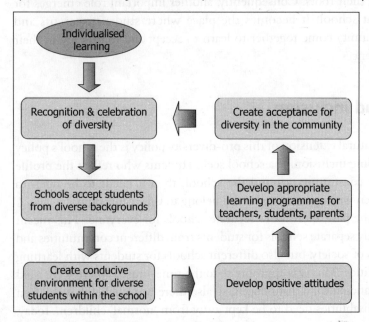

The second step is to create an environment where these diverse students thrive. We live in an increasingly mobile and fluid world. From year to year, as the community around the school changes, the profile of students also changes. Each year therefore brings with it new challenges. As a learning organisation, the school, its teachers and students learn to deal with these changes and constantly remain in a learning mode. They learn to develop the right attitudes towards diversity. They accept differences and recognise that these differences are not barriers, but are in fact, enablers of cooperation, friendship and harmony. The school ensures that all students learn together and learn from each other.

In order to make this possible, the school develops learning programmes that are sensitive to the needs of each of its students. The curriculum is not pre-defined but changes in response to the requirements of the changing student profile. Dealing with diversity is a major part of the school's long-term and short-term plans.

Yet, the world around is still in the midst of a transition towards an acceptance of diversity. The great school accepts that many people still tend to stay within the safe barriers of community and society. There are many with closed minds who do not wish to mix with those who are different. There are many more who may have open minds, but do not know how to adjust to this constantly changing world without losing their roots. Consequently, another important role emerges for a great school. It becomes the place where students, parents and community come together to learn to accept and to find joy in their differences.

...and inclusion

As a natural extension of this pro-diversity policy is the school's policy regarding inclusion. If a school seeks students who reflect the profile of the community around the school, then it needs to be open to children with special needs who belong to this community.

In the past, there were separate schools for everyone. This meant not only separate schools for students from different communities and classes of society, but also different schools for students with learning disabilities. This was appropriate to the time—just as there were rigid social and cultural distinctions, so also there was a belief that children with disabilities need to be kept away from 'normal' children. Today, the increasingly fluid society we live in does not exclude anybody. Everyone is a 'normal' and integral part of this society. Everyone has a part to play and has a need that has to be satisfied.

Much has already been written on the science of inclusion. Without going into what has been said elsewhere, let us accept the wisdom that educational and social development of students with special needs is far better in inclusive education environments. Inclusion also develops positive attitudes of non-disabled children towards children with disabilities.

What is an inclusive environment? In very simple terms, this means that schools educate children with disabilities in general education classrooms. Support services are brought to the child within the general education classroom. The basic premise is that every child in the community has a right to be accepted as a part of the school learning community. All students in a school will always benefit by inclusion—by learning together, they will learn to live together. The school will develop a detailed Individual Education Plan (IEP) for each child in the school, including those with special needs. This plan will define the level of inclusion that is most appropriate for students with special needs.

Let us move on to two aspects that affect the learning programme for learning and development of students with special needs. The first is development of the right attitudes, skills and abilities in teachers, students, parents and the community. The second is the development of learning programmes tailored to these special needs.

The most important role in the implementation of effective inclusive policies will be played by the teachers of the school. The teachers of the school have to manage this diversity and inclusion. They have to develop learning programmes at the individual level (IEP) as well as develop the right attitudes for the entire group. The first task of the school is therefore to orient their teachers and the first part of the orientation is to develop the right attitudes in the teachers. These teachers also belong to the community and therefore their views will reflect commonly held prejudices and perceptions. Once teachers develop positive attitudes, the school then needs to give them the freedom to develop flexible programmes. The school also needs to give the teachers the facilities and infrastructure to implement these programmes.

A great school should create spaces for students of varying abilities. In the example that follows, I have tried to illustrate how the teacher made a constant effort to integrate a student with special needs with

Children with special needs are not just children with disabilities of the body and the mind. Some are children with economic disabilities—they may not be able to afford the cost of education in the school. Others may be children with social disabilities—such as girl students and students from minority religious backgrounds.

the rest of the class by understanding his limitations but trusting his abilities.

Avinash was entering into senior school. This meant confronting a whole new environment, a new building, new desks and most importantly new teachers. He was suffering from Autism. Autistic children show deficit in social interaction, verbal or non-verbal communication and repetitive behaviours. They often have unusual responses to sensory experiences. He had a little trouble in learning to read and exhibited extremely poor social interaction. He felt and heard things which normal students did not, and these abrupt feelings distracted his mind and did not allow him to focus.

For such students, special educators use a technique called 'sensory integration' where efforts are made to minimise the distraction and channel the energy appropriately. Conscious of the condition, his teacher used to take him out to other rooms for his special therapy classes. Among other things, there was a trampoline in the room where he was asked to jump on whenever he showed signs of aggression.

Avinash studied all the subjects, enjoyed mathematics and was very proficient with the calculator. His teacher made an effort to modify and simplify the notes to his level of understanding. Classes usually began with loud reading or spelling which was his area of strength. He was popular among his peers and like any regular kid of his age, idolised film stars and followed popular Hindi film songs. He was especially close to one of his classmates, Tanish. However, he would be with Tanish all the while and also distract him between classes or even make phone calls to Tanish's home after school. In the process, he was denying space to Tanish. The teacher held counselling sessions with both Tanish and Avinash separately as well as together, to address this issue. Avinash's teacher also made a tiny booklet for him that had a story about a boy and his friend and which described socially accepted behaviour among friends in a school. Whenever any traits of aggression were seen in him, he was made to read the book, and it always calmed him.

Moreover, Avinash's condition was described to the students in the class and they were made to understand how they should behave around him. At the same time, stories about disabled people were read out in the class to make the other students aware of their condition.

Creating the right mental environment

Perhaps sometime in the future, attitudes towards children with special needs will not be an issue of importance. Today, many people are confused—they do not know which attitude to adopt. A part of this is because the entire issue of children with special needs has been bogged down by political correctness. A new term is coined to describe these children, and as it becomes a label with a negative connotation; it is discarded in favour of a new term that will suffer the same fate. The point that many people seem to miss is that it is not the descriptive term that needs to be continually changed, but the attitude. Once differences of all kinds are accepted as normal, the label will be no more than a useful description of the child.

In the not very distant past, attitudes were much simpler. The 'bad' attitude was ridicule and contempt, the 'good' attitude was pity. Current wisdom does not believe in pity anymore. It is as much a negative attitude as contempt. Every child is source of joy to her parents, to her friends and her teachers. Every child is special. The only difference is that some children have more complex needs than others do.

Developing the attitudes of teachers

Teachers need to cultivate the attitude that all children, though different, are equal. Every child is a child with special needs. Once she accepts this truth, she will then have a positive attitude towards those children who need learning inputs that are more complex than that of other children in the class. For these students, the attitude that is needed is one of acceptance and of looking for solutions. There is no need to pity a left-handed child. There is a need to teach her how to place her notebook correctly so that she can write comfortably. There is need to teach her how to change the right and left click buttons on the mouse in her computer.

Whatever may be the level of disability, teachers need to cultivate this same matter-of-fact attitude towards the needs of all their students. A child may detest history (she needs to be given a project that links history to the music she loves; perhaps she needs to see the school counsellor). She has a tooth cavity (she needs to go to the dentist; it does not affect her IEP). She has a hearing disability (she needs a more complex IEP, a speech therapist and the teacher needs to co-ordinate her learning and medical programme with her parents).

While the teacher needs to cultivate this objective attitude, it cannot exist without empathy. The teacher needs to have the ability to look at the world through a child's eyes in order to understand her point of view, in order to do what is best for her. Objectivity does not mean that she should not form an emotional link with her students. What is important is that this emotional link exists equally for all her students.

Figure 10.2 The two aspects of a teacher's attitude, empathy and objectivity, help a class to achieve learning goals in an atmosphere of oneness

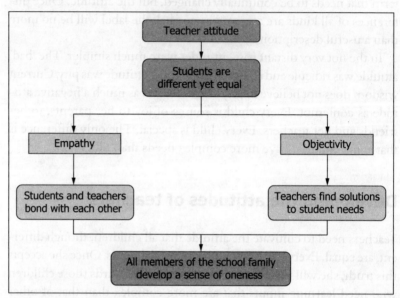

All students need to understand that their teacher finds joy in their achievements and that she understands their needs. She needs to convey the message that they are all equally important to her, even though the time she spends with each may differ. Once all students understand this attitude, those with disabilities will become an integral part of the class. They will no longer see themselves as different and nor will the students without disabilities see them as different.

When a teacher cultivates these attitudes, inclusion of all children becomes an essential part of her routine. It is no longer considered an additional burden that disrupts the rest of the class.

Developing attitudes of parents

Once teachers begin to understand and develop the right attitude, they need to learn how to develop these attitudes in others. An important part of their duty as teachers is to 'teach' these attitudes. They have to develop positive attitudes towards both diversity and inclusion in students as well as in parents.

Developing the attitudes of parents is important, as students in the school will reflect the attitudes of their parents. Parents may have negative perceptions towards all people from a minority community; others may have negative attitudes towards people with disabilities. These attitudes will naturally affect their children. This is one area of the learning programme, where the support and understanding of parents becomes crucial.

Teachers have to first influence the attitudes of parents who have children with special needs. One of their most important tasks is teaching parents acceptance. Many parents who find themselves in such situations withdraw into a shell of denial. This can have a negative influence on the child's learning programme.

The curriculum for teachers, therefore, needs to include methods by which they can deal with parents. They need to learn how to interact with parents with tact and how to help them to accept their child's abilities with realism. They also need to be sensitive to aspirations that parents have for their children. Sometimes this interaction with parents of children with disabilities may even have to include helping them learn how to love and how to find joy in their children.

For parents with children who do not have disabilities, teachers may need to sensitise them and help them to develop attitudes of acceptance. They need to be taught to love and not pity and certainly not to ridicule.

Developing attitudes of students

Very young students have the right attitude towards everyone else. Unless something happens to frighten them, they tend to accept everyone. As they grow, and become more aware of their surroundings, they receive indoctrination from several different sources—the most important being their parents, their friends and the media.

However, students of this age do listen to their teachers. This is the age when teachers can very effectively develop positive attitudes in their students. In fact, it can be said that this development of attitudes in very young students is a very large and important part of the students' academic curriculum. Attitudes developed at this age will be difficult to change later.

Inclusion of children with different abilities is also easier at this age. These very young children are just learning to communicate and to think. Therefore, children with special needs do not stand out as being 'different'.

Developing attitudes in children has two aspects. One is direct and the other is indirect. Active attitude development can be achieved through programmes in the curriculum that will teach all students to respect, love and accept each other. These could be through group activities where students of different abilities are included in the group and each is a given a task according to her abilities. Apart from this, there can be direct methods such as stories and candid discussions with students on how to behave with equality towards all.

The indirect aspect is the attitude of the teacher herself. She needs to be very careful about how she talks about students to other students and how she behaves with each one. All students will subconsciously register her body language. This perhaps is the most effective method of developing attitudes. Teachers are role models and are closely watched and imitated by their students. Especially, very young students will do anything to be like their teachers and do things that they believe will make them liked by their teachers.

Figure 10.3 Teachers need to use both active and passive methods to influence student attitudes. Methods needed for different age groups will vary.

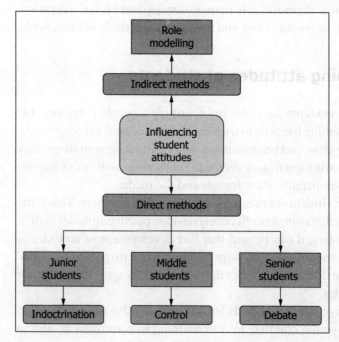

Interestingly, these techniques work for students in the higher classes too. Fifteen- and sixteen-year-olds will be open to new ideas suggested to them by their teachers despite parental prejudices. An obvious difference between the very young and young adults is that the level of discussions on inclusion and diversity will be at a much higher level. There will be a greater awareness among students while participating in activities that include students with different abilities. The students themselves may distribute responsibilities in the group according to different abilities. These are young adults with an adult understanding of issues and need to be treated as such.

A not-so-obvious difference between these two age groups is that while very young students will listen to all that their teachers say, the older group will listen only to teachers they respect. These students recognise a great teacher when they see one. Teachers who wish to influence the attitudes of older students will have to develop not just the right attitudes themselves, but will need to develop all the qualities of a great teacher.

The other factor that teachers need to contend with in students of this age group is peer pressure. They will consciously need to work on students who are leaders. Influencing the attitudes of these natural leaders will affect the entire class. They will also need to create new leaders deliberately by recognising students who have the right attitudes and setting them up as role models for the rest of the class.

Dealing with the students in the middle classes is perhaps the most difficult task. These are the young pre-teens and teens. They are of an age when they are most rebellious and least amenable to direction. This is when teachers need to be most watchful to end the bullying of 'different' children. Frequent, open discussions on what is right and what is wrong are required. Constant reinforcement is also very important. Here too, peer pressure is very important and influencing the opinions of the class as a whole is an important part of the teacher's duties.

Creating the right learning environment

Creating the right attitude is the first step in dealing with children with special needs. The second step is in creating the right learning environment for these children. Their learning needs are more complex and therefore the facilities that they require will be complex.

Figure 10.4 Multi-dimensional planning is a very crucial part of the learning-teaching process. Teachers make plans for students with different abilities that are also sensitive to their cultural, social and economic background.

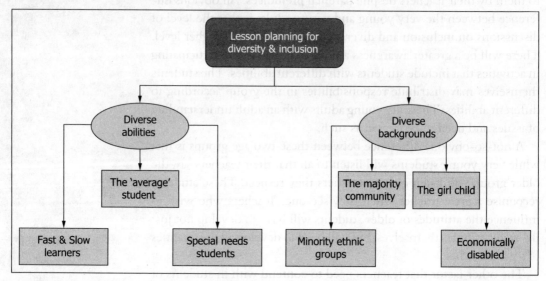

Lesson planning

A teacher in a great school does not plan a lesson that is suitable for an 'average' class. She makes multi-dimensional plans for different ability levels and for different types of reinforcement.

Thus, she may have some core activity in which all students can participate. Then she may divide the class into groups with members of each group working on different tasks. Finally, each student may be allotted some assignment or worksheet to work on alone. These assignments and worksheets may be different for different children. Teachers may also create small independent activities for children who are behind or ahead of the class level. These children will be occupied with these activities while the rest of the class listens to the teacher.

These multi-dimensional lesson plans need to be sensitive not only to students with different abilities, but should also recognise needs of students from diverse backgrounds. The teacher will use examples that will be culturally acceptable to the class and will specially include students who belong to minority groups in the class. Similar sensitivity is required for students who may have an economically weak background—projects will be designed in such a way that all children will be able to afford the additional expenses of the materials required. Activities will also be gender sensitive—for example, role-playing activities will make sure that girls and boys are not required to participate in stereotypical female and male roles. Examples used will consciously aim to narrow the gender divide.

Managing diversity and inclusion

Dealing with such diversity in the classroom is not an easy task. Even when students are from a homogenous background and have similar abilities, each child is very different from the other. Teaching for diversity and inclusion of children with special needs makes the task even more difficult. Teachers need to use a variety of techniques to reduce their task to manageable levels.

Support systems

One method is to reduce the curriculum to manageable levels. Inclusion does not imply that students with disabilities need to learn all that is being taught in the general education class. They only need to participate in the class. Yet, despite this, it may not be possible to teach an exacting academic syllabus when there are some children who cannot cope with this level of learning. Teachers will need to go through the curriculum carefully and remove any concepts that they feel are not required for the present. It may therefore be necessary sometimes to sacrifice academic learning for the social and emotional learning that will happen in an inclusive classroom.

Obviously, such modification in the syllabus by the teacher requires support from the school and the school board. Schools can also permit systems by which students are not classified by age in all classrooms, but rather by ability. Students who are ahead in a subject can learn with older students and students who are behind can learn with a younger class. What is important is that this facility is made available to all students, not just to those who are categorised as 'special' and there is no stigma attached to staying behind in some classes.

Teachers will also need to accept that classrooms that consist of students from diverse backgrounds, different abilities and age groups is likely to be more chaotic than a homogenous class. Therefore, it may be necessary to reduce the overall class size for such diverse groups. More than one teacher may be required in a classroom at the same time to manage the individual needs of different students.

191

Figure 10.5 Networking, diversity-friendly systems and infrastructure facilities are the three important factors that make the management of diversity and inclusion effective. All three need to be part of a single interdependent holistic plan for all students.

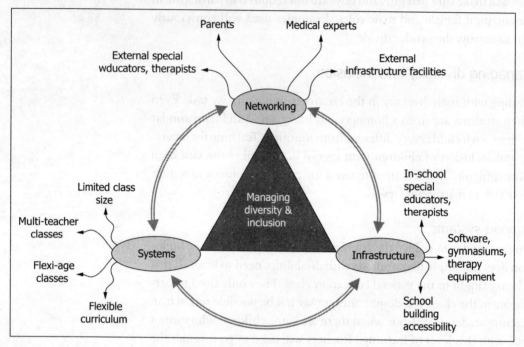

Facilities and infrastructure

Apart from this level of flexibility in curriculum and systems, the school also needs to provide some facilities within the school for students with special needs. Schools will need to provide basic services such as speech and occupational therapists, physiotherapists, special educators, psychologists and Braille experts.

The school building will need to be built to acceptable standards for disability access. Other infrastructure facilities will include software that is accessibility-enabled, gymnasiums that are disability-enabled, basic in-school medical facilities and so on. There may also be special equipment for different types of therapies in the school.

Networking

While it may not be possible for a school to provide every kind of expert that may be needed for a student, they should be connected to networks that will give them access to these experts when required. Schools may also not always be able to provide all facilities on their premises—but will know where to send a child for the type of therapy she may require.

Another type of networking is when teachers interact closely with parents of children with special needs. A child with special needs has a very complex IEP. Each step in her learning process will require more facilities, more time and more effort. Parents can be a major support to teachers in this learning process. They have the best understanding of their child's needs. They can therefore work together with the teachers to reinforce the skills taught in class.

All these support systems are required in addition to the training that the regular teachers get in handling students with special needs. The needs of students are so diverse that it will not be possible for the regular teachers to develop all the skills needed to teach these children. Yet, the special educators and parents will not replace the class teachers. They will work very closely with them and help them to understand how they can create well-integrated plans for children with special needs.

Finally, all these measures must be part of a single plan for all students. They do not function in isolation, they do not duplicate effort, nor do they work at cross-purposes. The school systems, the infra-structure support and the external network support need to form a holistic mesh that works together towards the same ends. Each co-operates with the other to fill any gaps that may exist.

Inclusion and acceptance

In a great school, inclusion and diversity are integrated into the general learning programme and curriculum of the school. This is not something extra that happens for the sake of a few students who are seen as different. This integration is not a statement for the sake of political correctness, but is part of the core philosophy of the school.

A great school, as we have seen, has a flexible curriculum and an indi-vidualised syllabus. In such circumstances, every child is special and therefore being 'special' is not a label.

However, while great schools do all they can to integrate all their students, they must also be realistic. It may not be possible always for children with special needs to learn all the skills they need in general education classes. Inclusion cannot be applied indiscriminately. For some children, skill development may be better outside the general classroom. Schools may then have to provide resources where some of their learning happens outside the mainstream and some within.

Sometimes, the teachers in the school may not be able to provide the kind of learning that a special student requires. This may happen despite all the efforts of the teachers and all the facilities available in the school. The school will then have to accept and tell the parents of the child that they cannot handle this situation. They will help the parents place the child in some other school that will be able to deal with her needs more effectively.

A teacher who cannot handle all the children with special needs who come to her does not become a bad teacher. A school that cannot provide facilities for extreme cases does not become a bad school. Even a great school has to accept at times that it may not be the greatest school for this particular child.

Summary

- Great schools welcome diversity as this is an extension of their philosophy of individualised learning.
- The student profile of the school reflects the diversity in the community around the school.
- Students with special needs who belong to the community around the school are welcomed into an inclusive learning environment.
- They create an environment within the school where diverse students thrive.
- They create an environment around the school that develops positive attitudes towards diversity.
- The right mental environment is created by influencing the attitudes of teachers, students and parents.
- Teachers learn to empathise and to be objective.
- Parents of all students learn to accept, rejoice and love.
- Students learn though direct methods—through indoctrination, behaviour control, debate and discussion.
- Students also learn through indirect methods—by observing the attitudes of teachers and role models.
- The right learning environment is created through:

  - Multi-dimensional planning—i.e. planning for diverse abilities and for diverse backgrounds
  - Wholistic management of systems and infrastructure and through effective networking

- Schools need to accept diverse students with different abilities and backgrounds not for the sake of political correctness, but as an integral part of the learning-teaching environment of the school.
- Yet schools need to be realistic and need to accept that sometimes they may not be able to manage all students who come to them.

11

Parents[1]

A great school works with parents to meet their aspirations

Despite the very fundamental causal link between parents and schools—the two often exist as two separate entities, with little in common and negligible interaction.

Schools exist in order to satisfy the need of the species to survive. They exist because parents want their children to be the fittest survivors. Schooling complements parenting; it is for survival, leadership and preparation for life. The purpose of a school is only to polish what happens at home, to provide varied additional exposure that parents on their own will not be able to give their children. It is very rare indeed for parents to have any say in key decisions made by the school and equally rare for schools to share with parents the processes by which they are guiding students to meet their aspirations.

Perhaps at the time of admissions, (some) parents do study the learning and teaching philosophy of the school; they look at the qualities of the students who study or have studied in this school; and if this is close enough to their personal philosophy in life they choose this school for their children.

However, given the admission scenario in Indian schools, often this does not happen at all. The government's monitoring and control of the pricing structure of the school has led to such a shortage of good schools that it has become a seller's market where few parents have any say. Parents have to take whichever school their children are lucky enough to get admission; they have to remain silent in the face of school policies and functioning even if they feel these are harming the interests of their children.

In such circumstances, there is very little incentive for schools to avoid the pitfall of becoming power centres that dispense admission favours to desperate parents. Even less is the incentive, once the child is in the school, to listen actively to what parents have to say and to act

[1] Everywhere in this book, the word 'parents' refers to the person or persons who have actively taken on the role of parenting a child, and not necessarily to the biological parents of the child.

Figure 11.1 Government control over fees and finances of schools has a detrimental effect on the parent–school relationship

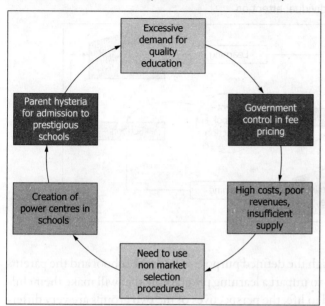

in a manner that will be in the best interests of each child. Great schools avoid these dangers and interact very closely with parents to work out an optimum learning development programme for their children.

Great schools do not just listen to parents—more importantly, they view their requirements objectively. Not all parents can be objective about their own children and sometimes may not be able to see exactly where the child stands with respect to her abilities and needs. These schools separate the 'wants' from the 'needs' and not only provide the latter, but also educate the parents so that they too will understand the latter.

On the other hand, since a school deals with very large numbers of children, they know that they can never know as much about any child as a parent can. They listen to parents in order to understand each individual child better and deal with each need of the child. Great schools join hands with parents to create a bank of resources for students that they can draw on later in life. This is a bank of life skills, inform-ation, values and happy memories and everything else that is required to make students into fulfilled and responsible adults.

No school can therefore achieve the goal of preparing students for life without communication with parents or without their active involvement.

197

Figure 11.2 Parent–school interaction enables sharing of strengths—schools help parents to become more objective, parents help schools to give better individual attention

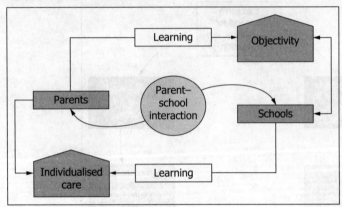

Even though the defined purpose of both the school and the parents is identical—to impart a learning programme that will make their children succeed in life, the perspectives of the two groups are very different; theirs is not a symmetrical relationship. Each needs certain inputs from the other, and each needs to communicate and participate in different ways in order to fulfil these wants.

Perspectives in school–parent relationship

What do schools want from parents?

Some schools want parental involvement to end with the payment of fees. Not so for the kind of schools we are talking about. Most good schools want parents to be closely involved with their children and to spend quality time with them. Schools get all kinds of parents—each parent will deal with their children differently and each child needs different types of parental concern.

Different parents have different approaches to parenting. At one extreme are parents who are so bogged down by their professional and other formal commitments that they fail to find adequate time for their children and may compensate for the guilt by trying to satisfy the child's material wants and meeting every demand of their child. At the other extreme are parents who might get so involved with their children that the child is not given any space to grow. Most of the time they are

Figure 11.3 Balanced parenting requires an appropriate mix of different parenting styles to meet the needs of different situations, family backgrounds and child needs

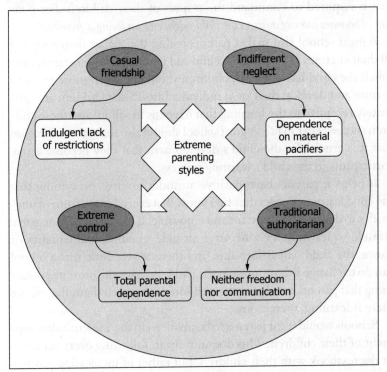

compensating for whatever they lacked in their childhood or are pushing their children to get ahead in the rat race and succeed in life. The former set of children cannot deal with the stresses and pressures of life because they have never been exposed to any form of denial, the latter set of children also cannot deal with the stresses and pressures of life as they have been exposed to too much pressure from far too young an age and are already burnt out. In the end, neither is going to be prepared for life.

Unfortunately, the pressures of modern-day existence mean that parents belonging to such extremes are growing day by day. A great school would want the parents to tread the middle path as both extremes are detrimental to a child's emotional and intellectual development. Recognising this predicament that we find ourselves in today, it should be the endeavour of a great school to make parents realise if they are falling into the trap of 'extreme parenting' of the types just mentioned. While all the time that parents spend with children should be quality

199

time rather than setting aside small capsules of time in the day for the child; parents should also avoid the trap of excessive informality with their children but instead guide, nurture and keep that little distance that is required to command the respect of their children. *For, if the parent becomes more of a friend the child might end up losing a guardian!*

A great school also makes parents realise that rather than focusing all their energies in pushing the child and in measuring constantly how much the child has achieved, children should be given more space to mature and develop their own individualities. Such children are ultimately receptive to the learning that happens in school and these children succeed later in life. A great school should also make parents realise that it is crucial for the child's development that they become active participants in the child's learning process.

It helps if parents have positive attitudes towards everything that the child learns and to let the child know that everything—from mathematics to dance—is important and enjoyable. If parents have a negative attitude to learning, or a negative attitude to either mathematics or dance, the child will absorb this, and there is very little that a school can do to change this mindset in the child. Perhaps the most important thing that parents can do for their children is to teach them that where there is learning, there is joy.

Schools would want parents to be involved in the academic development of their children. This does not mean following every sentence in the textbook with their children, but rather of inculcating positive attitudes to learning. Thoughtful discussions at home are far more useful, in the end, than sitting with textbooks. Parental involvement with the innovative aspects of learning is more important than involvement in the routine homework that children ought to be doing on their own.

Parents have left school long ago and branched out into their own specialisations. They often have no link with many of the disciplines that their children study, yet they can always find ways to participate in the learning process of any subject. They can be involved in the search for additional material, help their children in organisation of their work or teach them time management skills.

Schooling will always lead to stress—part of the lesson of life after all is in learning how to deal with stresses that one will inevitably face. Parents have to accept that this stress is part of the learning process—children do not go to school just for fun and games, it is serious work.

A student cannot reach her ultimate potential without being stretched, and this invariably leads to stress. Schools can ensure that this stress remains within the limits that the child can handle only if parents do not do anything to exacerbate the situation. Parents will thus have to deal positively with their own stresses—not only the stresses caused by their personal and professional lives, but also the stresses caused by their expectations from their children.

Figure 11.4 Schools expect parents to have certain basic qualities that have a positive influence on their child's ability to learn and adjust to the school programme. They also want parents to be involved in proactive and balanced parenting.

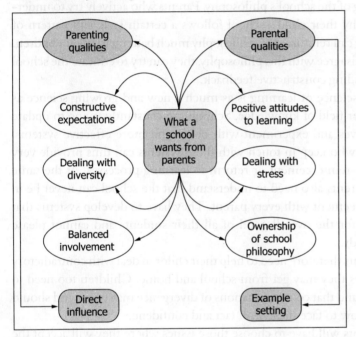

It helps if parents too make little sacrifices: for example, things as basic as giving up some family activities, like watching television, in order to help their children cope with school work; to ensure that their children manage their time effectively at home and at school. More important, it would send a positive message to the child that they take a genuine interest in her intellectual development and progress.

Most important, however, is that parents should not be worked up themselves. Often, children face hurdles in their path with greater confidence and less anxiety than parents do. Parents tend to get excessively worried about the competition in the external world, the syllabus load on their children and long study hours. They are affected by pressure from other competitive parents.

Parents need to enjoy and be excited about what their children are learning and not just to percolate this attitude to children, but also to reduce the stress in schooling. Many parents believe this enjoyment reduces as the child moves to higher classes. As the load increases, they would help their child much better if they inculcate (in themselves and in their children) an attitude of enjoyment and excitement at having to face and conquer new challenges.

Another aspect that parents need to be involved in is their understanding of the school's philosophy. Parents who actively try to understand why their child's school follows a certain style and pattern of learning can reinforce this philosophy much better with their children. If they disagree with this philosophy, they can try to educate the school by providing constructive feedback.

The science of learning is as much a new and growing science as any other field of knowledge. Schools are constantly trying to update themselves and experiment with better and more effective systems. Parents who keep in touch with these systems can thus provide very valuable reinforcement or reform to learning processes. At the same time, parents also need to understand that the school can never be in total agreement with every parent. They have to develop systems that will be for the overall good of all their students and cannot please everybody.

Parents therefore need to help their children deal with contradictory messages they may get from school and home. Children too need to understand that certain situations of divergence may occur and should know how to face these with tact and confidence.

Parents will have to choose those issues where they will accept the school line whatever their personal beliefs. For example, while they may not believe it is important for their child to learn music, yet they will ensure that she puts in her best effort in music because it is part of the curriculum. Schools that are attempting to remove gender biases in children will not succeed if parents treat girls as second-class citizens at home.

Another example where parents must co-operate with school policies is in school systems for discipline.

Parents do not need to agree with the school in every aspect. If there is an activity in school that goes very strongly against their principles— say the wearing of a particular type of dress for a school entertainment

> The sharing of values between parents and schools becomes very important—schools that are trying to reinforce values that parents do not believe in will never succeed in their task.

> Parents need to be very clear about communicating their own value systems to their children and to let them know that while differences with the school line on a particular issue may exist, these can be resolved without conflict.

programme, they can certainly work out a solution in consultation with the child's teachers. This co-existence of differences will ultimately help to make the school environment richer. Diversity is important for the learning process of the child and no good school is in the business of mass production of clones. Parents who differ very strongly with the school philosophy must consider placing their child in another school.

Ultimately, what schools want is that parents have the right kind of expectations from their children. Parents must expect that their children will put in their very best attempt in everything and try to excel in those areas that specially excite them. They must teach their children to cope even when young. They need to create an environment at home that is conducive to learning and an environment that respects achieve-ment and excellence. Finally, parents need to inculcate a culture of self-discipline in their children, the ability to work hard towards set goals, and the ability to deny or postpone enjoyment when needed.

What do parents want from schools?

The first and most important requirement of parents from the school is to develop the academic and intellectual skills of their children. In order to do this, parents want to know what the school's method and philosophy of learning is. Most parents will do their best to reinforce the school's philosophy with their children, but are often frustrated by a lack of communication with the school.

Figure 11.5 Parents want to participate in an effective learning programme for their children

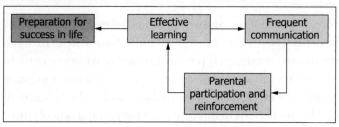

Some schools believe that the annual report card is all the communi-cation that is required. This may have been sufficient in the past, but today parents are far more involved in the learning process of their children. They would like very definite instructions from schools on how they can help their children at home. They also want far more information on their child's strengths and weaknesses and detailed profiles of their child's character and pace of development. For parents, academic progress and communication of academic progress go hand in hand. Parents today want to work with the school to ensure that their child gets the best possible education. They want to be aware of every gap in the school's programme and take proactive measures to fill these gaps either at school or at home.

Parents also want schools to go beyond academics and reinforce values that they believe in and are trying to inculcate in their children. They would like schools to deal with wide-ranging issues—from integrity to inclusion. Parents may talk to their children about different values, but these will not have the same impact as actual experiences. They would like schools to use situations that arise in school, as examples to reinforce these values.

When cheating in examinations happens, schools should use this opportunity to discuss honesty, or loss of equipment to discuss care for property. Schools should ensure diversity in their student profiles so that students learn to respect people of different races, religions, social backgrounds and abilities. Parents want that schools provide both separate forums for discussions on ethical issues as also their integration into daily lessons.

Parents also want schools to deal with this aspect with tact and sensitivity. Schools need to deal with universally accepted values and not with specifics that may hurt the sentiments of particular parents or communities. While it is acceptable to have discussions on the unacceptability of violence, it should never be used in the context of singling out a single community or religion as examples of perpetrators of violence.

Therefore, a school 'line' on current issues related to ethical situations will definitely need to be very tactfully formulated. In some cases where an issue is extremely sensitive, it may be wiser not to tilt in either direction. Yet this should never be a reason for schools to evade the responsibility of inculcating values in their children by avoiding all discussion. The discussions in this case must happen and schools must make sure that all students, whatever their parental background or predisposition, are exposed to both sides of the argument and are allowed the freedom to make their own considered judgements.

Parents recognise the overwhelming influence of the school in their child's life. Children often react faster to peer pressure and teacher recognition than to parental reinforcement. Children know that their

Figure 11.6 While parents want schools to reinforce core values they do not want interference in their personal way of life. This leaves the school with the task of dealing tactfully with issues that fall in the grey area in between.

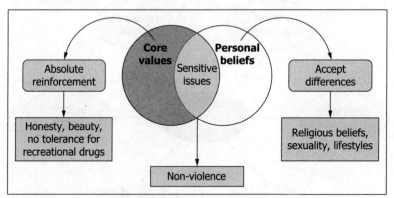

parents appreciate their abilities whatever may be their actual achievement. The same appreciation from a teacher or another student carries far more value as it is likely to be objective and with respect to a larger group of people.

Parents would therefore like teachers to be proactive about showing their appreciation for all the achievements of their child. They would like schools to guide peer pressure to put the right kinds of compulsions on their child. Schools need to recognise the good work done by students in a way that they become role models for other children.

Apart from developing the intellect and the values of their children, parents strongly feel that schools have a duty to develop the personality of their child. Today in the face of increasing competition, the person who communicates better has an edge over another person who may otherwise be equally competent. This ability to communicate well is not just in terms of language skills, but also in terms of body language.

Children need to communicate respect for others, confidence in oneself and an air of competence. Often in the midst of a heavy academic curriculum load and preparation for examinations, the development of these skills tends to be of secondary importance. This could lead to disastrous results when the students finally get on the stage of life and have to perform.

How are schools to achieve all this for their students? Each child is different; each has different abilities and needs. The only way is through individual attention. For every parent, his or her child is precious. Parents want that their child remains equally special to the school.

Figure 11.7 Parents want their child to be recognised as unique and to be nurtured by the school in a manner that is most appropriate to her as an individual

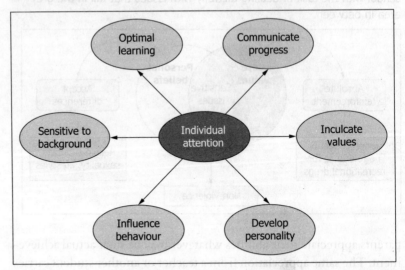

Schools therefore have to fight consciously the tendency to view students as an anonymous group, to look beyond those children who are at the top in terms of achievement, behaviour and personality and to look closely at all the rest, and understand the unique strengths of each.

Teachers need to understand that each child craves attention and often the ones who are creating trouble in school are, in their own way, crying out for help. Parents want the teachers and the school to notice what their children are doing and get back as soon as possible with their feedback so that they can deal with situations before they get out of control.

Enabling communication and interaction

In the present world of fast communication, schools have many tools by which they can enable communication with parents, teachers and others in the school. Communication relates to three different types of issues—feedback on student performance and ability, feedback on student needs and behaviour and communication of school policies and philosophy.

Feedback on student performance and ability has already been dealt with in detail in Chapter 4. The various instruments for this communication are periodic and consolidated reports on all aspects of the child's development, feedback in the form of comments in the corrections of the student's work and their scores in class assignments. Apart from this, most schools also schedule fixed times when parents can come to school and meet the teachers to review their child's progress in the course of the academic year. These parent–teacher interactions can also be constructively used to discuss not just issues of learning but also behavioural issues and progress.

However, schools should not restrict themselves to these scheduled meetings only for parent–teacher interactions. Teachers can send home notes through the children, send e-mails or make regular phone calls directly to parents both to express their appreciation of the child as well as to discuss remedies for problems they may have encountered.

What is important is that on the part of teachers, these communications should not take place only when there are problems, and these should not become forums for complaint. All communication must be either for appreciation or remediation—for positive and constructive feedback and sharing of a common interest in the growth of the child. Parents too need to react proactively to these overtures and respond promptly. Few teachers can raise the level of their enthusiasm for the child's good work if the child's parents are not interested.

Apart from these, other forums for communication are discussion boards on the school Website, parent networking groups, regular class meetings scheduled for discussions on specific topics and e-mails and letters sent out to parents to highlight special occasions and concerns. These forums could be used for discussion of issues related not to a specific child but to school policies and philosophy and for helping parents to become aware of all that is happening in the school.

Interaction between parents and schools needs to go beyond passive listening to each other. Parents can contribute a lot to school by actively participating in the everyday life of the school. Parents and teachers can work in tandem to help children deal with issues such as negative peer pressure, violence, exposure to graphic content in the media and so on. Parents can form groups to put positive parental pressure on other less involved parents or resolve problems with parents who are actively causing conflict in the school.

Parents could also take on the role of volunteers to stand in for teachers when they are on leave, to help with school transport arrangements for children, to manage the traffic at school opening and closing times. Parent representatives could take on the responsibility for different aspects of the school life—whether in helping out with routine daily tasks or on special occasions, either in administration or in academics.

The parent community is diverse and rich in varied experience. Sharing these experiences with the children can help them to develop a greater awareness of different points of view, different professions and different approaches to life. In some senses, this interaction is one of the most important types of interactions possible.

Schools have a tendency to build their own self-sufficient worlds, to live in enclosed ivory towers. Few schools actively interact with the outside world even though they have the resource bank of parents nearby. These parents are members of the community that students need to become a part of later in life. They can be the means by which students are gradually exposed to the outside world and to a variety of exposures.

A community of parents can therefore help in providing enriching experiences to all the students in the school—whether it is in the form of a visit of the youngest students to the orchid farm run by a parent in the school or whether it is the summer management training for senior students in the offices of another parent.

In all these interactions, the student must never be left out. As children grow in school, they too should be given more responsibility

Figure 11.8 Parent–school interactions relate both to communication and to participation. Students need always to be active participants of these interactions.

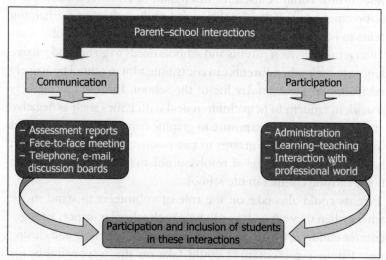

and involvement in these interactions between school and parents—they are after all the link between the two. They should be active participants in the discussions that take place between the school and the parents. They should be members of all the forums for discussion that are appropriate for their age and stage of intellectual and emotional development.

Thus, different types of interactions are possible that suit the different temperaments of parents. These interactions can help parents to become more involved and develop a sense of ownership in the school. Schools and parents have a lot to gain from closer interaction with each other—each has the same ultimate goal and any sensible school will ensure that this synergy is exploited fully.

Summary

- Schools complement parenting, yet parents have a very marginal role to play in schools.
- One reason for this marginal role is the fact that the demand for good schools far exceeds the supply.
- Great schools listen and learn from parents; they also positively influence parenting.

Schools want from parents
- Involved parenting that is not overly 'friendly' and neglectful of attention and discipline.
- Parenting that is not so obsessively close that the child has no space to grow.
- Positive and joyful attitudes to thinking, learning and challenges.
- Involvement in the learning of their children that is geared to developing skills knowledge.
- Acceptance that children need to face stress and assistance in helping them conquer stress.
- Understanding of the school's philosophy and support for school systems, especially systems for inculcating self discipline.
- To help their children understand diversity, to respect the different points of view they will encounter and yet remain firmly fixed to family values.
- Positive expectations from their children—that their child will always attempt to the very best she can.

Parents want from schools
- A learning programme that will make their child a success in life.

- Frequent and regular communication of the methods used by the school to prepare students for life.
- Assistance in reinforcing core values.
- Balanced approach to different perspectives—sensitivity in handling differences of opinion of children from different backgrounds.
- To use the influence of the teachers and student peers to make positive behavioural impact in their children—the creation of role models.
- Development of the personality of the child in terms of developing confidence and good communication skills.
- Individual attention for their children—to make each child feel special, to appreciate each child's strengths and to help each child overcome her weaknesses.

Forums for communication and interaction
- Academic and non-academic assessments at regular intervals.
- Formal and informal meetings with parents.
- Communication over telephone, e-mail, discussion boards.
- Interactions with school and parents.
- Parents can lead discussions in schools on various issues related to values and self development of students.
- Parents can volunteer to help the school in managing some simple administrative and managerial tasks.
- They could enable the interaction of the school with their professions and give students valuable exposure to life in the real world.

Management

12

The primary focus

A school (or, for that matter, any educational institution) as an organisation does not have the type of structure one finds in the corporate organisations. A school of average size is an organisation of a hundred or more employees and perhaps clients in the thousands. The principal employees are the teachers. Teachers have very few chances of 'rising in the organisation' in the commonly accepted sense of the phrase, that suggests moving on with some guarantee to higher designations, different work responsibilities or higher salaries.

Most teachers will remain teachers right until they retire, and their responsibilities will remain the same. The highest paid teacher is not likely to be earning disproportionately more than the lowest paid. There is very little scope for teachers to move on to managerial positions, which are few—those of principal and one or two vice principals. The half-a-dozen heads of department will continue to teach while carrying out their other responsibilities and may revert to being a 'mere' teacher when their term as head expires.

The clients too are different. There is some confusion here about who are the clients: The students with whom the school interacts closely and whose needs they are contracted to meet? Or, the parents who actually sign the contract and make the payments for services rendered? If parents are clients, the service is rendered to them indirectly; they have little or no contact with the school and do not interact with the organisation on a regular basis. If students are clients, they are minors who have almost no say in the manner in which the contract is executed and cannot stand up for their contractual rights.

Managing such a structure needs a very different mindset. The challenge is to give students what they need, though they may not even know what these needs are or how to communicate these needs clearly. The challenge is to give teachers a sense of fulfilment in their work despite the paucity of physical rewards.

Figure 12.1 The organisational structure of a school has effectively two layers. Department heads are also teachers. The clients too are in two layers—students who interact directly and parents with whom the contract is actually signed.

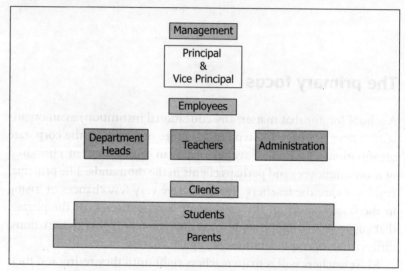

Then, there is the measure of success—a standard organisation would measure its success either by its profitability, or by its sales. In a great school, being able to charge high fees and make profits is not an indicator of success, nor is the ability to increase 'sales' by increasing the number of students.

These challenges can be met only by creating an environment that puts the highest premium on learning. This environment is one where all players are in the midst of an adventure, in pursuit of the unknown. The emphasis is on nurturing a learning organisation. The sense of achievement that a student has in conquering the unknown and creating new knowledge is the fulfilment of the contract for the student. For teachers, the reward is the sense of achievement in having helped a student onto this path of self discovery and independence.

Ultimately, it is neither profits nor sales, but the quality of the product that the school produces that will determine its success. For a school, the 'product' is the student. Unlike institutions of higher learning that can measure their success solely by the professional success of their students, a school measures student quality in a more comprehensive way. The students have to be a success in life—schools mould students intellectually, emotionally and ethically, apart from imparting a host of other skills.

Figure 12.2 A school creates a positive learning environment to deal with challenges of managing clients and employees

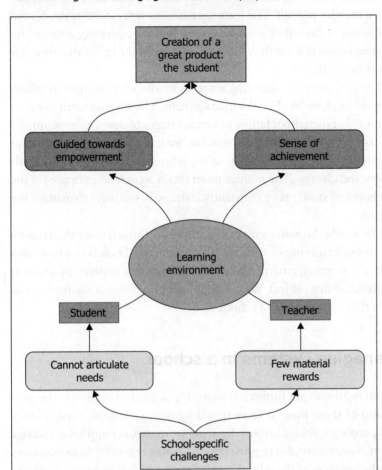

The task of the management of the school, therefore, is to ensure an environment that will create such outstanding products. The emphasis is on nurturing a learning organisation. The management of a great school provides a learning environment for its teachers. It gives them the space and freedom to follow their creative instincts. It gives them the tools to create outstanding students by giving them access to intellectual resources that will enhance their domain knowledge, cognitive skills, material resources and instruments that they will need to guide students during the learning process.

Great schools do this by creating and managing systems in the school that meet the goals of the school. They ensure that these systems run

213

effectively and unobtrusively. These systems give support to the teachers and ensure that focus and efficiency are not lost somewhere in an open-ended creative pursuit. The learning environment is further reinforced by these systems—they are not systems that are externally imposed on the employees nor are they followed blindly in the belief that time has tested their efficacy.

These systems are learning systems by the very manner in which they are implemented by the management. The management involves members of the school family in various stages of development, implementation and review of these systems. Systems do not exist in isolation but are dependent on the goals of the school and changed as the goals evolve and change. The management therefore sets an example for the teachers and students by constantly learning better ways to manage the school.

Obviously, the management of a school does much more than ensure the smooth running of systems. The aim of this book is not to write a treatise on management; there are innumerable sources of wisdom available on this subject. We will highlight only some of the managerial tasks that are unique to a school.

Managing systems in a school

When resources are limited, systems are needed to maximise the utilisation of these limited resources. In any organisation, time, money and people are always limited. Systems are therefore required to manage them. Systems are also required to ensure that repetitive tasks necessary for the business of the school are performed with minimum effort and maximum efficiency in order to let all the members of the school community focus on the primary task of the school—development of the learning abilities of the students.

A school cannot run without a timetable or calendar. Every system must have a goal—as goals change, so do the systems. Alternatively, systems change when the process of achieving the goal is not being met. Thus, no system is sacrosanct—it needs to be flexible.

Systems affect the stakeholders in the organisations. In a school, these stakeholders are the students, their parents, the teachers, the school management and the community that interacts with the school. Systems are affected by areas of concern (which are outside the control of the organisation; for example, the syllabus is given) and areas of influence (which are within the control of the organisation). If people were islands, then areas of concern would equal the areas of influence and there would be no need for systems. However, we have to function with or without outside influences and so need to have systems, even though they constrain us and force us to function within defined boundaries.

Balancing goals and systems

A school may have the following goals:

- Prepare students for success in life by:
  - Providing good academic education and understanding of concepts
  - Enabling students to score high marks in public examinations
  - Enabling entry into the best colleges
  - Inculcating excellence in non-academic fields
  - Developing well-rounded personalities
- Provide professional fulfilment to the teachers and all other staff
- Have a proactive involvement with the outside world—by reaching out to the community around and its environment
- Manage within limited resources

It is possible that a set of goals may require conflicting systems; it is also possible that the same goal could be achieved by different processes or systems.

Providing a good academic education and enabling students to be learners may conflict with high marks. It is possible that an inflexible system of drill will maximise marks in public examinations, but students may not have understood even basic concepts. Alternatively, spending time on understanding concepts may make it more difficult to cover all aspects of the syllabus within a given period and thus lead to lower scores in public examinations.

Conflicts occur not only due to goals that cannot co-exist, but also due to systems that may be inconsistent with each other. The system of providing varied experiential learning to all students may clash with the examination preparation drills required for students in the final year of school. Similarly, goals and systems may also be inconsistent— the school's stated goal may be conceptual learning, but all systems may be geared to rote learning.

However, it is not necessary that only a single system will lead to a specified goal. Drill is not the only way to help students get high marks in examination—it may only be the easier and faster option. A school that spends more time in experiential learning that strengthens conceptual understanding in students also enables students to score high marks—but at the cost of greater effort, time and teacher input.

While this system helps to meet two different goals, it may work only if resources are stretched and there is proper co-ordination and quality control of systems. Thus, it is possible to devise systems that enable multiple goal achievement—but at a cost. Most of the tensions and trade-offs caused by systems are due to limits of resource availability.

Figure 12.3 Conflicts are caused due to differing perceptions of stakeholders and due to limits in resources—time, finances and people

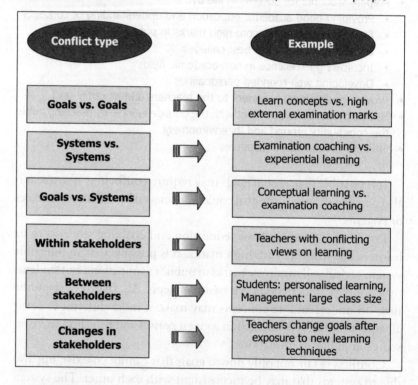

The other reason for tensions is differing perceptions of stakeholders. Conflicts occur when different stakeholders have different goals or want to use different systems. Students want a personalised learning system but the management may want to maximise the number of students in a class. Alternatively, among stakeholders, some parents want systems to focus on strict discipline while others want greater flexibility. Stakeholders change over time—and when they do, well-entrenched systems may become obsolete, but inertia may cause them to remain.

How then are these conflicts to be resolved? The first step is to decide on a hierarchy of goals. They must be ordered according to importance. Then the system may be decided based on a market force system of demand (the goals), supply (the resources available and their limitations) and the price (the system that brings equilibrium between goals and resources).

A conflict between goals and systems should not be a conflict at all. In such a case, the system needs to be changed. However, often schools have become so entrenched in the system or are so afraid of the cost of changing systems or in such state of inertia that the system actually continues without meeting the goals for which it was devised. An example is the examination system for students in the primary classes. The goal is clear—to assess the progress made by the students in the learning process. However, current wisdom and advances in pedagogy tell us that examinations are not a good measure of assessment for such young students (and in fact often even for older students). Other techniques of continuous assessment for students are far more accurate and less stressful to young minds. Yet, because many schools have always had examinations from Class I onwards, they find it simpler to continue with this system rather than change to one of continuous assessment. The additional effort and the required change in mindsets makes it very difficult to move to a new system, even though it is clear to most that the goals are not being met.

In fact, it also happens that the goal for which the system was made may be totally forgotten, but the system continues merely for historical reasons. Many schools in India continue to insist that their students wear neckties as part of their uniform even in the hottest weather. Very few would be able to justify the reason for this custom! The most important point that cannot be missed here is that systems are always subordinate to goals, and clarity and awareness of the goal of each system must always be kept in mind.

Conflicts between stakeholders are more difficult to resolve. The decision on whose goals are more important and whose are less important can be subjective. It depends on the differential influence of the stakeholders. The goals of the more influential stakeholders such as the management may in some cases be the more important goals and may at times unfortunately, ('let us maximise resources through a high student–teacher ratio') override the goals of the teachers and students ('conceptual understanding for each individual child').

Systems in a school

Every organisation has different classes of systems.

Figure 12.4 Some examples of systems and subsystems in a school

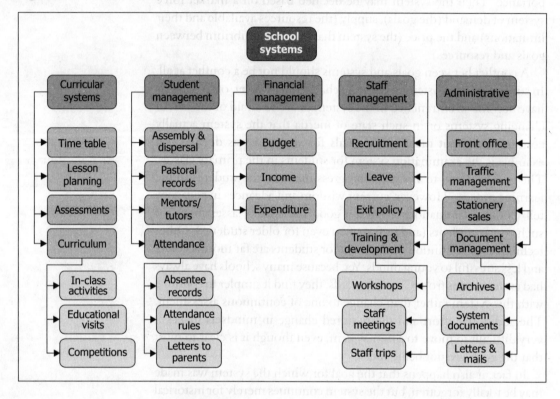

Need for clearly articulated systems

Clearly articulated systems benefit all. Often it appears that administrative systems lack clear articulation. This will not be so if administrative policies too are openly focused towards school goals. For very complex administrative procedures (that are often determined by outside forces such as financial laws and other legal regulations), the way to bring about greater clarity is by following policies and procedures transparently and objectively.

In all organisations, managing of finances is crucial—and therefore effective systems that manage finances are very important. Not only finances, but also all resources need to be used efficiently. Therefore, schools need systems to get rid of redundancy. Often in an organisation,

Figure 12.5 The problems in implementation of financial systems are that they are externally given and are difficult to understand. New systems for greater involvement and better communication can solve this issue.

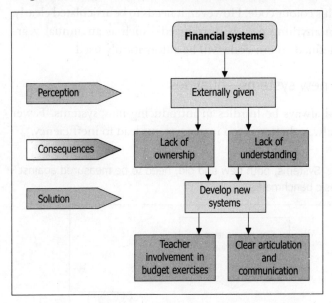

there are many people doing duplicate tasks: budgeting exercises are not added up and some systems are not directly efficient. It is in the interest of all stakeholders to be more efficient in cutting out deadwood.

Yet there is a perception that all administrative systems—especially financial ones are 'externally given' and that the school teaching staff has no control over or involvement in these systems. This need not be so; for, if the staff of the school actively co-operate in formulating the school budget, the finance department will have a better idea of the resource requirements of the school and can work towards optimal finance utilisation. For example, when the year is planned, the budget required for each activity is indicated by the heads of department for their respective departments. This results in the efficient implementation of the activities planned by the different departments as they know beforehand the budget amount at their disposal. The desired activity could therefore be carried out without any worry of long-drawn procedure for approvals while implementing the programme. An administration that articulates its systems clearly in order to facilitate all the staff to participate actively in its procedures will ultimately be more efficient.

Some systems in a school are often unspoken and are based on custom or school culture. These systems too need to be turned around and articulated objectively in a manner that the decision maker will appreciate. For example, a school may have a colour code. This is reflected in the student uniform, and all school furniture, stationery, etc. may follow this colour code. However, it needs to be articulated clearly, so that when anything new is introduced—such as an annual yearbook—the defined colour code will be automatically used.

Designing new systems—qualities

There would always be hurdles in introducing new systems. Fewer systems are always better as too many systems lead to inefficiency.

Figure 12.6 Systems, both new and old, need to be measured against these four basic benchmarks

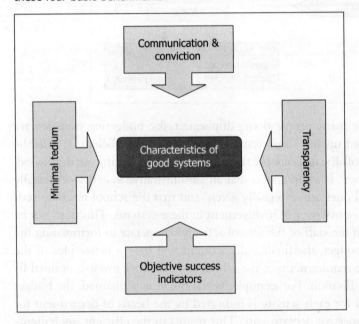

Communication and if possible, conviction

People who need to be part of a system should generally be convinced about it—but in reality, democracy does not always work. Therefore, while conviction is not always essential, communication is both necessary and crucial. Systems for communication are orientation, revaluation and the development of a knowledge base. Systems are also needed to handle those who do not follow systems and for conflict resolution.

Objective success indicators

The process of system design often requires hard decisions. Targets need to be based on efficiency in order to judge the success of the system. While values are incorporated in the goals of the systems, there are no values in the system itself. Therefore, it is possible to make system evaluation objective.

Minimise tedium

Tedium is inherent in all systems. It is necessary to choose systems that minimise tedium. Often systems prevent one from doing one's job. Therefore, it is necessary to weed out unnecessary systems. If teachers are recording attendance four times, it can be gathered once and delivered to those who need it. Systems need to meet goals without becoming taxing. Systems for different stakeholders need to be co-ordinated.

Transparency

Some systems are transparent while some are not. Conflicts that non-transparent systems cause can be resolved by assigning ownership for them—for example, exit policy is the prerogative of the head. At the same time, just because a system hurts does not mean that it should not be transparent. The credibility gain of a transparent system far exceeds the hurt it could cause.

The procedure for developing appropriate systems

It is crucial to develop a process that permits organisations to create transparent and appropriate systems. This process must also enable an organisation to let go of the systems that hurt and to give clear signals that the time has come to change a system. This process checks if over a period of time goals have changed; it checks if goals are not being met. It evaluates and reviews systems at regular intervals to remove complacency and inertia. *Thus, three core components of the procedure are the actual system processes, validation/monitoring and documentation.*

Defining system processes

A new system is created when a new goal arises or when an existing system is found not achieving an existing goal. The various processes and procedures need to be defined clearly based on the qualities of a good system mentioned earlier. Within this process is a built-in procedure that defines benchmarks, creates validation processes, enables communication and documentation and sets standards for success and parameters for failure of a system.

Validation procedures—ownership and monitoring

Apart from a well-established validation procedure based on logical arguments, all systems must be documented and distributed to those who have to carry it out. For this evaluation and review system to succeed, some conditions need to be met. Every system in the organisation needs to have an owner—usually the person who introduces the system. The reviewer of the system should never be the owner. This reviewer needs to look at the intended and unintended consequences of the system.

In the case of computerised reports for students, the owner will be the person who is in charge of ensuring timely data entry, generation of the reports and in charge of the software. The reviewer could be another staff member who evaluates if this system is actually leading to more informative and comprehensive reports than the earlier manual system. She asks questions to find out if this has reduced the workload on teachers due to the automated calculations (the intended consequences) and also checks whether there is a greater workload now due to the increased data entry load (the unintended consequences). Usually the owner will document the new system—and incorporate the reviewer's comments and suggestions in the documentation.

Documentation and communication of systems

The process of developing systems is not complete until a portfolio of all systems in an organisation is made, including the most obvious systems such as the morning assembly system. (What are the components of the morning assembly? The prayer, announcements and songs, where is the prayer and song book kept, who is in charge of collecting the announcements, who conducts the assembly on a daily basis and what is the order of those who are designated to conduct the assembly in the absence of the person who normally conducts the assembly.) Often systems exist but few know about. In a school where all educational trips are planned and budgeted ahead of time, there could also be a contingency fund available for unexpected outings. Teachers who are not aware of this fund may cause students to miss learning experiences that could not have been foreseen during the planning stage.

Thus, a school needs to document systems related to all aspects of the learning-teaching process. This includes how in-class and outside-class activities are conducted, how assessments are carried out, the types

Figure 12.7 Developing the system process is only one step in the development of a new system. Two crucial steps that tend to be left out in the process of creating a system are documentation and feedback.

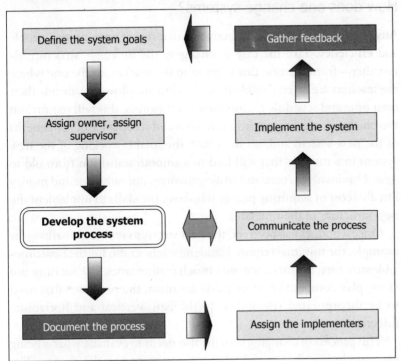

of pedagogical methods that will be used by teachers for different fields of specialisation and for different age groups, the behaviour norms for students and staff, the infrastructure and other resources that are needed and so on. There will in addition be documentation of systems for planning for each of the above processes and for debriefing on these processes at well-defined intervals.

Documentation in itself is not sufficient—people need to have easy access to documentation. While it would definitely help if the school has a comprehensive and well-developed computerised knowledge management system that is accessible to those who need to know, there are other simpler ways of creating accessible documentation. One of these could be in the form of an annual diary distributed to all staff that contains information on not just the calendar and timetables, but also on basic guidelines of behaviour for students and teachers. While it will not be possible to describe every system in the school in this diary, a list of people who are in charge of (owners) the different systems

223

in the school will go a long way towards helping those who need information to seek out the right person.

How does one change systems?

Any change in systems can be budgeted in terms of time, money, people and efficiency. Take the case of changing the timetable structure altogether—from the one that is given to the teacher, to the one where the teachers are given flexible time slots but are allowed to decide their own time and schedule requirements. Obviously, this will require, on the one hand, creating positive mindsets and acceptance of the benefits of the new system and, on the other, the total reworking of the new system in a manner that will lead to a smooth transition from old to new. This involves costs, and costing involves not only time and money but also cost of acquiring people who have the skills to implement the new structure of the timetable.

Once a budget has been set, the next step is to set benchmarks—for example, the minimal required student/teacher ratio for the new timetable structure, the list of activities (teach mathematics, take for museum visits, play competitive sports) that are must, the processes that need to be incorporated (flexibility, [w]holism, vertical and horizontal integration).

This process of changing systems also needs to evaluate what is being given up by the change and what is being gained by the change. The old timetable ensured the comfort of routine and order, the new system enables creativity and experimentation.

The entire process of changing systems needs to answer the following questions in sequence:

- Where are we and who is around us? (the current reality)
- Where do we want to go? (the new set of goals)
- What resources do we have?

The restructuring exercise will define:

- Activities that are a must
- Activities that one would like to do
- Activities not required

Answers will be found to:

- What is a budget? What is a financial reporting scheme?
- What are the resources, physical space and infrastructure required?

- How will changes be reported to stakeholders (*fait accompli* or discussion)
- What is impacted? (A new timetable structure impacts the class system, the appraisal system, the training policy, new recruitment policy)
- Who is impacted?
- How do decisions take place in the new system?
- Who is the owner of the system?
- Who will monitor and review the system?
- What are the success benchmarks and validation processes for this system?

The changes in the system are developed by answering these questions. Once the system is in place, the questions that need to be asked are:

- Have we achieved the goal or purpose of the system?
- How do we know we have reached the required destination?

Success indicators are part of the restructuring exercise and must be set in advance. It is also necessary to break up big goals into small steps through indicators. Schools will review if a system is working on the basis of these indicators. These benchmarks evaluate the efficiency of the system. The validation process tells us if goals have been achieved. For example, are students excelling in more activities now that the time table structure has changed? Are teachers meeting their targets more efficiently (in less time, or higher targets than the earlier system)?

Finally, the changes must be documented and made accessible to all those who are involved in the functioning of the system.

Need for following systems

Some systems are necessary, even though they may appear complex and unreasonable. It is sometimes necessary to live with certain systems in order to achieve a certain purpose. If the system is articulated clearly, follow it. Consequences for not following systems must be laid out clearly with transparency. Otherwise, it becomes very difficult to judge if rules have been followed.

Following systems leads to greater efficiency, even if they do not appear to be intuitively reasonable. Often it is necessary to follow what appears to be an unreasonable system in order to make a compromise due to resource limitations. If a large number of stakeholders feel that a system is unreasonable, then the system should be formally changed, but, until the new system is officially introduced, the old one must be scrupulously followed.

In a school, teachers may be creating multiple records of attendance—one for themselves, one to submit to the administration, another to submit to the department that generates student reports and yet another to submit to the head of the school. It may appear to be an unnecessary multiplication of work, but if these records do not reach the various people who require them, there will be chaos further ahead in the line. Until a new system is generated where, for example, attendance records are stored online in a database directly accessible to all those who need them, this inefficient system must continue to be followed.

Flexibility and creativity in systems

While it may be easy to decide on the kind of systems the school requires today, it is also necessary to put into place systems that will work tomorrow in totally changed circumstances. Planning for the unplanned requires flexibility, creativity and contingency plans.

Some systems do not lend themselves to flexibility—such as reimbursement policies. Only some systems can be planned for creativity. In a school, the systems related to the learning-teaching process are the ones that need to be devised with flexibility and creativity. Any school that believes that its primary goal is to prepare students for life—for the time when they leave the school 14 years from now, will have to build systems that will work for the students 14 and 40 years in the future. Yet we live in a world of constant change and often cannot envisage what the future will hold next year—let alone 14 years ahead. It is therefore important to keep in touch with the changing knowledge, because as knowledge changes, goals may change and systems to meet these goals efficiently will definitely need to keep changing. This is the reason for the continued emphasis on the system of regular and periodical review of goals and systems.

Ultimately, when learning how to deal with the varied systems in a school, the most important factor is never to lose sight of the big picture that is based on the school's fundamental value system and to look at the entire schooling process as a single holistic system.

Creating a system to assess whether a school has had a successful year

Just as students and teachers need to be assessed and their assessments used to modify their subsequent learning programmes, so also a school needs to assess itself annually and use the feedback from this assessment to improve its performance. A school needs to measure success very differently from other organisations. There are no managers available to schools to check the annual reports for success or failure of the school programmes.

The currency in which a school transacts its business is not money. Most schools tend to rely on subjective feelings to gauge whether a school has had a good year or not. At the most, schools may analyse the board examination results of their students and declare a school successful if its students have performed well. Few believe that much more is required for self-assessment, and fewer still have any system for an in-depth analysis of school performance, believing this to be an impossible task.

However, this task is not impossible. Systems can be devised that, while not having the same rigour as formal accounting practices, are still far more reliable indicators of success than dependence on emotions. In fact, these systems could be devised in such a manner that they will also show exactly where the strengths of the school lie. They will pinpoint the weaknesses that must be dealt with in the succeeding years.

The process of devising a system for assessing success

Step 1: Define the system
To devise a methodology that will enable schools to **assess** how **successful** the **preceding year** has been.

Step 1a: State the purpose of the new system
In other words, this system will analyse the reasons for success or lack of success and will find ways to improve school performance in the future.

Step 1b: Define the keywords and parameters in the purpose statement
Success is defined as creation and development of successful students—who are high achievers in a variety of spheres. Success also measures effectiveness of teachers, involvement of parents, atmosphere conducive to learning and successful systems and infrastructure for student learning programme.

Student success will measure their success in different dimensions— in class learning, outside class activities, physical development, external examination success and success in college and professional placements and finally and yet foremost, successful development of humane traits.

An assessment of teachers and their level of commitment and effectiveness is also needed. No school can succeed if the quality of teaching is not of high standards. A school that functions without the involvement of the parents cannot succeed as the entire purpose of the school is to meet the aspirations of the parents.

Along with the people involved with the school, systems and resources also need to be assessed. This is crucial, as the final assessment needs to correlate the success of the systems and the sufficiency and efficiency of the infrastructure with the success of the students. It will often be found that these systems are the direct cause for the level of success of the students. The success of systems will measure the deployment of various systems, their effectiveness and their efficiency.

Assessment: Different tools for assessment of each of the parameters to be measured will be described. Benchmarks will be defined to measure success and acceptability or non-acceptability of results. Once the benchmarks are applied, the results will be analysed and actions will

Figure 12.8 The first step in creating a new system to assess the success of a school in a given period is to define what is meant by each of the terms and also to indicate the processes and parameters of this new system

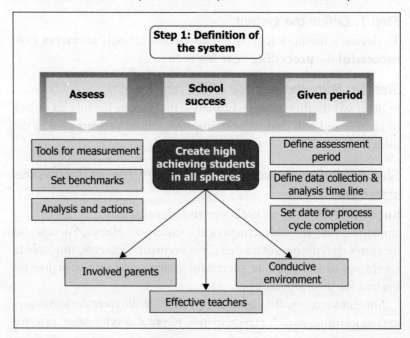

be defined for different types of results—reinforcement actions for good results and remedial actions for unacceptable results. These assessments will be described in greater detail in the Methodology section of the system.

Preceding Year: Two points need to be defined for the purpose of the assessment. This could be a calendar year starting at some random date and ending exactly a year later; it could be an academic year or a financial year. What is important is that there should be no confusion in the definition of the time period.

Step 2: Defining the owner and supervisor of the system

Once it has been decided that a certain system needs to be developed and executed, ownership must be assigned. It could be given to an outside agency, to a teacher, a parent or to a team of teachers or parents. This team or this owner decides on the methodology of constructing the system and the process of implementing the system. These owners are responsible for collecting the data and making the final reports and they will receive the feedback on the system.

The supervisor of this system also needs to be assigned—the person or team who monitors the functioning of the system, receives reports on this system and gives feedback.

Step 3: Defining the system process

The system process selects the parameters and assessment tools and defines the mapping of assessment tools to parameters. It also describes the methodology of creating assessment instruments and setting benchmarks and steps for collecting the data. This step is the core part of the system definition.

Step 3a: Mapping assessment tools to parameters

In-class learning: Results in the internal assessment of school. This internal assessment is not just a weighted score of performance in home work, assignments and tests, but also includes subjective assessments made by the teachers at regular intervals on student qualities such as punctuality, efficiency, class participation, etc. Thus in order to measure success in in-class learning, assessment mechanisms will need to be in place for comprehensive and holistic assessments that include not just the academic subjects, but also performance in arts, on the sports field and familiarity and ability to apply emerging technology in ones learning.

229

Outside-class activities: Performance of the school as a whole in outside class activities will require:

- Assessment of the range of outside class activities that students have participated in (across various disciplines—the school should not excel only in soccer and debates, but also in cricket, music and science quizzes, etc.);
- The level of participation of the students (do a large percentage of students get opportunities to take part, or do the same students participate every time?); and
- The quality of the performance—the number of prizes and other types of recognition received in proportion to the total events participated in.

Physical development: This could be measured by developing standardised tests that use different physical tasks to measure physical skill such as flexibility, balance, strength, co-ordination, power, muscular agility, etc.

Scores could be given to students based on their achieving different levels of achievement in each of these parameters.

External examination performance: Trends in examination scores of overall performance as well as individual subjects: Are overall averages rising or falling? Comparison of results with other leading schools is also needed for this analysis. Analysis of percentile scores to see in which percentile the majority of students are placed.

Placement in higher education and professions: To see how successful placements are, it will be necessary to divide all institutions of higher learning and professions into categories. The institutions and organisations with the highest reputations would be A-level organisations, middle levels get 'B' and the lowest 'C'. The school can use its own categorisation based on the school priorities and philosophy or they can use standard categorisations made by some other reputed agency. Once this is done students, who were placed in these organisations during the defined year, will be sorted by category. An analysis of the percentage of students in each category will reveal the success or lack of success of students once they leave the school.

In this context, it is necessary to put unusual and non-conventional placements in a higher category listing—there must be special recognition for students who make adventurous choices.

Humaneness: This is by far the most important parameter that needs to be assessed, and yet the most difficult to define. Rather than get into very complex measurement mechanisms, a simple way is to

Figure 12.9 Each success parameter is measured using a specific instrument. The instruments could be generated from existing systems or created specially for this task.

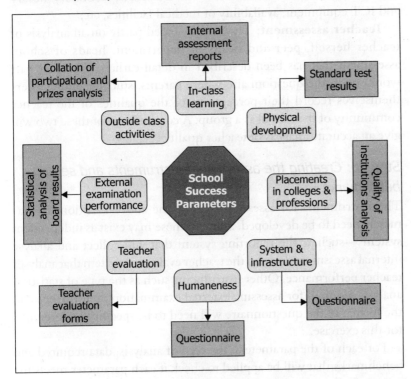

devise a questionnaire that measures the perceptions of students, teachers, parents and the outside community. While this may appear to be a very subjective way of finding out which humane traits the average student population of the school has, a scientifically constructed questionnaire can give very accurate insights. Also by giving these questionnaires to different sets of people the levels of agreement or disagreement between these groups can add to the accuracy of the findings.

Systems and infrastructure: These too are very difficult to measure; many of them will not directly relate to specific results. Thus, we fall back again on questionnaires and gather perceptions of various stakeholders on the effectiveness and efficiency of these. The school will need to decide which systems to measure in the questionnaire—some examples are: Planning for the academic and non-academic programmes, Continuous assessment system, Parent–Teacher meetings, School trips, Dispersal system, House system, Sport camps, Outreach programmes, Reading programmes and so on.

The infrastructure questions could relate to various facilities such as the school building—its size and spaciousness, layout and maintenance. Other infrastructure elements are sports, laboratory, library and ICT equipment, availability of medical facilities, etc.

Teacher assessment: This will be based partly on an analysis of teacher herself, peer and heads of department, heads of school assessment that has been described in detail earlier. The other part would be in the questionnaire where parents, students and teachers themselves record their perceptions of the qualities of the teacher community of the school as a group. A combination of these two will give an accurate analysis of teacher quality.

Step 3b: Creating the assessment instruments and setting benchmarks

The instruments for assessing each of the above-mentioned parameters need to be developed. Some of these may exist as independent systems—such as the reporting system that will collect and analyse internal assessment data and the teacher evaluation system that analyses teacher performance. Other instruments such as the type of statistical analysis required for assessing external examination performance and the format of the questionnaire will need to be specifically developed for this exercise.

For each of the parameters, the type of analysis, data required and benchmarks that will be applied to check if each parameter meets the criteria for success need to be formally put down.

For example, for the internal assessment result analysis, the criteria of success could be that at least 20 per cent of the students should get scores above 80 per cent and all students should score above 60 per cent. In case of external examinations, these benchmarks may not be in terms of absolute scores, but could be linked to percentile scores. Here the aim may be that in each subject 40 per cent or more students should be in the nationwide 80th percentile or higher. High absolute marks are not relevant for admission into good colleges that have limited number of seats.

In the questionnaire, the categories of questions, the actual questions that will be asked under each category, the scoring scheme needs to be defined. Once this is defined, the benchmarks will be in terms of agreement and disagreement in responses. A good score could be one where 80 per cent of the responses are positive and a poor score where less than 50 per cent of the responses are positive (implying that the majority of responders have a negative perception to this parameter).

Step 3c: Documenting and communicating the system and defining implementers

Once the system processes have been defined, it is time to start the actual implementation of the process. This requires first that the entire process described earlier is documented with clarity and stored in a manner that it is accessible to those who need to know. In addition, there must also be forums for discussion about this process with those who will be generally involved. Therefore, this step also includes the identification of the implementers of this process.

This is also the step where the owners can get opinions, feedback and ideas on improving the process that they have outlined. They can also gauge the reception they will get when the process is actually implemented.

Step 4: Implementation of the process

Step 4a: Collecting data

Once the instruments are ready and the analysis requirements have been laid out clearly, it is time to start implementing the process by collecting data. Some data will be available only at specific times—such as board examination results or placement data. Other data are within the control of the school. For each of these, time schedules must be drawn so that data collection happens in an orderly manner. Methods of storage of raw data, the persons responsible for collection and collation should also be clearly stated.

For example, the questionnaire data could be in the form of an online questionnaire that will automatically collate and calculate the required percentages, averages and standard deviations. This questionnaire could be available in the form of a password-protected page on the school Website for parents and others to access easily and submit.

Step 4b: Analysis of data and reports

The penultimate stage is the actual analysis. The analysis for each parameter is done separately, and the essential results and statistics are extracted from the raw data and these are put together to make the big picture.

The big picture requires the analyst to find the linkages in the results of different parameters, to find cause and effect. The purpose of the system is after all to find remedies to weaknesses and reinforcement of strengths.

233

Thus, English and science may show outstanding results—these could also be the two departments that have the highest levels of inter-disciplinary outside-class activities that have reinforced student concepts. This could also be reflected in the high quality of science-based placements at the college level and the success of students in communication-based professions.

The high success rate in the physical development tests may be reflected in good performance in the inter-school matches of various sports, which may help students at the margin in college placements. Similarly poor performance in social sciences may not be due to lack of activities, but actually due to an excess of activities that are not properly linked to the goals of the student learning programme.

The analysis must take into account that all parameters are linked and have cause-and-effect relationships with one another. The success or failure in a particular parameter has impacts on other parameters. The analysis will not serve its intended purpose if these inter-linkages and causal relationships are missed out. Every year, the analysis should also include the findings from the previous years and see if actions have been taken and if these have been effective in causing the required change. Once this is done, the analysis can be said to be complete and meaningful. The actions that will be taken because of the analysis will depend on the causes and consequences revealed. These actions are in fact the entire purpose of the system.

Step 4c: Action plan

Feedback is of two kinds. The first is the feedback generated by the system on the various parameters that have been involved which leads to the action plan. The second is the feedback on the effectiveness of the system.

Finally, we have the feedback loop. On one hand, we gather feedback from the findings of the analysis and plough them back into the school system. If excessive participation in social sciences outside-class activities is affecting examination performance, in the succeeding year these activities must be toned down or connected to the learning curriculum with greater care. The entire process of analysis is of little use if the findings are not translated into action. Thus, an Action Plan emerges from the analysis. This feedback is part of the system process implementation and is not to be confused with the feedback on the system itself.

Step 5: Feedback and debriefing

On the other hand, there is feedback on the system itself. Would parents prefer paper questionnaires to the online one? Would they like to change some of the questions? Would teachers like to add their participation

Figure 12.10 The steps in the development of the system for measuring the success of a school are closely related to the steps for the development of most systems. Step 3 and Step 4 of system process will be different for each system, the rest are common.

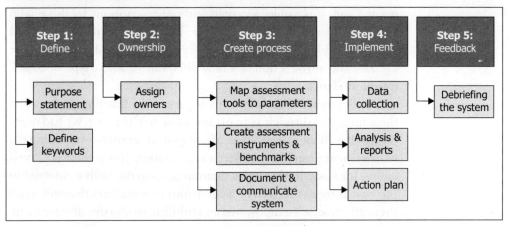

in various seminars and conferences in the preceding year to this analysis? After all, this too affects the quality of their teaching (too much leads to missing classes and too little leads to less awareness of better teaching techniques). In addition to these small details, the feedback of the system also asks questions on the success of the system:

- Was the system simple enough to be understood and implemented accurately?
- Was the analysis accurate, did it reflect reality?
- Did the Action Plan make practical recommendations?
- Were the recommendations made by the plan actually implemented in the succeeding year?

If the answers to any of these questions is 'no', obviously the entire system needs to be scrutinised and changes made to remove the weaknesses of the system. This feedback thus determines the success of the system. If the answers to these questions are still 'no' even after modifications over three or four years, then it may be necessary to do away with this system.

Thus, two sets of actions need to flow out of the analysis, which must never be seen as an end in itself, to be filed and forgotten.

A curriculum for school management

The development of the system to determine if the school has had a good year is just one example of how a new system can be developed.

235

Many old systems can be reworked or improved using similar methodology and similar sequential processes. The aim ultimately is to have systems in schools that lead somewhere, that are efficient, clearly enunciated and, if possible, accepted without reservations by those who are involved in making them possible. This type of methodology could equally be adopted for the timetable system, for attendance records or even for the introduction of a new discipline or a new type of course for the students.

Development of such systems is part of the learning process that the school goes through as an organisation. In Chapter 1, we had mentioned that all the stakeholders of a school are learners—including the management. Every learner needs a curriculum. Just as there is a curriculum for students that helps them to develop the skills to succeed in life, just as there needs to be a curriculum for teachers that will make them effective, self-empowered and fulfilled, so also this development, analysis and constant examination of systems is a part of the curriculum of the organisation as a whole. The existence of a system to review systems at regular intervals is one way of preparing for the future and for keeping pace in this constantly changing world. As new knowledge emerges and new developments take place in the science of management, these can be built into the systems that are being reviewed for change.

The analysis and constant reworking and improvement of systems is one way in which the management of schools escapes the trap of complacency, especially the schools that have been running like well-oiled machines for several years.

Summary

Part 1: Uniqueness of organisational structure of a school
- A school has an unusual organisational structure with a principal and vice principal (managers), hundreds of teachers (main employee) and thousands of students (clients).
- The lack of material benefits available to teachers can be compensated by giving them the joy that a sense of achievement brings.
- The inability of students to voice their needs implies that the role of the school is to lead them to self-empowerment.
- The success of the school as an organisation is not in expanding sales nor in making profits, but in creating an excellent product—this is the self-empowered student.

- Thus, the management needs to create a learning environment that is conducive to self-development.
- The role of the management is to smoothen the path of teachers by implementing efficient systems for the running of the school.
- They create the learning environment by making learning-based systems.

Part 2: Systems in a school

- Systems needed to manage limited resources—time, people and money.
- Each system needs to have a goal, and goals and systems should not be in conflict with each other.
- Conflicts are resolved by creating a hierarchy of goals and mapping systems to these goals.
- Systems need to be clearly articulated—there needs to be both understanding through communication and ownership through participation in all stages of the system, not just in implementation.
- The characteristics of a good system are communication and conviction, transparency, minimal tedium and objective success indicators.
- The process of developing a new system involves defining the new system, assigning ownership, defining system processes, documenting, assigning implementers, communicating the new process, implementing the system and gathering feedback.
- Systems need to be followed even if they are not efficient or not clearly understood—this leads to less chaos.
- Yet systems need to be built by creativity and flexibility in order to change with changing times.

Part 3: Developing a system to determine success of a school

- A system could be devised to assess if the school has had a successful year.
- The process involved is:

  Step 1: Defining the system and defining the key terms of the definition (assessment, success and year).
  Step 2: Assign ownership.
  Step 3: Develop the process by mapping assessment tools to parameters, create assessment instruments and benchmarks, collect data.
  Step 4: Analyse the data and write the report.
  Step 5: Action plan for the assessment as well as feedback on the system itself.

- Creating, renewing and implementing systems in this fashion becomes a part of the learning curriculum for the management.

13

Leadership

A great school, as we have seen, is a community of learners. All stake-holders of the school need to remain in the learning mode by focusing on the learning process, which has two functions. The first is to make each member of the school community an effective learner. The second is to ensure a certain amount of foresight—to choose the path of knowledge that will be relevant for tomorrow.

However, the question that has not been answered so far is, how does the school make such a foresighted learning process possible? Is there some driving force that points the school on to the right path? That force is leadership.

Leadership, in the context of a great school, has two meanings. One refers to the leader of the school who guides the school through the path that will lead it to greatness. The second refers to the leadership provided by a great school to other schools. A great school provides the leadership that will carry this world into the future. It is a leader for all other schools in the community. It also leads other learners and learning organisations in the community.

The leader of the school

An important characteristic of the leader of a great school is her vision for the future. In all organisations, this vision for the future relates to the future of the organisation and the future of the world with respect to the organisation. This vision looks at where the organisation sees itself several years into its future. It looks at those factors in the surrounding environment that are likely to affect the growth of the organisation in the future. Certainly, a leader of a school needs to have this vision. However, this is not enough for a great school.

The leader of a school needs to foresee how the world will develop in terms of changes in social structures because her students will need to live in that society. She needs to know what the economy of the world will be 20 years ahead because her students will need to earn

The leader of a great school needs to have a vision of the future of the world itself.

Figure 13.1 While all members of the school community contribute to and learn from the learning process, the leader of the school and leadership by the school give the right direction to this process

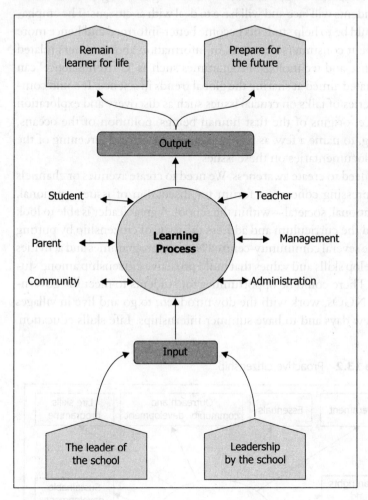

their living in that future economy. There is no aspect of the future world—scientific, technological, cultural or philosophical that—does not affect the students. If the leader needs to guide the school that will prepare students for life, she needs to understand what life will be like when they leave behind the protective fences that have sheltered them so far.

For example, the ever-growing importance of scientific issues in our daily lives demands that the young people who will be our future citizens have sufficient knowledge and understanding to follow science and scientific debates. One of the ways of empowering future citizens about matters involving science and technology is to consolidate students' understanding of science by directing learning towards issues that students will face and will have to deal with as citizens. The emphasis should be to help students become better-informed and hence more intelligent consumers and users of information about matters related to science and technology. Programmes such as 'Citizen Science' can be initiated aimed at sharing the global trends in science. It could comprise series of talks on crucial issues such as discovery and exploration of space, origins of the first human beings, pollution of the oceans, cloning, to name a few, as well as exhibitions on and screening of the latest documentaries on these issues.

We need to create awareness. We need to create avenues or channels for expressing concern, a forum for discussion of issues—national, international, societal—within the school. A great leader is able to look beyond the curriculum and address the issue of citizenship by putting in place several community-centred learning programmes and activities to develop skills and values that build proactive citizenship among students. There could be opportunities for students to meet the government, NGOs, work with the downtrodden, to go and live in villages for a few days and to have summer internships. Life skills education,

Figure 13.2 Proactive citizenship

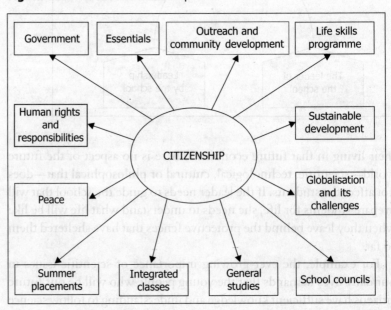

general studies and value-based education could be incorporated in the curriculum and leadership skills could be developed through school councils.

Besides the need for creating awareness, it is also vital to create a critical consciousness (reflection, enquiry and debate) that questions different ideologies, institutions, principles governing a state and extreme values among students. Students must acquire a sense of individual and community responsibilities and learn about their relationships with one another and with members of society. One of the fundamental tasks of education is to empower students, improve their quality of life and increase their capacity to participate in the decision-making processes leading to social, cultural and economic policies. A great leader recognises this and incorporates the issues of human rights, respect for others, equal dignity, globalisation and its challenges, sustainable development, peace and religious tolerance as an integral part of the school curriculum. Students could be provided opportunities to develop their understanding and skills to reflect on these issues through 'school life', that is, all aspects of school as a living, social environment with its collective rules, inter-personal conflicts, time and opportunities for co-operation, and through opportunities for spontaneous initiatives by the students outside the actual teaching activities. The methods and approaches chosen could be those based on discussion among students and between teachers and students. Modes of expression may be varied: in addition to discussions, drawings, songs, poems, reading and debating on different written material, researching a topical issue and analysing sources of information, using imagination to consider other people's experiences, participating in school and community-based activities and reflecting on that participation and so on.

An important trait of the leader is that she has the ability to convey this vision of the school's future to all members of the school community. She needs to convince them that her vision of the future is indeed an indicative picture of the future. She needs to develop in them a sense of ownership in this vision. At the same time, she also needs to make sure that no member of the school community converts this vision into a rigid and absolute truth. She ensures that as the world changes, this vision too keeps evolving. She makes sure that everyone understands the need for this evolution and the direction in which the change will take place.

Some basic values may never change—these relate to the inner self, interrelationships, humaneness and the individual as a learner. What

241

keeps changing is the path to these basic values. Therefore, the understanding that change is a constant is a core part of this vision.

The next step for the leader of the school is to develop and implement systems that will achieve this vision. These are the learning systems for the students: the learning process, assessment and curriculum. These include systems not only for high levels of student achievement, but also systems for development of student qualities and personal traits. The leader of a great school develops the systems in which teachers take the responsibility of creating an emotionally safe environment by encouraging students to share their views without the fear of criticism. Every teacher strives to ensure a climate of co-operation, healthy competition and friendship among students, creating an atmosphere of mutual respect and rapport in the classroom. Teachers are expected to provide varied opportunities to the students through group discussions, projects, lab work, field trips, etc., and also at the same time ensure that there is an extensive and appropriate use of technology. It is important for teachers to use differentiated instructions to cater to different learning styles and abilities of students in the class. 'Planning' is the keyword for such a system of teaching to be effective and efficient. Teachers take care to make plans for the year, each term and each lesson of the day. The plans are detailed enough to include assignments, remedial work, enrichment work and provide for enough time for reflection and assimilation. The teachers ensure that the students get comprehensive and prompt feedback on their work through report cards, diaries, letters, interactive sessions with parents, review meetings.

There are also systems for the development of teachers, involvement of parents and efficiency of administration. The leader makes sure that these systems are interpreted correctly and are implemented efficiently. She creates a positive atmosphere for constant development, improvement and evolution of these systems.

The leader is often just the catalyst that makes this vision happen. The actual implementation of the vision is delegated to the most competent members of the school community. She ensures the creation of a self-empowered community of leaders. These students, teachers, parents, administration and support staff will use their learning skills to find the way. Many will become leaders in their own right. The leader of the school creates the right conditions and atmosphere and then lets the growth of each individual take place. She creates giants within her school.

A great leader optimises each individual member's potential in the school by giving them a first-hand experience of multi-tasking. For example, every teacher should be given space in the school calendar to organise at least one event in her area of responsibility. Each department should plan two special events in the year that are spectacular. One of these events should be with the students and one with the teachers. There should be an additional event that involves students from other schools. Events should be organised in a manner that does not affect the classes and the centrality of the academic programme. The events planned should also promote the quality of interaction between teachers and students and teachers and parents.

The role of the administrative and support staff in all these programmes is like 'oil in an engine'. Though invisible, they make a significant contribution in smooth and effective implementation of school systems.

The leader's role is to interact and communicate with everyone in the school family and to learn from everyone. One part of this interaction is to understand the needs and abilities of everyone in the school so that they get a sense of ownership and take pride in what they do. She should take an interest in their activities, give them the space to utilise their skills, listen to them. For example, even support staff such as the gardeners in the school, have a perspective on the school that can give a great deal of insight into not only improving the school environment but also creating a positive atmosphere to realise it.

Efforts should be made to give the parents a sense of belonging from the day the child enters school. We should take every opportunity to infuse confidence in parents to entrust their children in our care from the very first day. In our school we have an orientation for parents and children wherein after a general welcome address by the head of the school, they are introduced to the class teacher and the other teachers who are responsible for helping them to learn, grow and evolve. On the first day of school, every parent is given a pouch containing a tissue, a tea bag and a personalised letter. The tissue and the tea bag, so that they can go back home and put their feet up and relax; and the letter to assure them that their child's emotional, physical and academic needs will be nurtured that will complement their parenting at home.

The leader of a great school understands how the needs of students change as they grow from infancy to adolescence to adulthood. She understands how parents change—the parents of very young children are far more involved in the small details of their children's upbringing. Over time, they step back. The leader understands that when young students join school, her clients are the parents and she has to deal

243

with their aspirations and their assessment of their child's abilities. As students grow older, her clients are now the students—they are now old enough to communicate their own aspirations and needs and assess their own abilities.

The leader also has to interact and communicate with her teachers—their development and growth is one of her chief priorities. The better their self-development, growth and satisfaction with working conditions, the better will be the level of learning guidance that they will give to the students. The leader also needs to motivate her management team, her administration and support staff to understand and implement the school vision.

The second aspect of the leader's interaction with the school family is to create a sense of belonging and bonding within all members of the community. This bonding leads to sharing of knowledge and the co-operation that is required to move ahead. It leads to ownership and understanding of each other's goals.

The leader ensures that within certain boundaries, every individual has the freedom to find her own way. There is a healthy mix of differing ideas, even if these ideas are in conflict with each other. She encourages differences but ensures that a sense of a common purpose unites all these differences. It is crucial that the leader of a great school establishes trust with candour, transparency in her teachers.

For example in our school, we have removed the time frame from the learning goals which we call the curriculum—academic, physical, emotional. So Foundation, Nursery and Class I are seen as one. Class II stands alone. Classes III, IV and V are together as are VI, VII and VIII; Classes IX, X, XI and XII are already together. In order to make a success of this we need a change in the attitude of teachers who will work together to take the process forward. After all, a teacher who is teaching E, F and G must have the confidence that the teacher before her has taught A, B, C and D. Otherwise the process is doomed to failure. What this means is that we need to have divisions but that these divisions are more fluid than before. In order to fulfil our learning process and goals, we need to empower students to understand the mechanics of learning and also develop their skills to create new knowledge.

The sense of bonding and sharing should not be limited only to members of the leader's school. She creates bonds and shares knowledge with the larger learning community. This includes other schools in the neighbourhood (or e-neighbourhood), institutions of higher learning and every organisation that affects and is affected by the school.

The leader of a great school should have the courage to make unpopular decisions and gut calls. The most unpopular decision in my career was the doing away with the school bell that is supposed to regulate and give a structure to a typical day in a school. Instead, we have only two bells in a day; one in the morning that begins the day's activity and one in the afternoon that brings the day to an end in the school. There is a clock in every classroom and students and teachers are expected to take upon themselves the responsibility to follow the class schedules. The reason is that instead of being dependent on an external stimulus like a bell, both students and teachers cultivate self-discipline and self-regulatory behaviour. This system initially met with a lot of resistance by the teachers as they felt that 'no bell system' would lead to chaos and anarchy. The general feeling was that students would not come to classes on time and also teachers coming in late would take longer to finish their lessons and disrupt the lesson of the next teacher. However, the system has worked remarkably well in the school and instilled a sense of responsibility and ownership in everyone.

Leaders inspire risk-taking and learning by setting examples. A student of Class X from our school was facing difficulties in her studies. Her problem was that she found mathematics difficult, and low grades in maths affected her overall performance. She was an extremely bright student otherwise and performed well in other subjects. In the CBSE curriculum that we follow in our school, there was no way out of her predicament as mathematics of a certain level is compulsory in Class X. In order to ensure that she does not lose interest in learning we encouraged her to shift to the National Institute of Open Schooling (NIOS) curriculum where she can choose the subject combinations she wished to study, all the while being a part of the school and taking her Class X board exams through the NIOS system. Once she cleared her board exams through NIOS she returned to the CBSE curriculum for her secondary education in Classes XI and XII, where CBSE allows one to choose a discipline one likes. The student opted for humanities; where there is no compulsion to study maths and came out with flying colours in her Class XII CBSE board examinations. It is heartening to know that she is now majoring in psychology in a leading college of our country for her undergraduate degree.

We trusted her abilities and took the risk of allowing her to shift to an alternative curriculum while being flexible enough to let her be a member of a school following the CBSE curriculum. This inspired her to be where she is now!

245

Leaders celebrate. Celebrating magical moments, however small, create an atmosphere of encouragement, recognition and positive energy. It helps tremendously in not only building the self-confidence of teachers but also raises the bar, stretching the staff to exploit their potential to the maximum. This could entail letters of appreciation, sharing an accomplishment with the rest of the staff, handing out book coupons, tickets for a cultural evening, celebratory lunches and so on.

Creating a community of learners

In the unification of differences and the sharing of knowledge lies the second main difference between leadership in an organisation devoted to the pursuit of learning and that in other types of organisations. Organisations that are in business in a competitive space will definitely co-operate and share knowledge to the extent that this sharing will help their growth. However, there are always internal processes that an organisation keeps to itself as these give it an edge over competitors.

Once a school establishes itself as a great school, what strategy will it use to remain a leader? In the context of the changing world that we have described earlier, a great school will continue to lead not because it keeps its secrets well-hidden, but because it has no secrets. If a school gives away all its knowledge, how does it then create the edge that it has over other schools?

In any race, it is very well known that records are broken only when the quality of all the players is very high and nearly level. By raising the level of the competition, the school sets even higher standards for itself. Great schools are not satisfied with relative greatness—they seek to be the best among great schools. They take proactive steps to help other schools. They create a community of schools where all others are close to overtaking them.

Since a school is in the business of creating new knowledge, its purpose is to create an environment that creates new knowledge. This environment is created when different perspectives are shared. As a great school learns, it must keep sharing this learning with others who are in the same business. The reason for the existence of the school is to give the best kind of education to its students. Therefore, the larger the boundaries of the learning community around it, the better the inputs it will get from learners everywhere.

The way forward for a great school is to create a community of schools. Yet, each school in this network needs to be autonomous. These are like servers on the Internet: inter-connected yet independent. Each server openly takes what it wants from the other and gives away its own knowledge with equal openness. The communication between servers is always open and available whenever needed. Each school in this network shares practices and processes with each other in order to boost each other.

This is especially true for schools that are not up to the great school's standards. These schools are given a greater push. A great school understands that schools that lag behind will pull down the entire level of learning in the community.

The principles used for developing the potential of each individual student in the school are equally relevant for developing the potential of all the schools that belong to this network. Great schools not only know that every student in the school has the ability and potential to become a great human being, but also that each school in the community has the potential to become a great school.

Great schools not only understand that every student has strengths and weaknesses, but they also understand that different schools have different strengths. They have the modesty to accept that in some aspects of the learning process other schools may be ahead of them. Therefore, a great school does not necessarily appoint itself the leader in this community of schools.

Different schools in this community take on leadership roles for different aspects of the learning process. Each school in the community is a role model for the others in some way. Other schools observe, interact and learn. There is healthy mix of both co-operation and competition.

A major advantage of this community of schools is that they draw from each other's resources. Schools are traditionally short on resources—an important characteristic of school education in this country. This often leads to poaching of resources from each other, especially of teachers. The existence of the alliance ensures that resources are shared and there is therefore mobility of resources without loss of resources.

In the process, each school in this community becomes like a living organism. It continuously evolves. It keeps re-incarnating itself in new avatars. It acquires new DNA and sheds redundant DNA. Over time, it may emerge as a completely different and new organism—but one that is most relevant to the time in which it exists. This evolution cannot happen in isolation, a necessary part of the process comes from sharing the DNA.

The structure of the learning network

For sharing to happen in an efficient manner, this network needs to have a certain formal structure. As each school is autonomous, other schools cannot invade their privacy at will. The formal structure helps each school to maintain its independence and yet not lose the benefits of sharing knowledge.

An example of such a structure is a set of schools linked to a central research alliance. The central research organisation coordinates the process of inter-school co-operation. This research organisation is not an external agency, but the staff and teachers of member schools are deputed to run the centre. There is therefore a sense of ownership. It is very important that this centre is not perceived as being 'outside' the school, but very much a part of the school. In some senses, it is a club where all members of the participating schools are equal owners. They rotate responsibilities from time to time.

The role of this centre is not to make rules for the schools to follow. It makes no policy recommendations. It has no authority to tell schools what to do. It is purely a learning organisation, where teachers take a break from their teaching duties for a few hours, for a few days or for longer periods. During this time, they may pursue serious independent research on any aspect of learning, they may attend courses given by leader teachers from other schools, or they may conduct these courses or workshops for other teachers. Teachers take back their learning to their own schools and implement what they have learnt after adapting it to the vision of their particular school.

Apart from the formal in-service training and refresher programmes, this centre is a forum for discussions on everything from teaching organic chemistry to managing an inter-school debate.

Though teacher development is a crucial function of this alliance, it is not just for teachers. This is one place where parents and teachers get together to share ideas and learn from each other. The management learns about school management practices and the administration shares administrative knowledge. There is a forum for each member of the school community to air their views. Students too will be represented

Figure 13.3 The research centre connects all types of organisations in a community that are interested in education and learning from each other

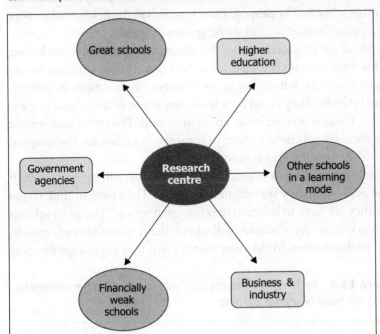

here. They will periodically speak to all the other players about their needs and aspirations.

Apart from sharing of knowledge, the purpose of this alliance is to create new knowledge. Research and development of new learning techniques will emerge from here. There will be greater stress on using technology to make learning more effective. New techniques of learning—e-learning techniques, using games and simulations to learn, further research into the biological understanding of how the brain learns—are some examples of the types of research that can be undertaken.

The centre will also help the schools to meet their social responsibilities. Financially weak schools and schools that serve students with economic disabilities will be part of this alliance. They will benefit by sharing the resources, the teachers and the extensive knowledge base of the richer schools in this alliance.

This organisation is also a link to other organisations related to education—CBSE, ICSE, and the NCERT and to higher education organisations such as the UGC, various universities and institutions of undergraduate and graduate learning. This centre could also reach out to business organisations that are future employers of their students. Each of these organisations helps to broaden the perspectives of the member schools. They expose them to trends in the fields of education, business, economy, management, governance, etc.

One of the characteristics of this alliance is that schools that belong to this alliance could belong to any school board. They could be private unaided schools, schools set up by religious organisations or government schools. They could be schools anywhere in the country or the world. There is no restriction on membership. The only characteristic that these schools need to have in common is a thirst for learning and a desire to give the very best to their students.

For such an alliance to succeed, all the schools will have to put their egos aside once they are within this centre. They have to understand that they are here to learn, to develop open minds. The great schools in this community of schools will take on the responsibility of smoothing out differences. In the same manner that they encourage diversity

> A great school becomes the leader of this alliance not through appointment but by the excellence of learning inputs that it gives to others and by the humility with which it learns from others.

Figure 13.4 Each research centre connects to several other centres to widen the base of shared learning

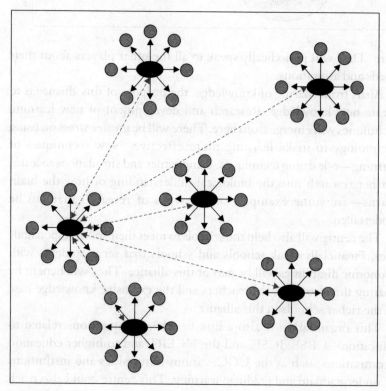

within their schools, they will ensure that though differences exist, these are accepted with tolerance and harmony.

This centre of learning is only part of a larger grid of many such centres that connect schools in different parts of the world. A school cannot be run efficiently once it crosses a certain size. The alliance too cannot survive if it has too many members.

The world of schools should in due course be connected to each other through such research and development centres, which are in turn connected to each other.

As in the case of member schools that belong to an alliance, each centre in this alliance of centres is an independent entity that is linked to other centres by the common bond—a desire to learn.

The future

Schools of yesterday had a 'one size fits all' curriculum. This type of school developed from the needs of the society of yesterday. In those times, schools were required to train students for a mass production-based, industrialised economy with rigid social layers. People from one profession did not interact much with those in other professions; and such lack of interaction was also marked among the different classes of society and different ethnic groups.

Schools in the past reflected the reality of their times. They remained isolated from each other. They developed their own systems to meet the needs of their students, and these systems remained in place through several generations. Students who started life with very different abilities were converted into homogeneous products by the process of education handed out by these schools. Students in a school tended to develop very similar skills.

Today, people are increasingly mobile. People with different backgrounds, cultures and abilities are no longer separated by geographic or social barriers. Social distinctions are increasingly fluid. The world over, there is an acceptance of differences and people have begun to realise the importance of learning to live in harmony with diversity.

In part, this change is a consequence of the fact that the world is moving towards a knowledge economy. The work area no longer consists of factory workers, all from the same social background performing similar tasks. The work area instead has become very complex; organisations today require people with very different skills and backgrounds working together in the same workplace.

Therefore, with the change in society, schools today are changing and developing new systems to meet these new needs. There is an increasing tendency towards greater individualisation of education. Schools are offering a more broad-based education to their students. It is no longer enough to excel in school board examinations; students also need to develop a portfolio of other skills and interests—whether in academics, art or sports or in community interactions.

Earlier, the only streams of specialisation that schools offered were the standard trio of Humanities, Commerce and Science. Today many traditional schools offer alternatives within these streams. This change is in response to the fact that students when they move onto higher education are no longer restricted to a professional degree in engineering and medicine, and bachelor degrees in science, commerce and arts. There are myriad other options available to service the changing world around them.

In addition, schools at the cutting edge—those that keep up with new challenges—offer almost any subject combination that interests a student. They offer students courses in newly emerging subjects and fields of specialisations. They know that more and more professions around the world require just this type of state-of-the-art and broad-based knowledge. The workers of tomorrow will be multi-skilled, flexible and adaptive to change. Students today have greater freedom of choice in what they can choose to study than they have ever had in the history of education.

This is just one example of the type of freedom of choice, and therefore of complexity, that has emerged due to the changing structure of the economy and of society. The schools that could look ahead and predict such a future 20 years ago and schools that could change their systems to keep pace with these changes are the ones that have produced the most successful students. These were the great schools of yesterday.

These great schools of yesterday were less isolated from the world outside than the other schools around them. They were different because they observed what was happening in this world and reacted to the changes that were taking place.

In a similar manner, great schools today are looking towards the future. In order to meet the challenges of the future, great schools know that they need to go one step further—they realise that an occasional change in systems or learning structure is not enough. They know that systems and learning need to keep changing to keep pace with constant change. They are aware that the pace of change itself is becoming faster. They know that no one school can meet this formidable challenge on its own.

Schools will meet this responsibility only when they realise that the future lies in co-operation. Survival of schools is not possible if they remain isolated from each other. To become the fittest, it is no longer enough to merely observe and react. Schools need to become proactive in sharing and creating knowledge. Science, technology and research in all aspects of knowledge have given them the tools to create seamless sharing of ideas. They need to use these tools to ensure that the challenges of the unforeseeable future can be met.

Summary

- We live in a world that is characterised by an ever-increasing pace of change.
- To survive, one must remain in the learning mode through life and develop abilities that will be useful in an unpredictable future.
- The leader of the school needs to set the school on the right path.
- This requires a realistic vision of the future of the world.
- The leader also communicates this vision, develops systems and people who will achieve this vision.
- The leader of a great school should have the courage to make unpopular decisions and gut calls.
- Leaders inspire risk taking and learning by setting an example.
- Leaders celebrate.
- The leader enables sharing of knowledge, as she understands that this is the only way to cope with the challenge of change.
- Schools need to form communities of learners—to share knowledge, to create an atmosphere of wholesome competition and co-operation.
- A research alliance that links independent schools is one way of co-operation.
- The alliance links organisations involved in learning and education.
- It enables creation of new knowledge and new techniques of learning and sharing of ideas and resources.
- The research centre in turn connects with research centres across the world.
- For survival and fitness, schools cannot function in isolation, nor can they be passive observers, they need proactively to work together towards meeting the challenges of the future.

About the Author

Arun Kapur has over 28 years of experience in the field of education. He started his career at The Doon School, Dehradun, and went on to join the British School in New Delhi as Principal. He is currently the Director of Vasant Valley School, New Delhi, which he started from scratch, designing and implementing processes, procedures, logistics, staffing plans and management systems. In a short span of time, Vasant Valley School became, and remains, among the most sought after institutions in the country.

As Executive Director of Learn Today, the Learning Division of The India Today Group, he conceptualised a learning-and-testing portal to bring quality education within the reach of students across India. Learn Today also advises on setting up new schools, which are centres of excellence, across the country. In 2002, he established Pallavan, an early childhood development programme for children between the ages of 2 and 5 years. He is a member of the core team of the Confederation of Indian Industries looking at innovative education interventions to improve the quality of school education.

Arun Kapur is the Chairman of Ritinjali, a non-governmental organisation he set up in 1995, which is a vehicle for community development through education and constructive work among marginalised societies across India. Children's shelters, schools and vocational programmes, youth programmes, libraries and community development programmes form the core focus of Ritinjali through extensive professional and volunteer networks. The singular objective of Ritinjali's various initiatives is to empower people through its various projects so that they may be able to contribute constructively to their own lives, their families, their communities and society at large.

The author is also actively engaged in building learning environments catering to a diverse group of learners—mentally challenged, physically challenged, rural and urban—across India.